THE FAMILY
Handyman®

*Landscape
Projects*

Landscape Projects

Planning, Planting, and Building for a More Beautiful Yard and Garden

THE READER'S DIGEST

Pleasantville, New Y

A READER'S DIGEST BOOK

Produced by Roundtable Press, Inc.
Directors: Susan E. Meyer, Marsha Melnick
Project Editor: William Broecker
Project Manager: Kathy Clark
Associate Editor: Abigail Anderson
Editorial Assistant: John Glenn
Design: Sisco & Evans, New York
Editorial Production: Steven Rosen
Consultant: Anne Halpin

For The Family Handyman
Editor: Gary Havens
Executive Editor: Ken Collier
TFH Books Editor: Spike Carlsen

Library of Congress Cataloging in Publication Data
Landscape projects : planning, planting, and building for a more
   beautiful yard and garden.
          p.   cm.
     At head of title: The Family handyman.
     Includes index.
     ISBN 0-7621-0047-8 hardcover
     ISBN 0-7621-0388-4 paperback
     1. Landscape gardening. 2. Garden structures—Design and
construction. I. Reader's Digest Association.   II. Family
handyman.
SB473.L36924   1998
635.9—dc21   97-27810

2 4 6 8 10 9 7 5 3 1   hardcover
   4 6 8 10 9 7 5 3 1   paperback

A Note from the Editor

This book contains a whole wheelbarrow full of landscaping, planting, and outdoor building information and projects. It includes garden planning, the planting and care of flowers, trees, and hedges; the installation of a watering system; the construction of retaining and landscaping walls; the building of footpaths, a bridge, a pavilion, and a gazebo. Plus much, much more.

What makes this book a standout? It contains hundreds of clear illustrations—photographs and diagrams—not only of completed projects, but also of how to get from beginning to end. The colorful illustrations and down-to-earth instructions walk you through every step of each project. And when you're ready to put down your shovel for a while and pick up your hammer, you'll find a section of uniquely designed backyard structures.

Landscape Projects reminds me of my new 33-inch, 7-horsepower, balloon tire mower. It's so easy to use, so well designed, so suited to getting the job done that I actually look forward to using it each weekend. The material in this book comes from the pages of *The Family Handyman* magazine. TFH, as we call it, was around when that 40- or 50-foot maple in your front yard was just a sapling in 1951. TFH will be around when your tree gets to 60 feet, too. That's because of our formula for success. We use only the best experts, we build and rebuild every project ourselves, we love to get dirt under our fingernails—and best of all, we love to share our enthusiasm, experience, and knowledge with you, our readers. So here you are: dig in and have fun!

Gary Havens
Editor in Chief, *The Family Handyman*

Landscape Projects

Trees, Shrubs, and Hedges

Walks and Walls

Garden Structures

Introduction

Your home is much more than a house; it is the sum total of everything within the boundaries of your property—the natural surroundings as well as the house, patio, garage, deck, and other structures. The charm and character of your home depend largely on how well the house and the surroundings fit together, how well they complement one another.

Landscaping is the context in which your home exists. Depending on your preferences, it may be a tailored setting or it may be loose and free. The choice is as much a matter of personal taste as the furniture you buy, the clothes you wear, the car you drive. Whatever kind of landscaping you want to have, this book has a wealth of information and ideas that you can use to beautify your property.

The twenty-four chapters of the book are divided into five sections corresponding to the topics that most concern homeowners when they discuss or ask about landscaping: Lawn Care and Maintenance; Beautiful Gardens; Trees, Shrubs, and Hedges; Walks and Walls; and Garden Structures. Some chapters, such as Alternatives to Grass, and Foundation Plantings, explain how to make landscaping design decisions and choose the appropriate plants for that design. Other chapters, such as Restoring a Lawn, Planting Flowering Bulbs, and Pruning Trees, highlight specific gardening and landscaping techniques. Still other chapters—Creating a Water Garden, Laying a Flagstone Footpath, and A Garden Arbor, for example, provide detailed instructions for adding various features and structures to your landscaping scheme.

In every chapter, you'll find both the information and the instructions you need to maintain or improve the landscaping of your home. Step-by-step illustrations, construction plans, and shopping and cutting lists are included to help you accomplish each project as easily and efficiently as possible. So choose what appeals to you, have a good time doing it, and then relax and enjoy the results of your work for years to come.

Lawn Care
& Maintenance

Caring for Your Lawn

A beautiful lawn enhances your home. With the right grass for your region and the proper care in each season, you can have a first-class lawn year after year— without a lot of hard work.

12

Restoring a Lawn

Blazing sun, drought, freezing weather, or neglect can cause serious damage to a beautiful lawn. There's more than one way to bring a damaged lawn back to health and beauty.

22

Laying Sod

Sod is "instant grass." There's no faster way to create a lush, green lawn in large or small areas of any shape. It's great for slopes, too, because it won't wash away like newly sown grass seed.

28

Alternatives to Grass

Green grass isn't a perfect fit for every home or community. Transform your landscaping with the colorful variety of wildflowers and graceful native grasses. They're virtually maintenance-free.

32

Caring for *Your Lawn*

A beautiful lawn creates the backdrop for all your other landscaping projects. But you can't leave the lawn to itself—it needs care. Here's what you need to know to keep your lawn in first-class condition.

Lawn Basics

To have a healthy lawn you must plant the proper grass for your region or climatic zone, as explained on this page. You also must give grass the proper care. General techniques for lawn care are explained on pages 14–18; seasonal procedures are on page 19.

Grass Zones

Lawn grasses in North America and the Hawaiian Islands can be divided into types suitable for one of two major growing zones, northern and southern.

Northern or cool-season grasses thrive in cooler climates, yet can take high daytime temperatures. These grasses usually look their best when the daytime temperature is about 70°F (21°C) and evening temperatures are 10° to 20°F (5° to 11°C) cooler.

Southern or warm-season grasses can survive temperatures into the 90s F (30s C), but do not grow well in cold ground and may not withstand freezing. Of course, some tropical and semitropical grasses will grow only in Florida, other Gulf Coast states, and Hawaii.

The grass zone map *(below)* shows the northern and southern zones and a transition zone between them. If you live in the higher elevations of the transition zone, plant northern grasses. Plant southern grasses in the warmer sections of this zone, where full sun exposure is more common.

This map is a general guide to the types of grasses that will do best in your area, but some are better than others. Local climate and soil conditions play a significant role in how well certain grasses will grow in any geographic location. Whatever zone you are in, check with a local nursery or county or state agricultural extension office for specific recommendations for your area.

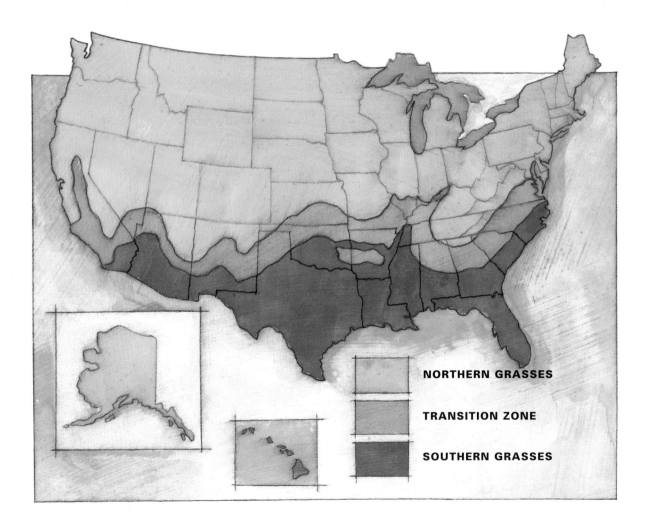

NORTHERN GRASSES

TRANSITION ZONE

SOUTHERN GRASSES

Lawn Care Techniques

The techniques for maintaining a healthy lawn include mowing, raking, fertilizing, watering, spot seeding, weed control, dethatching, and aerating. That may seem like a lot, but don't be overwhelmed. The following discussions of each technique are limited to the common-sense care needed to bring an existing lawn to a healthy, good-looking state without unreasonable cost or effort. Of course, if you want golf-green quality, or the sort of lawn that might grace an English manor house, you'll need to invest far more time, work, and money. Or if your present lawn is a total disaster, turn to Restoring a Lawn (pages 22–27) and Laying Sod (pages 28–31). Then, after your new grass is established, use the information on this and the following pages to keep it in excellent condition.

Mowing

The basic mowing rule is: Don't mow too often. Grasses grow at different rates, depending on the season, so adjust your mowing schedule accordingly. Your lawn might need mowing every week if you have fertilized it and there has been plenty of moisture. But under hotter, drier conditions, once a month is enough.

Northern zone grasses grow fastest in the early spring and late fall and need more frequent mowing then, but in the hot months root growth slows. The roots become weak and shallow in their growing patterns, and will not reach as far down into the ground for moisture and nutrients. To avoid permanent damage to the root systems in the summer, mow less often than early and late in the growing season.

Southern grasses have a similar growing pattern, but root growth is more constant during the summer. Even so, adjust your mowing schedule in these months.

When you mow, make sure the grass is dry; that means no early morning cutting if there is dew. Wet grass sags and curls, and mowing may rip many blades; dry grass stands up straight, so you can cut it cleanly. Also, clumps of wet grass clippings decompose slowly and smother the grass beneath them.

Keep the mower blade sharp (a replacement blade is cheap) so it leaves straight, not jagged, edges. Jagged edges slow down recovery from cutting shock—physical stress to the growth system.

Don't cut the grass too short. Scalping can send a lawn into shock, and it exposes more soil, encouraging weeds. A good rule is never to cut off more than a third of the grass height in one mowing *(below)*. In spring and fall, cut to a height of about 2-1/2 inches; during the hot, dry summer, cut a bit higher, about 3 inches. If the grass has gotten quite tall, cut off just a third at a time. Wait a few days each time for the grass to recover from cutting shock before mowing again. It may take three cuttings to return a badly overgrown lawn to its proper level.

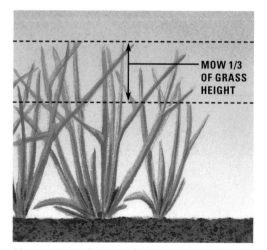

Mow your lawn often enough so you never need to take off more than 1/3 of the green growth to keep it at the proper height. Make sure the mower blade is sharp, to avoid tearing the grass.

Raking

Grass can't grow when it's buried under leaves or clumps of moist clippings, or when a layer of dry clippings and leaf fragments—thatch—covers the soil, blocking moisture from reaching the grass roots. Using a bag to catch mowing clippings helps, but in some seasons clippings ought to be left where they fall, to feed nitrogen to the lawn. Leaves must be raked away throughout the autumn. If they are left on the lawn, leaves will form heavy, wet piles when it rains and prevent sun and water from reaching the grass plants. This leads to winterkill.

Raking does more than remove leaves. The vigorous scratching of the rake tines down between the grass blades and into the soil removes excessive thatch. Some thatch is all right, but more than 1/2 inch will block water, sun, and nutrients, causing the grass plants to develop weak, shallow roots.

Use a "broom" rake, one with long, flexible tines, to remove leaves and grass clippings without damaging the grass. A metal garden rake with short, rigid tines is likely to tear and pull up grass plants. Use it only to roughen soil for spot seeding (page 16), or to remove stubborn spots of thatch. If you have a thick thatch buildup overall, use the de-thatching techniques explained on page 18.

Fertilizing

Fertilizer is lawn food; it adds nutrients to the soil that grass needs to grow well. There are both chemical and organic (natural material) fertilizers, but all usually contain three major nutrients: nitrogen (N), which promotes leaf formation and deep color; phosphorus (P), which helps seeds germinate and helps root growth in established grass; and potassium (K), which makes grass more resistant to heat and cold, drought, disease, and traffic.

Most fertilizer bags are labeled with numbers that indicate the percentage of each nutrient, N-P-K, in relation to the bag's weight. For example, a 25-lb. bag labeled 5-2-3 has 5% (1-1/4 lbs.) nitrogen, 2% (1/2 lb.) phosphorus, and 3% (3/4 lb.) potassium. The rest of the fertilizer is usually made up of fillers and minor nutrients that enrich the soil.

Choosing the right fertilizer can be a challenge because of the many brands and formulas available. Ask someone at a reputable local nursery, lawn and garden or home center, or agricultural extension office for fertilizer recommendations for your area.

In the southern zone, apply fertilizer in the spring and summer; in the northern zone, fertilize your lawn in the fall. Especially with northern grasses, if your lawn needs fertilizing more than once a year, it is better to do it in very early fall and again in late fall, rather than in early spring. Use a broadcast or "cyclone" spreader *(below)* for good coverage with less chance of excess droppage, which will cause burning. If you need a combination lawn food and weed killer, apply it in the spring in both northern and southern zones for the weed killer to be effective. However, don't use this kind of product unless you have weeds to kill; it is a high-powered weed killer plus fertilizer, not vice versa. Check the package to make sure it is safe for use above tree and shrub roots. (Some products contain dicamba, which can be deadly to large trees that have a main root under a treated lawn.) Don't use more than the recommended amount—fertilizer runoff from lawns is a serious source of water pollution.

Apply fertilizer or spread seed with a broadcast spreader to ensure uniform coverage and reduce the risk of fertilizer burn.

Watering

A lawn's watering needs depend on whether the soil it grows in is heavy (clayey) or sandy.

Heavy soil soaks up moisture but is slow to dry out. So you need to water it slowly for a long time to let the water reach the root zone of the grass. Applying water too quickly on heavy soil will result in a lot of waste.

Sandy soil absorbs water up to ten times faster than heavy soil, but tends to let it drain right through. So you must water more frequently—every three to four days—but for shorter periods of time.

The key to watering any kind of soil is depth of penetration. The water must reach a uniform depth of about 6 inches—the equivalent of about 1 inch of rainfall a week—to encourage deep roots and a healthy lawn *(below)*. Less water depth or uneven coverage promotes shallow, weak roots that cannot feed the grass plants adequately. To

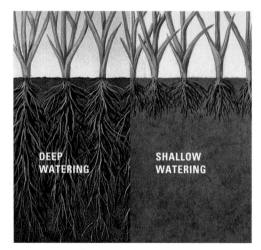

Water slowly and deeply, to a soil depth of 6 in. so your lawn can develop a strong root system *(left)*. Short, shallow watering leads to shallow roots that cannot feed the grass plants adequately *(right)*.

check the moisture depth after watering, drive in a shovel and spread back the soil. You'll soon know how much rain or sprinkling is needed to go 6 inches deep in your soil. In most parts of North America, rainfall provides less than half the water your lawn needs during June, July, and August, so be especially attentive in that period.

Although there is no particular best time to water a lawn, mornings are good, before the day's heat accelerates evaporation loss. Avoid watering on a windy day or at night. Wind can result in an uneven watering pattern; wet leaves overnight make plants more vulnerable to disease. In general, whenever your lawn is noticeably dry, water it. But be sure to observe any restrictions your community places on water usage.

A sprinkler makes watering easy. There are three basic styles of above-ground sprinklers: rotating, oscillating, and pulse.

▶ A *rotating sprinkler* is stationary and has two or more revolving arms. Coverage is not very uniform. A traveling version provides better coverage. It has wheels and moves along the path of the hose to which it is connected.

▶ An *oscillating sprinkler* sprays water back and forth over a rectangular area. The spray pattern can be modified to go in only one direction, if desired. However, the water has a tendency to pool at the end of each sweep before reversing direction.

▶ A *pulse* or *impulse sprinkler* shoots water through a spray head that can be set to cover a full circle or a smaller section. This type generally has a good range and distributes water relatively evenly.

If you have an in-ground watering system, see pages 20–21 to learn how to adjust and maintain it.

Spot Seeding

Planting grass seed in bare patches or where growth is noticeably weak is called spot, patch, or fill-in seeding. If an area is bare because it is walked on a lot, do something to reroute the traffic before seeding. Similarly, if there are bare spots where your dog has buried bones, dig up the bones first (and do a little canine training). If there is some sparse grass in the area, mow it short. Then proceed as follows for small areas and individual spots.

Loosen the soil in each spot by scraping it with a metal garden rake or hand cultivator. You don't need to go very deep, but the surface must be crumbled well. Then sprinkle seeds onto the loosened soil *(below)*.

Spot seed by dropping seeds by hand in bare spots and patches of thin growth after roughening the soil surface. Then cover thinly with topsoil, and keep moist until the seeds sprout.

About 15 to 20 seeds per square inch is enough, but you don't have to be exact. The type of seed to use will vary among regions and the part of your lawn that you're patching. Check with your nursery for the best type of seed to use for your conditions.

Lightly drag an inverted rake or cultivator over the seeds to work them about 1/8 to 1/4 inch into the soil. It's a good idea to add a thin layer of topsoil, but don't bury the seeds deeply. Gently firm the covering soil with your foot or a wood tamper (see page 23), but don't compact it.

Sprinkle the area thoroughly (don't flood it) and keep it moist until the seeds begin to sprout, which should be in about two weeks. Then water as for the rest of the lawn. Be careful not to step on the new spots when you mow—the new blades are delicate and need time to reach full strength.

To fill in larger areas of thin growth, where there are fewer than ten to twelve grass plants per square foot, mow the grass short, rake thoroughly to remove thatch, and break up the surface soil. Then sow seed with a spreader (the same as you use for fertilizer). Cover the seeds lightly with topsoil, burlap, or weed-free straw and keep them moist—not sopping wet—until they sprout.

Weed Control

By far the best defense against weeds is a healthy lawn, one that is fertilized, watered, and mowed. When lawn grass is thick and lush, weeds don't stand a chance. But if they do appear, get rid of them before they go dormant. If you don't, they will grow back bigger and stronger the next time, and most will spread as well. How you deal with weeds depends largely on the degree of infestation in your lawn.

If there aren't too many weeds—that's an individual decision based on how much work you want to do—you can pull them up individually. Water first, so the roots will let go more easily, and pull straight up with a slight twisting motion. A useful tool is a "weed digger," a 9- to 12-inch rod with a narrow V-shaped blade at the end. Insert it beside the center of the weed, along the root, as far as possible and twist it as you pull up on the plant. Try to avoid breaking or cutting off the root underground; it will just send forth new growth.

Most broadleaf weeds—dandelions, clover, chickweed, creeping charlie, and the like—can generally be dug out successfully. Or you can spray them with a spot-treatment herbicide *(right)*. To get complete coverage, spray each weed individually. You'll probably have to spray at least twice a week until the weeds are dead. Use a glyphosate weed killer as a first choice. It breaks down quickly after application, minimizing pollution, but is effective.

Dense, grasslike weeds, including crabgrass and quackgrass, and large areas of broadleaf infestation need a chemical treatment such as spraying with a weed killer to get the lawn into shape for fill-in seeding. You can rent a sprayer to treat large areas.

To select a chemical weed killer for either spot or area application, ask local experts for recommendations. A preemergence herbicide applied early in the spring is probably the most effective way to control crabgrass. Area-spray for broadleaf weeds in the fall. Be sure to follow the product instructions. Many herbicides are combined with lawn food; those that are not are very potent and work quickly (usually in a few days). Some kill grass too, so watch where you spray.

Spray summer weeds with a spot-treatment herbicide. Buy it in a spray container, or add a spray cap to a thoroughly washed household bottle. Spray carefully; some products can kill grass too.

Dethatching

If your lawn has a layer of thatch buildup more than 1/2 inch thick *(below)*, you should get rid of it so nutrients, water, and oxygen can flow to the grass roots.

Remove thatch buildup that is more than 1/2 in. deep above the soil line. It can starve roots.

Cut through the thatch with a power dethatcher, a vertical-blade mower. Rake up and dispose of the thatch afterward.

While you can remove thatch from small areas with a metal garden rake or hand cultivator, you ought to rent a dethatcher for working over large areas of grass. This power tool is a kind of vertical mower *(bottom left)*. Its vertically positioned blades cut into the turf and bring the thatch to the surface. Then you rake it off by hand. The recommended time for dethatching—also called power raking—is early fall. When you have finished, give the lawn a light application of fertilizer to speed its recovery. Spread about 1/2 lb. of nitrogen per 1,000 square feet, and water thoroughly to carry the fertilizer into the soil.

Aerating

Aerating the soil is the best way to loosen it and develop a deep grass root system. The quickest way to do this effectively is with a power aerator, which you can rent. Aerating with hand tools is a lot of work and is really suitable only for an area a few feet square.

An aerator *(right)* has hollow metal tines that plunge into the soil and remove plugs or cores of compacted soil 3 to 4 inches long. This permits more nutrients, air, and moisture to reach the grass roots. And using an aerator is less work than using a dethatcher, because you leave the aerator soil plugs where they fall. The plugs will crumble and return nutrients to the soil. Make several passes with the aerator in different directions, to make sure that you aerate the entire lawn.

If there is thatch buildup in the grass, the aerator cuts through it and helps break it up. This is important not just because it promotes lawn health. Power raking (dethatching) produces a huge quantity of dead grass that is difficult to dispose of. Most landfills won't accept dead grass, and it doesn't do well in a compost pile either.

Rejuvenate your lawn with an aerator, which cuts soil plugs 3- to 4-in. long. Leave the plugs to crumble and feed the soil. Run the aerator in several directions for complete coverage.

Seasonal Lawn Care

A lawn needs attention in early and late spring, summer, and fall. In all but the most southern zones, it is dormant in the winter months. Here's a season-by-season rundown for using the techniques explained on the preceding pages. Dates mentioned are for mid-America; figure two to three weeks earlier in the south, and two to four weeks later in the north.

Early Spring

Grass comes alive with a spurt of growth in early spring. If you did all the right things last fall, you shouldn't have much to do other than the following:

▶ Fertilize only if you didn't do so in the fall, or if winterkill has been severe. Spring fertilizing will feed the grass leaves more than the roots, so be prepared for early mowing.

▶ Rake all debris off the lawn. Seed any bare spots around mid-April.

▶ Attack crabgrass or quack grass before it can germinate. Check with a local nursery to see when germination occurs in your area. Use a fertilizer spreader to spread a preemergence herbicide before that time.

▶ Water only if rainfall is so light that there is not 6 inches of penetration in a week.

▶ Mow to about 2-1/2 inches in height. Rake up the clippings. They will be dense and can overwhelm the lawn if not removed. Dry them to use as mulch if you wish.

Late Spring

By the first weeks of June it is too late for major renovation, seeding, and fertilizing, but during late spring you should:

▶ Rake lightly to remove dead grass and old leaves. Grass can't live under such debris.

▶ Hand-seed small bare patches. Late spring isn't the ideal time to seed, but you need to get grass instead of weeds into the bare spots.

▶ Water thoroughly once a week if it doesn't rain. Check for 6-inch penetration and adjust your watering schedule as necessary.

▶ Fertilize only if you did not do so last fall or in early spring, or if your lawn looks like it is not doing well. A slow-release organic fertilizer is best at this time of year.

▶ Mow often, but not too short. Cut to about 2-1/2 inches high, and frequently enough so you never need to remove more than one-third of the green growth at a time. Bag thick, moist clippings; if left on the lawn they can smother growth beneath them.

Summer

Lawn care in late June, July, and August is much the same as in late spring, with the following exceptions:

▶ Water more frequently during hot, dry weather. The soil needs a 6-inch penetration about every five days. This is especially important if you're growing a rich lawn with more than one or two fertilizer applications a year. In addition, in very hot weather a light sprinkling just after the hottest part of the day, only enough to thoroughly moisten and cool the lawn, can help relieve heat stress.

▶ Mow a bit higher—about 3 inches is ideal. Taller cutting increases the grass's food-producing capacity and encourages deeper, more drought-tolerant roots. It also helps the lawn hold moisture and discourages weeds. You should be able to let the clippings from summer cutting remain, to put nutrients back into the soil.

▶ Spot-spray to keep dandelions and other invasive summer weeds in check.

Fall

Around the first week of September, lawns in most areas of the country begin a new growth spurt after the hard times of summer. Water and mow as in the late spring, and do most seeding, fertilizing, and weed control now. If your lawn needs more than basic maintenance, this is also the time to dethatch or aerate it.

▶ Use patch and fill-in seeding to take care of bare spots and areas where grass is thin.

▶ Fertilize your lawn around mid-September to get the best results. Leaf and stem growth slows in the fall, so the nutrients you add will mainly feed the roots. The type and amount of fertilizer to use depends on your lawn's condition and partly on the severity of winters in your area. Be sure to get advice from local experts.

▶ Attack dandelions and broadleaf weeds if spot-spraying in the summer failed to wipe them out. Apply either a combination weed killer and lawn food or a separate broadleaf herbicide. In areas where crabgrass and other weeds have taken over more than half the surface, spray with a nonselective herbicide. Wait a week or more (as prescribed on the herbicide label), then clear away the dead growth, loosen the soil surface with a garden rake, and sow new seed.

▶ Dethatch your lawn to remove accumulated layers of grass plants and roots if thatch buildup is more than 1/2 inch thick.

▶ Aerate the lawn to promote healthy root growth and prevent thatch buildup. The best time is from late August to mid-September, but aerating at other times can be successful.

Troubleshooting In-ground Sprinklers

An in-ground watering system is a great convenience, but sometimes the pop-up spray heads need adjustment and the nozzles or filters need to be cleaned or replaced. Whether your system has rotor or fixed spray heads, you can do these things yourself. To get replacement parts, you need to know the system brand and model—usually marked on the top of each spray head. If your home or garden center doesn't have parts, look under "Sprinklers, Lawn and Garden" in the Yellow Pages for an irrigation contractor. Most sell parts as well as repair sprinklers.

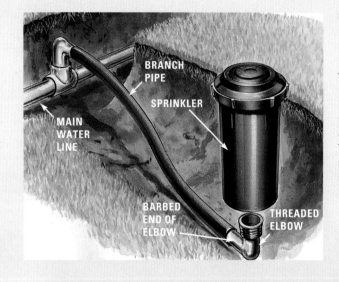

BRANCH PIPE

SPRINKLER

MAIN WATER LINE

BARBED END OF ELBOW

THREADED ELBOW

Replacing a Spray Head. Puddling around a spray head can mean a leak at the elbow or a defective head. Dig a hole to expose the head and elbow, probably about 12 inches down. Unscrew the head from the elbow, then pull the elbow out of its pipe. It has barbs, so you may have to pull hard to get it free, but don't pull the branch pipe out of place or loosen it at the main line. Install a new elbow and screw a new sprinkler head onto it. Do not use pipe dope, plumber's putty, or Teflon tape on the threads or connections. They aren't necessary for a tight seal and they could damage internal parts.

Rotor spray head   Fixed spray head

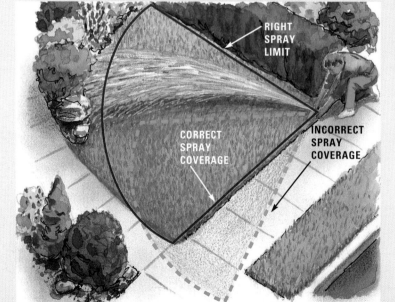

RIGHT SPRAY LIMIT

CORRECT SPRAY COVERAGE

INCORRECT SPRAY COVERAGE

Spray Pattern Adjustment. Put on old clothes or a bathing suit: you'll have to do this with the water on. With a rotor head, stand behind it as it operates and grab the head nut, which is at or just below the ground. Twist it all the way to the right, the 0° position. Then turn it back to the left until the right edge of the spray falls where you want it. Set the left edge limit with the adjusting key as illustrated on the opposite page *(top left)*. With a fixed spray head, simply turn the head nut left or right to position the spray as required.

Rotor Spray Head Adjustments

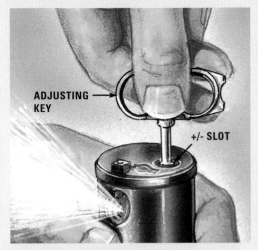

1. Set the left spray limit with the adjusting key. Insert it in the +/- slot and turn in the marked direction to increase or decrease the arc. One 360° turn of the key usually changes the arc sweep 90°.

2. To replace a nozzle, with the system off, insert the adjusting key in the lifting slot and pull the pop-up section up out of the head. Hold onto it and use the key to loosen the set screw in the nozzle adjustment slot.

3. Grab one of the nozzle "ears" with a needle-nose pliers and pull it out. Insert a new nozzle into the spray head—make sure the ears are on top—and reinstall the set screw to secure it.

Fixed Spray Head Adjustments

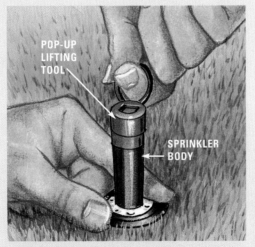

1. To clean or replace the filter in a fixed spray head, turn the system off and use a screwdriver to unscrew and remove the nozzle.

2. Screw the pop-up lifting tool into the nozzle opening. Use the ring on the tool to lift the pop-up sprinkler body out of the spray head.

3. Remove the nylon filter and rinse it clean; use a nylon toothbrush if necessary. Then reinstall it or install a replacement. You can also install a different size nozzle to change the spray coverage and trajectory.

Restoring
a Lawn

*Whether the ravages of weather or neglect
by a previous owner have left your lawn
in the last stages of survival, there's more than
one way you can make it healthy
and beautiful again.*

Choosing Restoration

Like all things in nature, a lawn is a product of its environment. When that includes season after season of hot and cold, torrential rains, and scorching sun—plus human abuse or lack of care—it's no wonder the grass begins to show its age. It gets tired and starts to wither and die.

But you don't have to let the patient expire. Using the proper procedures, you can rebuild your tired lawn and bring it back to a healthy, vibrant condition that is both beautiful to look at and easy to maintain.

To do that, you first need to know the present condition of the soil where your grass is trying to grow. Then you need to choose an appropriate method of restoring it to health.

Soil Condition

Just as turf grows old and needs revitalizing, the soil under it needs some help, too. Perhaps your soil will need nutrients for a new lease on life. To find out, the soil should be tested. You can do basic acid/alkali (pH level) testing yourself with a simple kit (see page 29). But for a thorough analysis, submit samples to your county agricultural extension service or a soil lab recommended by your nursery or garden center. The analysis should include advice about what specific steps to take to get your soil in shape for restoring the lawn.

Restoration Methods

There are four ways to restore a lawn: patching, seeding, plugging, and sodding.

▶ Patching—patch or spot seeding—is suitable when there are large areas that need help scattered throughout your lawn. The basic steps are outlined below; more detailed information is included in Caring for Your Lawn, pages 12–21.

▶ Seeding and plugging are the methods to use when the entire lawn needs renewal from the soil up. Seeding takes the better part of a growing season for the grass to become fully established and plugging takes longer, but each method is economical and requires little work after you have completed the initial stage. Both of these methods are explained on the following pages.

▶ Sodding is by far the most expensive way to restore an entire lawn. It gives immediate results and requires a lot of work at the very beginning, but only ordinary attention from then on. This method is explained in Laying Sod, pages 28–31.

Patching a Lawn

When only small areas of a lawn need to be restored, treat each one as illustrated below.

1. Mow the damaged grass as short as possible to expose the soil beneath.

2. Loosen the top inch of soil thoroughly with a metal rake, then rake it smooth.

3. Scatter grass seeds so they are about 1/8 in. apart throughout the patch.

4. Tamp the area lightly, just enough so the seeds make contact with the soil.

5. Cover with burlap or weed-free straw and keep the area moist until the seed has established itself, usually in two weeks.

Seeding a New Lawn

An excellent method to bring your lawn uniformly to peak condition is to prepare the soil and sow new seed throughout the entire area. There are seven steps in the process leading to the point where only watering and, eventually, mowing are needed. The steps are explained here and illustrated on the opposite page.

Get Rid of Weeds

Killing off weeds is essential in order to restore your lawn. The best method is to spray all weeds with a herbicide prior to turning over the soil *(Figure 1)*. Check the label of the herbicide to determine how far in advance to spray. Most products require at least seven to ten days to work before fertilizer can be applied or grass seeded.

Turn Over the Soil

For seed to take, you must break up the soil, turning under old sod, lawn, or turf—the words mean the same—and flattening uneven peaks and valleys into a level surface *(Figure 2)*. Don't try to do this task by hand; rent a rotary tiller. It will do a better job with far less work.

Begin by cutting the grass very short and removing the clippings. Save the clippings for later use. Then run the rotary tiller over the existing lawn. This may seem like a slow process, but the tiller will break up the grass and turn the soil over at the same time. It may take a number of passes to do the job properly. Go over the entire area from one direction, then again from another angle, and another until the soil is level and uniformly broken into 3- to 4-inch clumps.

Now spread the grass clippings from the short cutting and use the tiller to mix them into the soil, adding their natural nutrients. This is also the time to add other nutrients, as determined by your soil test results.

Add Topsoil

This step can make the difference between a lackluster new lawn and a green, healthy one. A layer of black dirt will provide excellent topsoil for the seed to sprout and take root *(Figure 3)*. Spread the dirt over the entire area. You can do this alone, but having a helper will save time. One person can haul and dump the dirt while the other spreads it in a layer of uniform thickness.

The amount of topsoil you need depends both on the size of the area and on how thick the layer will be. Check with the nursery where you buy the dirt or peat to determine how much you will need.

Whatever you have to pay for topsoil, having it delivered can double the cost. If you are willing to do some work, you can save a good deal by renting a trailer and hauling it yourself.

Mix the Growing Layer

Use a metal garden rake to mix the topsoil into the tilled soil underneath *(Figure 4)*. Don't bury the topsoil; make a uniform mixture. Then give the soil a light watering, so the seed will hold on to it.

Sow the Seed

When the hard work is done, you can spread the grass seed *(Figure 5)*. Use a drop spreader for even distribution, and follow the directions on the package for the recommended spreader setting. Don't sow the seed too thick; new seeds need room to take root. Too much seed in one area will thrive for a few weeks, but then will start to thin as the seedlings compete for space.

To avoid waste, and perhaps seeding your neighbor's lawn too, avoid sowing grass seed on a windy day. Even with moist soil, there's a good chance the seed will be blown about by the wind, losing some and causing uneven coverage and growth density.

Work the Seed into the Soil

You need to work the seeds into the soil so they can take root *(Figure 6)*. Turn over a leaf rake and use a light raking motion with the backs of the flexible tines to mix the seed into the layer of topsoil.

Cover the Surface

Spread a shallow layer of weed-free straw over the entire seeded area *(Figure 7)*. The straw will help hold the seed in place and keep the soil moist after each watering.

Final Stages: Watering and Mowing

Water, water, and water the straw-covered lawn to keep it moist. You may be watering two, three, or even four times a day in hot, sunny weather. Have the sprinkler cover as much area as possible in each position, to eliminate walking on the new seedlings.

Although it may look a bit shaggy as it comes up, don't mow the new grass until it's at least 2 inches high. Before the first mowing, gently rake out the straw you put down earlier. In subsequent mowings throughout its first season, leave the grass on the long side to help it establish strong roots.

1

Get rid of weeds by spraying with a herbicide, usually seven to ten days before turning the soil. Check the herbicide label for instructions about dilution and application.

2

Turn over the soil after cutting the existing grass very short. Make passes from different directions with a rotary tiller to break the earth into 3- to 4-in. clumps.

3

Add topsoil—either black dirt or peat—before sowing grass seed. Dump wheelbarrow loads at intervals and spread the topsoil in a layer of uniform thickness.

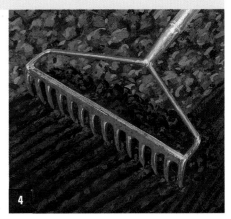

4

Mix the growing layer by raking the topsoil into the tilled soil. Use a metal-head garden rake and remove twigs, branches, and stones as you work. Then water lightly.

5

Sow the seed using a drop spreader. Work in a crisscross pattern to ensure complete coverage. Check the seed package for the spreader setting, and work on a calm day.

6

Work the seed into the soil with a leaf rake turned so the tines point upward. Use a light raking motion to mix the seeds just below the surface of the growing layer.

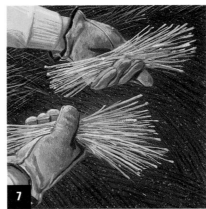

7

Cover the surface with weed-free straw to keep seeds from blowing away and to hold moisture. Water after covering and keep the area moist during the initial growing period.

Plugging a Lawn

Planting a lawn by inserting plugs of growing grass and letting them grow together is a method that originated in southern climates but is equally usable in the north. Many nurseries and large garden centers sell grass plugs, or flats of grass suitable for cutting your own plugs.

There are two major stages in plugging a lawn, planting and growing. The planting stage includes preparing the area and inserting the plugs into the soil. The growing stage includes watering, fertilizing, and caring for the plugs to get them well established.

Cut the Lawn Short

Set your mower to cut the existing grass very short, just 1 to 1-1/2 inches high *(Figure 1)*. Bag clippings as you mow. Clippings will interfere with cutting holes for the plugs, and long grass would compete with them as their roots take hold.

The day before installing the plugs, soak the area you intend to plant with a thorough watering. It may take two or three days to plug an entire large lawn.

Dig Plug Pits

Use a plugger or auger to dig pits—holes—for the plugs *(Figure 2)*. Most outlets that sell grass plugs also sell or rent a plugger. This is a kind of cylinder-spade with a long handle and a crossbar. You step on the bar to drive the cylinder into the soil. Apply even pressure; don't jump on the crossbar. If you meet resistance, rotate the handle back and forth to twist the cutter as you push it down. Then lift up, removing a plug of dirt. A plugger with a push-rod ejector to empty the cutting cylinder makes the work go faster.

Cut pits 3 inches deep, spaced about 12 inches apart. The spacing can vary, depending on the type of grass plug. Check with the supplier. Break the work into stages: Cut pits in one area several feet square, plant plugs in them, then go on to the next area.

Fertilize and Plant

Most plugs need a starter fertilizer, available where you buy the plugs. Put about 1 teaspoon of fertilizer into a hole and then insert the grass plug *(Figure 3)*. Make sure the plug is even with the existing lawn. Press it in firmly around the edges. If you are cutting your own plugs from flats, do so just before planting, using the plugger.

Cut the lawn short to prepare for plugging. It should be only 1 to 1-1/2 in. high so you can plant easily. The day before starting, thoroughly water the area to be planted.

Dig plug pits with a plugger/auger. Step on the crossbar to drive it into the ground, then twist and lift up. Space holes about 12 in. apart, or closer for faster fill-in.

Fertilize and plant in the holes one by one. Add 1 teaspoon of starter fertilizer, then insert the plug. Press the edges to get the plug level with the surrounding lawn.

Check the Checkerboard

Just after plugging, your yard will look like a giant checkerboard dotted with tufts of grass *(Figure 4)*. This will gradually disappear as the plugs send out shoots and runners and fill in the gaps. How long that takes depends on the spacing and on the care you give the lawn as it grows. You can shorten the time a bit by planting plugs at intervals of less than about 12 inches, but be sure not to get them closer than the minimum distance recommended by the nursery. In any case, it can take from one to four years before the checkerboarding is no longer noticeable.

Your main concern is to check that the growth proceeds evenly and to make sure that the lawn is properly watered and fertilized. Give extra attention to any spots that grow more slowly or weakly than others.

Water the Plugs

As soon as the plugs are in, divide the lawn into sections of the size that your sprinkler can cover, allowing for a slight overlap to avoid dry strips between *(Figure 5)*. Water each section every day for approximately 45 minutes at a time if you have a sprinkling system, or 1 to 1-1/2 hours if you use a hose and sprinkler (see page 16).

Follow these watering recommendations for about two weeks. After that, the roots usually are established and you can reduce watering time to the level suitable for the time of year or weather conditions.

Feed the Plugs

Fertilize the new plugs and the existing lawn with a high-quality lawn food every six to eight weeks. Use a drop spreader *(Figure 6)*, or a cyclone spreader with whirling vanes to throw the fertilizer in a circular pattern as you push it.

Once the plugs are established and the gaps between them have filled in, maintain the grass like a normal lawn.

PLUGGING A LAWN: GROWING STAGE

4

Check the checkerboard pattern of plug tufts for uniform growth every time you water. Give extra attention to spots that are filling in more slowly than the others.

5

Water the plugs right after planting and regularly thereafter. Water all sections 45 minutes with a sprinkling system or 1 to 1-1/2 hours with a hose and sprinkler.

6

Feed the plugs and the lawn with fertilizer. Use either a drop spreader *(above)* or cyclone spreader to apply the lawn food recommended for the plugs planted.

Laying *Sod*

Sod provides an "instant" lawn. You don't have to wait weeks for a lush carpet of grass to grow; it's there as soon as you finish the job. Laying sod is strenuous work, but not difficult. Here's how to do it the right way.

Preparing for Sod

With proper preparation, laying sod is the fastest way to get a new lawn. It costs about three times more than seeding or plugging (see pages 24–27), but you have a great-looking lawn immediately.

The recommended time to lay sod is early spring or late fall. Either season allows for strong root growth, so the roots can get established firmly in the soil before hot summer sun or winter ice can damage them. This helps ensure the continued health and good looks of your lawn.

Spring or fall, the first things you must see to are soil testing, collecting tools and materials, and surveying the site. You'll also have to plan for ordering sod once you have actually prepared the soil. These preliminary concerns are discussed here. How to lay the sod is explained on pages 30–31.

Soil Testing

To protect the investment you will make in sod, check the soil in your yard. Dig some random soil samples and have them tested for their pH level. The pH indicates whether the soil is sweet (alkaline) or sour (acid), and those conditions affect how well grass will grow. Most county extension services will make a pH test for a small fee, but you can do it yourself with an inexpensive kit, available at your local hardware store or nursery.

The pH scale ranges from 0 to 14; pH 7 is the neutral point. Most lawns do best when the soil pH is between 6.5 and 7. For starting sod, pH 6.5 is a good level. If the pH is lower than that, the soil is overly acidic and you should add ground limestone (gardening lime), which is alkaline, to raise the pH. If the pH is higher than 6.5 or 7, the soil is alkaline and you need to add powdered (dusting) sulfur, which is acidic, to lower it.

You can get lime and sulfur at nurseries and garden centers. The amount to add depends on the pH of the soil and the square footage to be sodded. Use the chart on page 30 to determine how much to add to your soil. The best time to adjust the pH is when you're adding topsoil.

Tools and Materials

You'll need a metal garden rake, a utility knife, a hammer, and some heavy work gloves and work boots. You'll also need two pieces of equipment: a gas-powered rotary tiller to turn under the old grass and to work topsoil and lime or sulfur into the dirt, and a drum roller to flatten or tamp the sod into place once it has been laid. You can rent the equipment.

For materials, in addition to sod, you'll need topsoil and some starter fertilizer. If there are any hills or slopes to be sodded, you'll need some short wood stakes to secure the sod on the hill until the roots take hold. Buy topsoil instead of black dirt. It is pulverized and virtually free of clumps, so you'll spend less time tilling it into the old soil. Black dirt has clumps and takes longer to work in.

Surveying the Site

Measure the dimensions of the area you will be sodding in order to work out the total square footage involved. You need this figure to order the proper amounts of topsoil, lime or sulfur, starter fertilizer, and sod.

If you have an in-ground sprinkler system, note the location of the pipes and spray heads. And check with your local utility companies (gas, electric, telephone, cable TV) for any underground wires, pipes, or cables. You won't be tilling deeper than 5 or 6 inches, but it's best to be safe. Most utility companies mark the locations at no charge.

Ordering Sod

Your nursery or garden supplier can recommend the best species of sod for your region, and tell you how much you will need. Sod is sold by the roll or "yard"—a roll covers an area equal to 1 square yard (9 square feet), and often measures 18 inches by 6 feet.

Before ordering, check that the sod will be freshly cut, and don't buy it too early. Plan to pick the sod up or have it delivered the day you will start laying it. Rolled-up sod won't last for more than a couple of days. You'll need to keep the rolls moist by misting them with a garden hose, especially if you can't get them all laid in a day.

When you do receive the sod, don't take it if it's dry, wilted, or yellowed—all signs that it is not freshly cut. Unroll a couple of rolls to check before accepting the order.

Adjusting Soil pH

Soil that is too acidic or too alkaline inhibits growth and can even kill plants and grasses. A recommended level for laying sod is pH 6.5. If a soil test (page 29) shows that your soil has a higher or lower pH, you can adjust it by adding ground limestone or powdered sulfur. The amounts to add per 100 per square feet of sandy or clay soil are given below. For ordinary soil—loam—add an amount midway between those shown for each pH.

To raise tested soil pH to 6.5

Soil pH	Lbs. of ground limestone per 100 sq. ft.	
	Sandy Soil	Clay Soil
5.5	2-1/2	5
5.0	5	7-1/2
4.5	8	10

To lower tested soil pH to 6.5

Soil pH	Lbs. of powdered sulfur per 100 sq. ft.	
	Sandy Soil	Clay Soil
7.5	1	2
8.0	2-1/2	3-1/2
8.5	3	4

Sod-laying Procedures

There are six steps to laying sod. Each step is described below and is illustrated in the photographs on the opposite page.

Turn Under the Old Sod

Using a rotary tiller, make several passes in a crisscross pattern to chop up the turf and turn over the soil *(Photo 1)*. Once the sod and soil are thoroughly mixed, add the topsoil and pH amendments—lime or sulfur, as required—and work them in with the tiller. Keep tilling until the soil is completely free of clumps.

Smooth the Tilled Soil

Use a metal garden rake to get the soil as smooth as possible *(Photo 2)*. If the bed is uneven, you'll end up with a bumpy lawn. This is the time to change the slope or grade of the land, if desired. When the bed is smooth, spread lawn starter fertilizer on top of the soil. This will stimulate rapid growth of the grass roots.

Lay the New Sod

Put down one roll, then butt the next roll tightly against it to minimize the seam *(Photo 3)*. Continue in this way, cutting some rolls short so the end seams in adjacent rolls are staggered, as in a brick wall. Staggered seams reduce erosion and runoff. Use a utility knife to cut the sod.

Lay Patches as Needed

You'll have to lay sod patches to fill along a driveway or sidewalk, and around trees and other landscape elements. Do this after laying full-width rolls. Cut the smaller pieces to fit as needed *(Photo 4)*.

Roll the New Sod

Use a drum roller to seat the sod on its bed the same day that it's laid *(Photo 5)*. Don't fill the roller's drum with water; that would be too heavy and could damage the sod. The empty weight is enough to push the sod firmly onto the topsoil so the roots will grow well.

Stake Sod on Slopes

Drive 6- to 8-inch long 1x2 stakes into any sod on a slope or hill to hold it in place until the roots can take hold—about two weeks. A stake at each end of a roll and one in the middle is enough *(Photo 6)*.

When the sod is all laid, water it repeatedly—you can't overwater new sod. Stay off the lawn for at least three weeks. Walking on new sod will create depressions, weaken the root structure, and slow root growth. And wait four to six weeks before mowing for the first time. When you do mow, don't cut more than one third of the grass blade length at a time. Cutting too much at once stresses the grass and the roots.

Turn under the old sod with a rotary tiller and mix it with the soil below to a depth of 5 or 6 in. Then mix in topsoil, and lime or sulfur if needed.

Smooth the tilled soil with a garden rake to eliminate all lumps and valleys. Do any necessary grading at this time, then spread on lawn starter fertilizer.

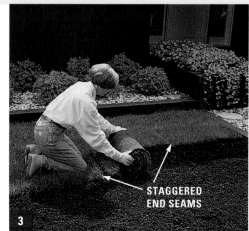

Lay the new sod one roll at a time. Butt each roll tightly against the sod already in place. Cut some rolls in half so you can lay staggered end seams.

Lay patches to bring sod neatly up to a driveway, sidewalk, flower bed, or other landscape element. Cut patches to size and shape with a utility knife.

Roll the new sod to ensure firm contact between its dirt base and the topsoil below. An empty drum roller is heavy enough; you don't need to fill it with water.

Stake sod on slopes. Drive stakes so the sod won't slide or creep downhill. Don't overdo it—two or three stakes are enough. Remove the stakes after about two weeks.

Alternatives
to Grass

The beauty of wildflowers and lush native grasses can completely change the character of a yard. In addition, they don't require the time-consuming maintenance that lawn grass demands. Here are some great options to consider.

Your Own Kind of Yard

Just because everyone else has one is no reason to lock yourself into the perpetual care that a standard-issue, regulation green grass lawn requires. There are a number of alternatives that will give your home a character and beauty unlike any other in your neighborhood.

It's not necessary to replace your grass lawn completely. But changing portions of it will reduce the amount of maintenance you have to provide. And combining different kinds of landscaping will give your yard attractive variety and interest.

For example, if you want to reduce but not completely eliminate the area devoted to grass, you could put down one or more walkways to various points in the yard (see Laying a Flagstone Footpath, pages 110–113). Or you could convert a section to a water garden (see pages 56–62).

To change larger areas, consider replacing the grass with other plantings (see Growing Ground Covers, pages 69–72). That's the kind of alternative considered here.

These pages tell you how to create a great-looking yard with minimal time and effort using native grasses and wildflowers. Every area of the country has wildflowers, native grasses (called prairie and ornamental grasses), and green ground covers (shrubs and leafy plants) that are beautiful alternatives to golf-course green grass.

These plants are colorful, easy to maintain, and—more important—use less water, because they adjust their needs to match the amount of rainfall. When things get really dry, they adapt and survive, and generally bounce back once the dry spell ends.

Large or small, at a summer home or year-round residence, shrubs, wildflowers, and native or ornamental grasses can combine to add texture and color in an attractive alternative to a traditional-looking yard.

Advantages of a Yard without a Lawn

There are many reasons you might want to consider wildflowers and native grasses as alternative yard covers. Here are some of the most important:

▶ Every yard has an area or two that is difficult to maintain—for example, a steep hill or a narrow strip between the sidewalk and driveway or the sidewalk and the street.

▶ Growing grass under trees can be hopeless, especially if the trees are pines. The dense shade and high acidity of the soil—indicated by the tested pH level (see page 29)—make it impossible to grow good-looking grass in these spots.

▶ Wildflowers, with their variety of colors and shapes, let you personalize your yard. Those shown on the opposite page and on page 36 are just a few examples. Check with a local nursery to identify the wildflowers that will grow well in your area.

▶ Yard maintenance time is cut enormously, because native plantings usually need nothing more than a springtime cleanup and periodic weeding. Only non-native or cultured grasses and plants that have not adapted to your region need constant care.

▶ Natural plantings use whatever amount of water nature provides. Not having to supply additional water means a lower water bill and less demand on your spare time.

▶ Overall maintenance expense is about one-quarter of that for a grass lawn. The initial investment in plants is usually all you will have to spend.

Ornamental and native grasses offer a wide variety of textures and colors, especially when left to grow to their full height and "ripen" to the seed-producing stage.

Shrubs and low ground covers are especially effective on hills and slopes, because they eliminate the need for mowing. The varying heights of the shrubs and the different shades of green make an attractive landscape.

Some Drawbacks of a Natural Yard

There are some potential disadvantages to consider before deciding to create a natural yard. They include:

▶ The initial cost can be considerable; it may be as much as $3,000 to $5,000 for even an average-size yard, depending on the plantings you choose.

▶ Your yard won't be covered with colorful flowers and lush grasses right away. It can take two to three years for the plants to establish themselves, fill in, and then look good. You'll have to weed during this initial period, to promote growth. Once the plants are established, however, you can take cuttings from existing plants and use them to fill any gaps. You can also divide ornamental grasses every two or three years to get more plants.

Blossom shapes and sizes are as diverse as the colors of wildflowers.

Wildflowers come in hundreds of varieties, each with striking blossoms and colors. This is *Linaria maroccana,* commonly known as toadflax.

The brilliant yellow petals and dark centers of rudbeckia are very attractive to birds. This perennial is very easy to grow.

▶ You won't want to eliminate all the grass in your yard. Wildflowers and shrubs won't stand up too well to your children's neighborhood soccer games and similar hard use. However, natural plantings and lawns can work well together.

▶ There may be local restrictions on the use of native plants of certain species, especially those that spread freely or produce unusual types or amounts of pollen, spores, or seed pods. So before starting, check with your city planning or zoning department about restrictions on native plantings.

▶ Finally, neighbors may be surprised and register some objections if they see you changing the character of your property but don't know what you are doing. Every homeowner is touchy about conditions that may affect the value of his or her property. To avoid misunderstanding, inform your neighbors about your intentions, show them pictures of what you intend to plant, and stress the beauty you will be adding to the neighborhood—at no expense to them.

What to Use and Where to Use It

Every yard has sunny and shady areas. You shouldn't try to plant the same things in both areas—they won't do well everywhere. Here's what works best in each area.

Sunny Areas

Where there is sun all or most of the day, you have plenty of choices, including:

Native grasses and wildflowers. The grasses that are native to your region will do well. In the Midwest they are commonly called prairie grasses, but there are native grasses in all areas. Some varieties are mentioned below.

The flowers that grow wild in your region are the ones that will survive almost everything. Since there are literally hundreds of species of wildflowers, it is impractical to give specific recommendations here. Instead, visit a nursery or consult a local horticultural group for advice on varieties that grow well in your area. Make sure the varieties you choose are sun-tolerant.

Buffalo grasses. There are a number of varieties, but all buffalo grasses are considered both sun- and drought-tolerant. They are extremely tough and do well almost everywhere.

Ornamental grasses. Some non-native grasses are very colorful and graceful. Your local nursery can tell you which ones will do well where you live. Typical examples of ornamental grasses are fountain grass and Japanese silver grass. Some grasses are invasive, so you may need to pull up unwanted seedlings to keep things in line.

Vines. As long as they don't have supports such as fences and trees to climb, many vines will trail along the ground. They make excellent ground cover and can help control soil erosion on banks and steep slopes.

Shrubs. Massing shrubs—planting them in small or large groups—is an excellent way to accent a path or patio. Most shrubs are low-maintenance plants that require only periodic trimming. Group them in islands with mulch or ground cover underneath to cut maintenance even more.

The cape marigold is a drought-hardy flower that will thrive in any soil.

Despite what its name implies, evening primrose thrives in full sun. Its vibrant color can range from pink to yellow.

Shady Areas

The parts of a yard that get little sun are generally more troublesome than sunny areas. Many varieties of plants will do well there, but advice from a nursery is especially valuable, because local conditions have a great effect on shade-growing plants. Some choices to consider are:

Perennials. Shade-tolerant varieties of leafy and flowering plants that come up year after year are an excellent choice. Leafy plants are perfect for adding texture, and they require little maintenance. Ferns and woodland wildflowers are also good choices for shady locations.

Moss. The wide range of rich greens and different textures available in mosses offer a chance for striking beauty and contrast in shady areas. A carpet of moss requires moist, well-drained acid soil, but moss is a low-maintenance ground cover if you have the growing conditions it needs.

Shrubs. Many varieties of shrubs have great shade tolerance. They are especially effective when massed in groups of different size. Native shrubs grow best, especially in shade.

The slender grace of variegated oat grass is accentuated by the dark green stripe down the center of each long blade. This native grass tolerates dry soil well.

Getting Rid of Grass

You can't just dig holes in a grass lawn to add natural plantings, and simply turning the grass over at a shallow depth is not enough. The grass will just take root again and compete with the new plants—and often win. However, the following four methods are virtually sure to get rid of grass permanently.

Dig It Up

Go to work digging up the sod and getting rid of it. This is the quickest, but also the most expensive, method. There's the cost of renting the equipment to strip the sod if you do the work, or the additional cost of paying someone else to do it. The most difficult part, however, may be disposing of the sod: most landfills won't accept it. You can compost sod by stacking it in grass-to-grass layers and letting it sit for a couple of years.

Use Chemicals

This method is less expensive than the dig-and-dispose approach, but not as quick. You spray the grass you want killed twice with a vegetation-killing herbicide such as Round-Up, then wait seven to ten days. If any grass survives, spray those spots again. Wait two weeks, then turn the dead grass into the soil with a rotary tiller, which you can rent.

When you till the soil, work in soil additives or nutrients. Have the soil tested by a soil lab or county extension service to determine what to add and how much. Then you'll be ready to plant.

Bury It Deep

This is very labor intensive, but also very cheap. Don't bother to kill the grass with chemicals. Instead, dig troughs about 10 inches deep at intervals across the lawn and turn over the soil and sod into them. Burying grass that deep deprives the entire plant—blades and roots—of sunlight so it won't take root.

Cover It and Wait

In this method, you cover the grass with black, 6-mil polyethylene film and wait for at least two months. That's cheap and easy, but slow. With no sunlight, the grass dies. When it has expired, turn it under with a rotary tiller, adding to the soil if needed, as described for the chemical method above.

Beautiful *Gardens*

Planting Flowering Bulbs

From earliest spring until late fall, various species of bulbs can keep your garden alive with color. They're easy to plant and grow, and will bloom for you year after year.

40

Planting Roses

A rainbow of colors in a wide range of types—bushes, climbers, trees—make roses the gardener's favorite flowering shrubs. Proper planting and care ensure rich blossoms and long life.

50

Creating a Water Garden

A pond brimming with water plants and goldfish—perhaps even a fountain or waterfall—can be a unique landscaping feature. Adding such a water garden to your yard is a fascinating project.

56

Container Gardening

For a "movable garden," plant flowers and shrubs in containers. That way you can have plants anyplace—yard, patio, porch, or deck—and rearrange them freely throughout the year.

63

Growing Ground Covers

Low-growing plants can provide a carpet of blossoms during part of the year, and a rich profusion of green at other times. There are varieties suitable for all kinds of conditions and terrain.

69

Drip Watering System

Make thorough, properly timed garden watering a sure thing—install a drip watering system with a timer. It's easy and inexpensive to do. Start with a simple system and add on as needed.

73

Planting
Flowering Bulbs

*Bulbs produce the earliest blossoms
of the spring, often before all the snow is gone.
They also produce beautiful blooms later
in the season—and year after year as well,
because they are perennials. Those are all
good reasons to make these easy-to-grow
flowers a feature of your garden.*

Beautiful, Versatile Bulbs

Bulbs are outstanding for the great variety of beauty, sizes, and blossom shapes of the flowers they produce. Few plants equal some species of bulbs for hardiness, longevity, ease of growing, and low maintenance. It's no wonder that bulbs are the delight of most gardeners as well as the outstanding feature of many gardens.

A bulb is a kind of underground bud that looks somewhat like an onion or head of garlic. When planted, it develops roots from its wide base end and sends shoots up through the surface of the soil, which develop into stems, leaves, and blossoms as the plant matures. Among the best-known flowers that grow from bulbs are tulips, daffodils, hyacinths, narcissus, and lilies, but there are many, many more.

Several other species of flowers grow from underground bulblike forms called corms, tubers, tuberous roots, and rhizomes. Because they are planted and grow pretty much as bulbs do, they are commonly included when speaking of bulb gardening. Among the flowers produced by these bulb relatives are crocus, gladiolus, some varieties of iris, and dahlias.

Selecting a Site

You can grow bulbs in a bed of their own, mixed with other kinds of flowers, or among ground covers or grass—a technique called "naturalizing." All of these approaches are shown on the following pages.

However you choose to plant them, bulbs grow best in a sunny or partially shaded location. When picking a spot, remember that in the springtime, when many bulbs bloom, trees may not have leafed out. So an area that is typically shaded in the summer could very well be sunny in the spring.

Locate a bulb bed next to a fence, near a house, or along a sidewalk. You can plant on level or sloped ground, or in a raised bed.

When choosing a site, here are some considerations to keep in mind:
- Soil must be well drained. Bulbs will rot if they sit in too much moisture. If necessary, lighten the soil for better drainage by mixing in organic matter.
- Keep bulbs at least 2 feet away from the foundation of a house or other structure. Those planted too close may be flooded by rainwater dripping off a roof. Or if the structure has wide overhangs, the bulbs may not get enough moisture when it rains.
- Take into account the spacing required between bulbs to allow for full growth. Different species need different spacing. The size of the area will determine how many bulbs you can plant, or the number you want to plant will dictate how big an area you need to prepare.
- If you choose a site in the middle of your yard, plan to plant a circular grouping with the tall-growing flowers in the center. To see how to plan bulb distribution in beds of any shape, see pages 42–43.

Buying Bulbs

It is important to choose bulbs suited to your location. For example, in warm climates hardy bulbs may not get the cold winter dormancy they need. Research varieties you can grow well before making any choices.

You can buy bulbs from a local nursery or garden center, or by mail from major suppliers. Bulbs are often put on sale, so you can save money with some careful planning and shopping. However, a cheap bulb is no bargain if it never blooms.

Whatever the price, look for strong, healthy bulbs—the larger the better. They should feel heavy, not light or dried out, and firm when squeezed gently. And they should be free of nicks, soft spots, and decay. (A light surface mold, which can develop when a bulb is stored, is common and does not harm it.) Any bulbs that do not pass inspection should be returned to your supplier.

For added insurance, buy from a reputable source that promises replacement or a refund if the bulbs don't grow and produce flowers in their first season.

Designing a Border Garden

There are many different ways to use bulbs in your garden. You can intermix them with other kinds of flowering plants, or you can plant several different kinds of bulbs together in a bed, or group beds to form a distinct floral area. Grouping beds is the approach in the garden design explained here.

The flowers shown below are part of an all-bulb border garden that is 8 feet long and 4 feet from front to back. The brightly colored flowers, which bloom in mid-spring year after year, are jonquils, two kinds of brightly colored tulips, two kinds of hyacinths, and jumbo crocuses.

The plan of this garden is shown in the diagram on the opposite page. It uses the taller flowers as background and framing elements. The yellow jonquils are in the rear, against the fence. Apricot Beauty tulips are grouped at the left side, Red Emperor tulips at the right side. Medium-height Blue Jacket hyacinths are in the center, between the tulips. The front row has the shortest flowers: Blue Grape hyacinths at each end of a long bed of jumbo crocus.

To give you an idea of how many bulbs are needed for a garden this size, the garden plan lists the number of bulbs of each variety, their spacing, and the planting depth. You'll find step-by-step instructions for planting bulbs successfully on page 44.

Developing Your Plan

You can use the principles shown in this border garden plan to develop a different design of your own. On graph paper, mark out the size and shape of your beds at a convenient scale, say, 1 inch equal to 1 foot.

Mark dots to show the placement of the bulbs, with their required spacing. That makes it easy to count how many bulbs you need in each section, so you can make up a buying list. To get an idea of the color massing in your plan, mark the dots in colors you intend to plant, or mark the dots in black and color in their section on the plan.

This all-bulb border garden was planted from the plan on the opposite page.

Plan for a Border Garden

Bulbs

	Carlton Jonquil	Blue Jacket Hyacinth	Jumbo Crocus	Apricot Beauty Tulip	Red Emperor Tulip	Blue Grape Hyacinth
No. of Bulbs	40	20	40	15	15	40
Spacing	6 inches	6 inches	3 inches	6 inches	6 inches	3 inches
Depth	6 inches	6 inches	3 inches	6 inches	6 inches	3 inches

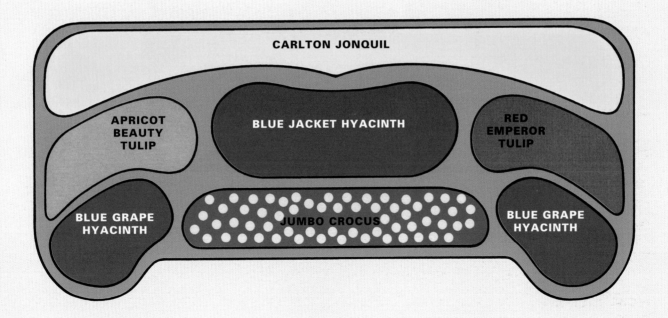

Planting Bulbs

Bulbs that bloom in early to mid-spring are hardy and can be planted in the fall, before the first hard frost. In areas where winters are mild, you can plant as long as the soil is workable. Late-spring and summer-blooming bulbs are tender and can be damaged or killed by frost. Plant them after the last frost in spring. Use the table on pages 46–47 to help you choose bulbs for the seasons in which you want blooms, and to determine when and how deep to plant them. Here are the steps for planting the bulbs:

First, dig up the entire flower bed to a depth of at least 12 inches to loosen the soil (Photo 1). If the soil is heavy and doesn't drain well, add organic matter such as peat moss to lighten it. In clayey soil, also mix in some sand.

Second, spread general-purpose bulb food over the bed and work it into the soil (Photo 2). Use a three-pronged hand rake or a garden trowel. Follow the instructions on the package.

Third, dig holes in a random pattern, not in rows, and place a bulb in each hole (Photo 3). Place each bulb pointed end up. Make sure the holes have the proper depth and spacing.

Finally, fill each hole with dirt and tamp down the soil (Photo 4). Water immediately, and as necessary until the first fall freeze. Then cover the area with 3 to 4 inches of noncompacting mulch such as shredded leaves. For spring planting, mulch is not necessary.

Planting Tip

For a freer, more natural look, space bulbs randomly, not in aligned rows. This will help to create a mass color effect while making each blossom individually visible.

1

Dig up the entire bed to loosen the soil to a depth of at least 12 in. Add organic matter to heavy, poorly drained soil, and add sand as well to clayey soil.

2

Spread bulb food over the bed and work it into the soil with a hand rake or garden trowel. Apply as recommended by the manufacturer.

3

Dig holes of the required depth and spacing and plant the bulbs. The pointed end of the bulb must be at the top. Seat the bulbs firmly in the soil under them.

4

Fill each hole with dirt. Tamp the soil lightly, then water immediately. Keep watered during early growth and dry spells. Cover with mulch after the first fall freeze.

Growing Bulbs

When the weather begins to warm in the spring and the first shoots are visible, gently remove any mulch from the bed. Rake the surface to break it up a bit, sprinkle bulb fertilizer over the bed, and water immediately to help carry the fertilizer into the soil. Spring rains and melting snows may provide early irrigation, but the bulbs need plenty of water as they begin to grow each season.

Most hardy bulbs need relatively little attention during the growing season. Remove weeds by hand or with a hoe as soon as they appear. During prolonged dry spells in spring and summer, water thoroughly to improve growth. When the plants are in bloom, water around the base rather than from above to avoid damaging the blossoms. A drip watering system (pages 73–75) provides excellent results. Continue watering in dry spells even after the flowers have faded. The growing cycle does not end until the leaves turn yellow and die.

If you are growing gladioli or similar flowers for cutting in the summer, you'll grow larger flowers by feeding the bulbs liquid fertilizer every three weeks after the buds form and until they open. For the best way to treat cut flowers, see page 49.

The blossom stems produced by most bulbs do not need support if the bulbs have been planted deep enough. But in a windy, exposed location tall varieties of hyacinths, gladioli, alliums, and dahlias may need support. Use bamboo or other canes, and loosely tie the stalks to them with raffia or strips of soft cloth. To support gladioli grown in rows for cutting, insert stakes at the front and back at both ends of each row and tie strong string tautly between the stakes.

After the blooms have faded, cut or snap them off to prevent seed production, which diminishes the bulbs' ability to produce blooms for the following year. This is called deadheading. Leave the foliage alone, however; do not knot or otherwise tie the leaves together. The plant needs the maximum amount of leaf surface exposed to the sun to continue providing nourishment to the bulb so it will produce strong growth the next year. When the leaves have yellowed and dried, you can remove them when they come free as you gently pull up on each one. If you have to tug to pull a leaf from the plant, it's too soon.

Each fall, tender bulbs can be "lifted": dug up, dried, and kept in a cool, dark place for replanting next spring. Ask your garden center about the best lifting procedures for the kind of tender bulbs you have planted. To get hardy bulbs through the winter, treat the bed with a general-purpose bulb food and spread mulch (see sidebar at right) after the ground freezes. (For more details, see Mulching Your Garden, pages 101–107.)

If you find as your garden ages that it produces fewer blooms, the bulbs are probably crowded and need dividing. Dig them up and replant only the larger ones. Throw away the small bulbs.

Making No-cost Mulch

Various materials are sold as mulch, including salt hay, straw, peat moss, buckwheat hulls, or pine needles. But if you have leaf-bearing trees in your yard, you have a source of mulch that will cost you nothing.

Chopped leaves make excellent mulch. Rake small piles in front of a sheet of plywood you have propped up as shown above.

Run your rotary mower onto or through the pile, shooting the bits against the plywood. Then shovel them up and spread them on your garden beds. Wear eye protection and keep the area free of people and pets when you run the mower. If you end up with more than you need, put the leftovers in your compost pile.

Planting Popular Bulbs, Corms, and Tubers

Flowers are listed by popular names; Latin names are given to distinguish varieties when helpful. In warm climates, flowers appear in the earlier of the two blooming seasons listed. In cold climates, bulbs usually should be planted in the earlier season listed, but always check with a local supplier; planting conditions differ widely, and instructions included with packaged bulbs are usually for average mid-U.S.A. temperatures, sun, and rainfall. For plant spacing, see the note at the end of the table.

NAME	BLOOMS IN	PLANTING Depth (in.)	Season
African corn lily (Ixia)	Late spring/Early summer	5	Early fall
Allium, Ornamental onion	Early summer	8	Early/mid-fall
Amaryllis	Early/mid-fall	8	Mid/late summer
Anemone, Windflower	Late winter/Midsummer	5	Mid-fall
Angel's tears (see Dwarf narcissus)			
Autumn crocus (Colchicum)	Fall	5	Late summer
Begonia	Midsummer/Fall	2	Spring
Bluebell, Spanish	Late spring	5	Early fall
Buttercup (Ranunculus)	Winter/Early spring/ Early summer	5	Late fall Early spring
Calla lily	Early/midsummer	8	Spring
Camassia	Late spring	6	Early/mid-fall
Crocus, various	Winter/Spring/Fall	5	Summer/Fall
Cyclamen, hardy	Midwinter/Mid-spring	5	Mid/late summer
Daffodil (see Narcissus)			
Dahlia	Mid/late summer	6–8	Mid/late spring
Dwarf narcissus (Angel's tears)	Late winter/Mid-spring	5x bulb size	Early/mid-fall
Fritillaria/Guinea-hen flower	Mid/late spring	8	Mid-fall
Gladiolus: Cold areas Warm areas	Summer Spring/Summer/Fall	5 5	Spring Spring/Summer
Gloriosa/Glory-lily	Early spring	5	Spring
Glory of the Snow (Chinodoxa)	Mid-spring	5	Early fall
Grape hyacinth (Muscari)	Mid/late spring	5	Early/late fall
Harlequin flower/Wandflower	Fall	5	Mid-fall
Hyacinth: Large-flowered, Dutch, Roman	Early/late spring	8	Mid-fall

NAME	BLOOMS IN	PLANTING Depth (in.)	Season
Iris, bulbous:			
Juno	Mid-spring	4	Early fall
Dutch, Spanish	Early spring/Midsummer	2 1/2–4	Mid-fall
English	Early/midsummer	6	Early fall
Jonquil (*see* Narcissus)			
Lycoris	Late summer/Early fall	5	Midsummer
Narcissus: Trumpet/Daffodil, Large/small-cup, Jonquil	Early/late spring	8	Mid/late fall
Oxalis	Late spring/Midsummer	5	Mid-fall
Snowdrop (Galanthus)	Late winter/Early spring	5	Early fall
Snowflake (Leucojum)	Mid/late spring	8	Early fall
Spider lily (Hymenocallis)	Midsummer	8	Spring
Spring starflower	Early spring	5	Early fall
Summer hyacinth (Galtonia)	Mid/late summer	8	Late spring
Tigerflower	Mid/late summer	5	Spring
Trout lily	Mid/late spring	5	Late summer
Tulip, various	Mid/late spring	8	Mid/late fall
Wood hyacinth (Endymion)	Late spring	5	Early fall

Spacing

A rule of thumb is to space bulbs a distance equal to their planting depth. In general, bulbs that produce short stems and flowers can be spaced more closely than those that produce tall flowers. However, some bulbs need plenty of room to grow fully, and soil composition and moisture affect spacing as well. It is best to check with a knowledgeable local source.

Planting for Continuous Color

Many common fall-planted bulbs like crocuses, daffodils, hyacinths, and tulips bloom beautifully, but early and briefly. In the rest of the growing season they display only stems and foliage. Here are some ways to have color throughout the summer.

▶ Mix early-blooming bulbs with later-blooming varieties. For example, snowdrops *(below)* are the earliest bloomers of all, while bulb irises bloom later—many in spring. Dwarf iris *(center)* and others bloom in early summer, and still other irises in late summer or early fall. Many lilies also bloom in summer or fall and will provide color after the spring-flowering bulbs have added their beauty to your garden.

▶ Plant bulbs in flower pots or boxes. That way, when the blossoms are gone you can move them out of the way and replace them with containers planted with other flowers. (See Container Gardening, pages 63–68.)

This also makes it easier to grow tender-bulb flowers. Instead of digging up the bulbs before the first frost each year, simply move the containers to a suitable location inside for the winter.

▶ "Naturalize" bulbs by planting them randomly in areas of grass or ground covers, so they look like part of the natural landscape. Daffodils are especially pretty when planted in this way *(below)*. Just cover the holes with turf you remove for planting. You won't be able to mow the grass until after the bulbs have bloomed and turned brown, but the area will be covered with growth at all times.

Daffodils are among the best bulbs for naturalizing. Planted in grass, they will eventually multiply, spread, and bloom early each spring.

Snowdrops bloom earlier than any other bulbs, often before winter snow has melted. They wither by late spring, so combine them with later-blooming bulbs.

Irises bloom from spring through early fall, depending on the variety. Plant them to provide color after earlier blooms are gone.

▶ In addition to bulbs, plant annuals in the bed; for example, pansies along with grape hyacinth *(below)*. The annuals will continue to bloom after the bulbs have finished. You can do this after the bulbs have begun growing. Place the annuals between the bulb positions, but don't dig so deep that you disturb the bulbs.

Grape hyacinths can provide rich color. They are especially effective when planted along with annuals such as pansies, which will continue to bloom long after the hyacinths have faded.

Cutting Flowers from Your Garden

For the best results when cutting flowers for display indoors, do the following:

▶ Cut flowers in the early morning, and immediately place the stems in water. Select flowers that have just opened, or are about to open.

▶ Once inside, cut the stems to length under running water *(right)* or below the surface of the water in a sink or bucket. Make a diagonal cut to keep the stems from resting flat on the bottom of the container, where they can't absorb water. Use a sharp knife, not scissors, which tend to pinch the end of the stem closed.

▶ To help the flowers last longer, place them in a vase of water containing floral preservative, available from florists and garden centers. Or make your own from equal parts of warm water and nondiet lemon-lime soda—for plenty of sugar—and a few drops of chlorine bleach.

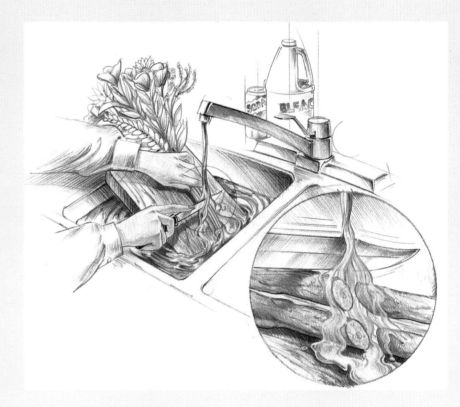

Planting *Roses*

Roses are America's most popular flowering shrub. There are large, small, and miniature varieties of climbing, low-growing, bushlike, and treelike plants; some are delicately beautiful, others have robust, vibrant colors. Roses require care but are not hard to plant and grow successfully. Here's how.

Roses for Your Yard

Landscaping with roses is no different from landscaping with other plants, but what you choose depends on the climate you live in and how much care you are willing to give.

Growing roses is not a plant-and-forget matter. Roses need watering, fertilizing, and pruning like other plants, and many require spraying and winter protection. But the beauty, color, fragrance, and interest that roses will bring to your yard year after year are well worth the extra time you'll need to spend caring for them.

Choosing Roses

The secret to successful rose gardening is to plant varieties that have care requirements you can meet willingly. If you dislike using pesticides, plant roses that are disease resistant. If you don't want to go to the trouble of providing winter protection, plant roses that can survive without it. Your choices will be more limited, but you won't dread having to care for your roses.

Selecting the types of roses to plant depends on how you intend to use them. If you want cut flowers for arrangements, plant

roses like the hybrid tea varieties *(opposite page)*. They produce elegant buds on long stems that open into high-crowned flowers.

For masses of color in your yard, plant a type like the floribundas *(below)*, which bear large clusters of flowers throughout the summer. These medium-height roses are also good for borders, hedges, and foundation plantings.

Plant size and growth habits help answer the question of where to use roses. Low-growing varieties, such as the miniatures *(right)*, are an excellent choice for edging walks and flower beds, and they even make good ground covers. Additional choices are shown on the next two pages.

Miniature roses range in height from only a few inches to over 18 in. Plant them as edging for walks and flower beds, or in masses as ground cover.

Floribundas are some of the most useful roses for landscaping. They provide masses of color and are commonly used as informal borders and hedges. They are fairly hardy and disease resistant.

Additional Varieties

Among the many types of roses are shrub varieties, climbing or trailing roses, and tree roses, shown on these pages.

Shrub Roses

Like floribundas (page 51) shrub roses can be used for foundation, border, and hedge planting. The shrub varieties are hardy, tough, low-maintenance plants that can tolerate less than ideal growing conditions.

Bonica *(below)* is a shrub rose that produces a thick profusion of blossoms and dense foliage. It is excellent as a hedge or as a planting to divide yard areas or mask such things as low storage bins.

Golden wings *(top right)* is a hardy shrub variety well suited for use as borders and foundation plantings as well as hedges.

If you live in an area that has severe winters, consider Parkland and Explorer shrub roses. These Canadian-bred roses can survive winter temperatures as low as −30°F (−35°C) unprotected, and they are very disease resistant.

Another type of shrub rose that excels in hardiness is the rugosa rose *(bottom right)*. As a rule, rugosas have crinkled, shiny, dark green foliage and fragrant flowers. Most also produce bright orange-red fruits, or hips, that provide fall color as well as food for wildlife.

Golden wings is a hardy shrub rose that can be used for borders, hedges, and foundation plantings. Like most shrub roses, it does well in less than ideal growing conditions.

Bonica is a hardy, low-maintenance shrub rose that tolerates less than ideal growing conditions. Its profusion of flowers and free-shaped bushes lends a natural, informal air to the landscape.

Rugosa roses, a hardy, disease-resistant shrub variety, produce fragrant flowers and bear bright orange-red fruits, called hips, which provide winter food for wildlife. They are excellent for sandy soil and seashore gardens.

Climbing or Rambler Roses

If a fence, arbor, trellis, or similar structure is part of your landscape, consider planting climbing or rambler roses along it *(below)*. These varieties don't actually climb, but they have long canes (branches) that can be trained and attached to grow along fence rails, up and around posts, on walls, arches, trellises, and other supports.

Some climbers with long, limber canes also make good ground cover for banks and short slopes. Such plants are also called trailing roses.

Tree Roses

If you want your home to have a rather formal look, you might incorporate standard, or tree, roses into your yard *(right)*.

Tree roses have an elegant beauty, but they do require special care. Their trunks must be supported by driving tall stakes alongside to which they must be tied until they twine around them. Good winter protection against ice and snow loads is also essential. Consult your local nursery or garden center for any special care that is needed for tree roses in your area.

Tree roses offer a formal, even classic look. They require staking for support, winter protection, and careful pruning to retain their form, but they will add impact and drama to the landscape of your home.

Climbing roses can be trained or attached to grow along many kinds of landscape structures, such as fences and arbors. The long, trailing canes of some varieties also make good ground cover on slopes.

Planting Rosebushes

Rosebushes you buy to plant will be either bare-root or container-grown. Instructions for planting both types are on these two pages. You can plant bare-root roses throughout a mild winter if the ground doesn't freeze. Plant them in late fall or early spring if the winters get no colder than 0°F (–18°C), but only in the spring if winters are colder. You can plant container-grown roses any time you can dig a hole in the ground.

Planting depth also depends on winter cold. In a mild climate where temperatures are usually above 32°F (0°C), set the bud union of the plant—the swollen area where the top joins the rootstock—even with the soil level *(below left)*. In colder climates, set it 1 to 2 inches below the soil level *(below right)*.

Planting Bare-root Roses

A bare-root rose has short-cut canes (stems) with no leaves, and no dirt around the roots.

Soak the plant for several hours in a tub or pail of water before planting. Keep it in the water while you prepare the hole.

Dig the hole approximately twice as wide as the root system and deep enough so none of the roots will be crowded *(top right)*. Form a mound or cone of soil in the center of the hole with your hands.

Remove the plant from the water and cut off any broken or shriveled roots with hand pruning shears. Then position the plant so the root system spreads over the cone of soil in the hole.

Lay a shovel handle across the hole to mark the soil level as you set the depth of the bud union as explained at the left. Make the center mound in the hole taller or shorter to get the right depth for your climate.

Begin adding soil around the roots, gently firming it with your hands. When you're finished, the rosebush should be firmly anchored. Then water thoroughly to settle the soil and soak the root area.

Mound soil over the canes *(bottom right)* to protect them from dehydration and cold snaps. When new leaves have grown to 1 inch long, wash the surface mound away with a gentle stream of water.

Dig a hole twice as wide as the rootstock of a bare-root rose. Mound up soil in the center of the hole and place the roots over it. Prune off shriveled or broken roots before planting.

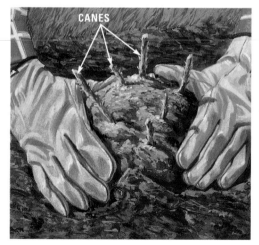

Add soil around the plant and firm it with your hands. Water thoroughly; when the water has soaked in, mound soil over the canes. Rinse the mound away when new leaf growth is 1 in. long.

Set the bud union at soil level *(left)* if the winter temperature is usually above 32°F. Set it 1 to 2 in. below soil level *(right)* where winters are below freezing.

Planting a Container-grown Rose

A container-grown rose is a plant with leaves, growing in a disposable pot or other container.

Begin by digging a hole twice the width of the pot, but no deeper. Remove the plant from the pot without shaking off the dirt around the roots. Slit the container to make removal easier *(below)*.

Put enough soil in the hole to set the bud union at the proper depth (see opposite page), and fill with soil around the root ball, firming it with your hands, to about two-thirds of the depth of the hole *(below)*. Then fill the hole with water and let it soak in. Finally, fill the hole with soil up to the top and water again thoroughly.

For a container-grown rose, dig a hole twice as wide as the container. Remove the plant by holding it at the bud union and pulling up. Slit the sides of the pot to make the plant easier to remove.

Set the plant so the bud union is at the proper depth for your climate. Fill the hole two-thirds with dirt and then with water. Finally, fill to the surface with soil, firm gently, and water thoroughly.

Rose-growing Tips

Roses, like all plants, have basic needs—sun, water, nutrients. Here's how to meet those needs to be rewarded with beautiful, productive rosebushes:

Plant roses so they won't have to compete with trees and other shrubs for water and nutrients.

Make sure they get sufficient sunlight. Most roses need at least six hours of direct sunlight a day to flower well.

Give rosebushes plenty of room. Most spread to about two-thirds of their mature height.

Plant bushes where they are protected from wind but get good air circulation, which will keep diseases at bay.

Plant in well-drained, slightly acidic soil (see Soil Testing, page 29). Before planting, work a lot of organic matter (peat or compost) into the soil to improve its aeration and water-holding capacity. To test drainage, dig a small-diameter hole about 18 inches deep and fill it with water. If the water doesn't seep away in about two hours, choose another site or consult a nursery about methods of improving drainage.

Give roses at least 1 inch of water a week. If the soil is sandy, they'll need more. Water at the base of the plants rather than from above with a sprinkler. A soaker hose works well. You can rinse the foliage periodically to wash off disease spores, but do so early enough in the day so it will be dry by evening. Damp leaves overnight encourage diseases.

Provide 1 to 2 inches of summer mulch to encourage high-quality growth. The best choices are organic mulches such as partly decomposed leaves, cottonseed hulls, pine needles, dry lawn clippings, and bark.

Fertilize regularly with a special rose fertilizer. Most roses are heavy feeders.

Protect most roses in the winter. Cover them with Styrofoam rose cones, or mound soil around the base of each plant after the first frost but before the ground freezes. Lay climbers or tree roses on the ground and cover them with soil. Tip plants for maximum protection: tie the canes together; dig a trench deep enough for the plant; loosen the soil around the roots with a spading fork; tip the plant into the trench and cover with soil.

Use a regular spray or dusting program to ward off insects and leaf diseases. Check with your local nursery or garden center about the best measures for disease prevention, as well as necessary winter protection, in your area.

Creating a
Water Garden

Relax and enjoy the calm beauty of lily pads,
colorful fish, and gently gurgling water.
You don't have to hike to Walden Pond or
a spring-fed mountain lake—you can
create a pond that is a living garden
in your own yard. It takes some work
but is well worth the effort for the years
of enjoyment it will give you.

Planning a Pond and Water Garden

The basis of a water garden is a pond. Ensuring that a pond has the proper flow of water and is the right size to sustain water plants and fish will allow you to transform the pond into a unique small garden. To do that successfully, first consider the work involved and the choice of a location.

Making the Work Easy

Building a backyard pond is mostly a muscle job. Working like beavers, you and a helper might be able to do the whole thing in a couple of weekends. But such intense effort would make work out of the project. Make it a pleasure instead: Plan ahead and don't force yourself. Do the work in easy stages so that when you're finished you can relax with enjoyment, not exhaustion.

The greatest effort will be digging a hole for the pond. Depending on its size, there can be a great deal of dirt to move. For a pond only 6 feet by 4-1/2 feet by 18 inches deep, you'll need to dig out 1-1/2 cubic yards of dirt. And unless you intend to pile it up to create a bank around part of the pond, you'll have to move the dirt somewhere. If you're going to create a pond of any size, make sure you can get some help, or consider renting or hiring a backhoe.

Fortunately, after the digging is done, the rest of the work is much easier. There are several things to be done—putting down a liner, installing a pump, adjusting the water flow, adding water plants—but none of these tasks is very strenuous.

Choosing the Pond Location

There may be a spot that seems perfect for a water garden in your yard, but before you start digging, check the following points:

▶ What is allowed? Local codes may limit the depth of open water permitted without a protective fence. A toddler can drown in only a few inches of water.

▶ Is there anything in the way? Without fail, call your utility companies to make sure there are no buried pipes or cables where you want to dig. And large tree roots can make digging a nightmare. Cutting them can affect both the health and the stability of the tree.

▶ Is there wind protection and sufficient sun? Plants will do better when sheltered from the wind, and both plants and fish need at least four hours of direct sun on the water each day. Make sure nearby trees don't provide too much shade. Also, trees will drop leaves and other debris that must be skimmed off.

▶ Will there be enough surface area? To permit sunlight to penetrate the water for healthy plants and fish, no more than half to two-thirds of the surface should be covered by lily pads or other plants. A rule of thumb for keeping fish is 1 square foot of pond surface for every 1 inch of fish. For example, a pond that has 12 square feet of surface should be stocked with no more than four 3-inch long goldfish or other species.

▶ How deep must the pond be? Fish need water at least 18 inches deep. If they are to survive in winter, the pond must have some spots that are deep enough for the water to remain unfrozen. Check with a local garden center or a landscape or pool contractor to determine the proper depth for your area.

Once you have worked out these things, you can go ahead with your water garden, as explained on the following pages.

Fish and plants transform a pond into a water garden, but there must be ample water to keep both healthy.

Anatomy of a Water Garden

The key to creating a water garden the easy way is to line an appropriate hole with durable waterproof material and install a pump to circulate the water. But there must also be provision for plants, and a way to aerate the water, in order to bring needed oxygen to the ecosystem that lives in the pond. The diagram below shows the anatomy of a water garden with these and other important features.

The liner is heavy-duty flexible material, which is both cheaper and much easier to install than a rigid preformed liner of fiberglass or thin, flimsy plastic. For more about choosing a liner, see page 60.

The hole should have various levels to provide shelves for plants, adequate depth

for fish, and a niche in one bank for a container that helps keep the submersible pump free of materials that might clog it. Electrical power for the pump comes from an exterior outlet with ground fault circuit interrupt (GFCI) protection. All electrical codes require properly installed GFCI outlets in exterior locations. Do not sidestep this requirement—it is essential for protection against serious injury and even death from electrical shock.

The water in the pond does not flow out, it is recirculated by a pump (see page 62). Fresh water comes only from rainfall, or from what you must add to make up for evaporation during extreme dry spells. For aeration, the water is pumped through a flexible plastic pipe to a fountain in an upper

holding pool at the other end of the pond, as far from the pump as possible in a large pond. In a small pond, you could use a pump with a fountain fitted directly over it. The spillway and small waterfall illustrated in the garden below also help to aerate the water, but they are not essential if you don't have room for them.

You don't need a detailed plan to create a water garden, but it's a good idea to make a rough profile drawing of the hole and mark the depths of the various levels you want in the pond. You can't change the levels once the liner is installed, so you need to make some decisions ahead of time about the size of pump and fountain you will use and the depths needed for various plants. These factors are discussed on the following pages.

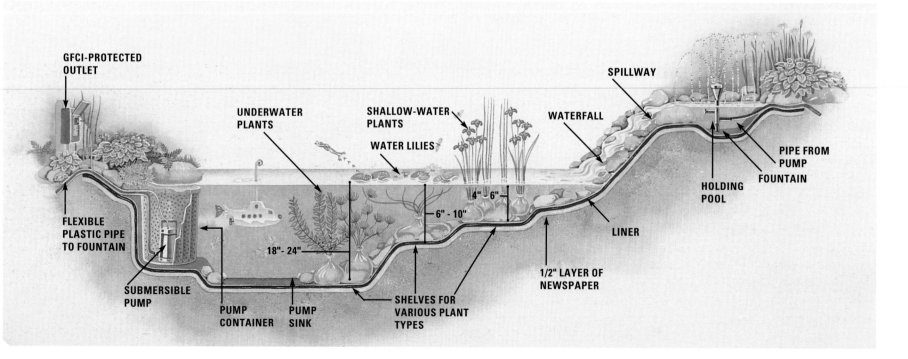

Digging the Hole

In your chosen pond site, lay out a garden hose to establish the size and shape of the pond that seems most pleasing to you *(right)*. The hose is flexible so you can make adjustments and changes easily until you are satisfied. Then start to dig.

Cut down all along the hose line and slice off the sod or turf. If you can use it elsewhere in the yard, transplant it immediately (see Laying Sod, pages 28–31); it won't last until the pond is finished. Next, remove the first few inches of topsoil. Transfer that to other parts of your yard or garden, or save it on a tarpaulin for later use around the pond. Finally, dig the hole into the lower soil. You must remove all exposed rocks, tree roots, and anything else that might damage the liner. If you are going to build up a sloped bank around part of the pond, pile the dirt there; otherwise, cart it out of the way. Refer to your profile sketch to reach the approximate levels you want.

When the entire area has been roughly dug out, check the banks of the pond by setting a level on a board long enough to span the hole *(near right)*. Build up low spots and cut down high spots to level the banks with the surrounding ground.

Measure the depth of the hole and the various levels or shelves from the bottom edge of the board laid across the banks *(far right)* and remove or add dirt as necessary. Remember that the water level will be a few inches below the banks of the pond. For example, if you want the water to be 24 inches deep at a certain spot, make the hole there 27 inches or so deep.

Lay out the shape of the pond with a garden hose. Then remove the sod and topsoil before starting to dig the hole in earnest.

Planning Ahead

A small depression in the deepest part of the pond floor will provide a spot to move the pump to if you should ever need to empty the pond completely.

Check the banks with a long 2x4 and a level. Build up or cut down the banks to make them level across the hole and uniform with the surrounding soil.

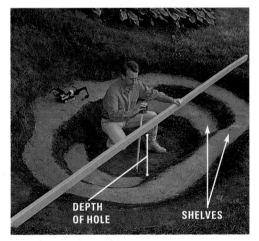

Measure depth from the bottom of the 2x4 to the bottom of the hole and the shelves for plants. Allow for the water to be a few inches below the edge of the hole.

Choosing a Liner

A flexible liner allows you to make your pond any size or shape. Liners are large sheets of rubber or plastic. Synthetic rubber liners, which are usually considered more durable, are made of butyl or EPDM (ethylene propylene diene monomer). Plastic liners are made of HDPE (high-density polyethylene) or PVC (polyvinyl chloride).

When buying a liner for your pond, follow these guidelines:

▶ Ask about warranties, which usually range from five to thirty years.

▶ Buy a thick liner. Thickness is measured in mils (thousandths of an inch). Pond liners are usually 20 to 60 mils thick. Thicker resists damage better.

▶ Choose a dark color; black is best. The dark color makes the liner easy to hide along the banks, makes the pond look deeper, and accentuates the colors of plants and fish.

▶ Calculate the size you'll need. Measure the length, width, and maximum depth of the pond. Figure liner length as the length of the pond plus twice the depth measurement. Then add 2 feet to allow for edging the pond. Use the same formula with the pond width to figure the width of the liner.

▶ Don't forget the waterfall and holding pool. Figure the holding pool liner size as you did for the main pool. For a stream or waterfall liner, measure the horizontal and vertical distance from the holding pool to the pond. To calculate the length, add those measurements, plus 2 feet to overlap the other liners. For the width, add 2 feet to the width of the waterfall or stream bed. If the holding pool is wider than the stream or waterfall, use a single piece of material.

Lining the Pond

To line the pond bed, first put down a layer of newspapers 1/2 inch or so thick *(below)*. This layer acts as a cushion under the liner to help prevent punctures. It will eventually decompose, forming a claylike layer that will hold water even if the liner does develop pinholes or other small leaks.

With the newspapers in place, lay in the liner so that it loosely conforms to the contours of the hole *(below right)*. You may want some help to spread the sheet if the hole is very wide or long. After getting it generally in position, lay rocks along the edge on one side while you work the excess toward the other side. You'll have to step into the hole to do this, so wear soft shoes that won't damage the liner. Don't try to make it fit snugly into every variation in the hole; the weight of the water will do that, and any overlapping wrinkles at the bottom of the pond won't be visible.

When the large pond hole has been lined, put the liner for the stream or waterfall in place, and line the holding pool for the fountain last. That way the edges will overlap down into the pond. Don't rely on that alone, however; bond the edges with cement or adhesive. Ask the liner supplier which product to use with your type of liner.

There will probably be excess liner material around the edges of the pond. You can trim it off with scissors or a utility knife later, but wait until the pond is full of water and encircled with rocks.

Line the pond bed with a layer of newspapers 1/2 in. thick to help prevent punctures. They will decompose into a waterproofing mass under the liner.

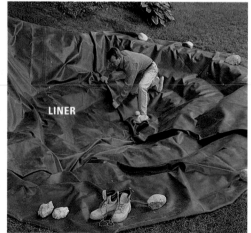

Spread the liner into and across the hole. Anchor it with rocks along one long side and work across to the other side. Wear soft shoes to avoid damaging the liner.

Completing the Installation

Make a container for your submersible pump from a small plastic garbage can or similar container. See page 62 for information about selecting the right size pump. Drill the container full of 1/4-inch holes so that water can flow in and out, put the pump inside, and set the container in place. Run flexible plastic pipe in through a large hole at the top and connect it to the pump discharge port. Run the waterproof electrical cable from the pump through another hole and up to the location for the GFCI outlet. To camouflage the lid of the pump container to look like a rock, set it on newspaper, give it a thick coat of expanding foam sealant (available at home centers), then spray paint it with a mix of black, gray, and brown.

Install a GFCI outlet with a switch, or have an electrician do it. Use only cable approved for underground installation to connect to the service panel in your house.

Put the fountain in position in the holding pool or pond location and connect it to the flexible plastic pipe from the pump. Run the pipe along a path where it can be concealed by rocks and plantings.

Next, using a garden hose, fill the pond about half full of water. This will weight the liner down into all the variations of the earth beneath and will probably pull a bit of the excess from around the edges. Then line the banks with rocks *(below)*. The water will hold the liner in place so you can lift up the edge where necessary to dig out cavities for the largest rocks to rest in.

Adjusting the Water Flow

Complete filling the pond with a hose, then plug in the pump and turn it on. Watch the water level in the container. If the level falls, there aren't enough holes in the container; water is being pumped out faster than it can flow in. This means that the container could run dry and the pump burn out. Simply make more holes until the level stays constant as the pump operates.

The water inlet to the pond—fountain, waterfall, or stream—should be as far from the pump as possible. If you have a stream or waterfall, locate the fountain or the end of the pipe from the pump in a holding pool, so the water spraying out slows down and spills lazily into the pond.

Getting the water to move down the waterfall or stream the way you want takes a lot of trial and error. If your garden hose provides enough flow, use it to make test runs when filling the pond, or fill a large bucket and pour it into the holding pool and observe the flow. Water has a frustrating tendency to flow invisibly under or between rocks instead of pleasantly over them. Prevent this by filling hidden passages with expanding foam sealant.

When you have the water level and rate of flow adjusted, turn off the pump and let the water sit in the pond for at least two weeks. This will let any chlorine in the water, which could kill plants, evaporate. Then add your plants and turn the pump on again. Wait six to eight weeks more before introducing fish into the pond.

Fill the pond half full before placing rocks all around the edges. Lift the liner to dig cavities for large rocks. Trim off any excess liner after filling the pool and adjusting the water flow.

Choosing a Pump

Many home and garden centers and industrial supply stores sell submersible pumps suitable for ponds, as do many swimming pool suppliers. You need a pump that will create a steady, gentle flow of water out of the holding pool.

The amount of water a pump moves is measured in gallons per hour (gph) or gallons per minute (gpm). To compare a gpm-rated pump with a gph-rated pump, either multiply or divide by 60.

A pump's actual output will vary with the diameter and length of the discharge hose or pipe and the vertical distance between the pump and the holding pool. Make a note of those measurements so the dealer can tell you what the pump's output will be. However, don't buy a pump until you've built the waterfall or stream and made some tests to estimate what flow you will need.

To do that, fill the holding pool, then time yourself as you pour a 2-gallon bucket of water into the pond at a rate that creates the right amount of flow out of the pool down the waterfall or stream into the pond. The time it takes to empty the bucket roughly determines the pump size:

1 minute	120 gph
50 seconds	144 gph
40 seconds	180 gph
30 seconds	240 gph
20 seconds	360 gph
12 seconds	600 gph

Before you shop, make some phone calls to find dealers who will let you return a pump if it's too big or too small.

Adding Water Plants

There are three kinds of plants you can add to a pond to create a water garden: those that are anchored in a container or root ball, those that float on the surface, and those that grow underwater. The last type, called oxygenators, are essential if you are going to have fish in your pond. They take up carbon dioxide and provide oxygen that will help prevent the growth of algae and scum. Various popular choices are listed below. When you buy water plants, ask the supplier for planting instructions and advice.

You can anchor plants in pots or baskets designed for aquatic growing, or you can make your own. Buy open-mesh baskets or drill 1/4-inch holes all over plastic containers and line them with burlap. Then add moist, heavy dirt and place the plant at the recommended depth. Do not use potting soil in your pond. Its high nutrient content encourages algae growth. If you plan to have fish in the pond, cover the soil with coarse sand or pea gravel, to prevent the fish from burrowing into the roots.

You can also place the roots of each plant in a "root ball," a mix of gravel and soil in a nylon stocking, tied with wire solder. Root balls make the plants easy to move and keep fish from disturbing the soil.

Lower the containers or root balls into the pond to place the plants on the various shelf levels you provided when you dug the hole.

You may also want to choose plants that grow in shallow water and boglike soil to plant around the edges of the pond, and rock-garden plants for the dry banks. Ask for suggestions at your garden center.

Popular Water Garden Plants

Deep-water Plants with Floating Leaves and Flowers
Floating heart
Water hawthorn
Water lily—species include:
  Hardy
  Pygmy or miniature
  Tropical day blooming
  Tropical night blooming

Oxygenating Plants
Anacharis
Cabomba
Curled pondweed
Eelgrass
Ludwigia
Sagittaria
Water milfoil

Free-floating Plants
Azolla
Duckweed
Water chestnut
Water fern
Water lettuce

Container
Gardening

Growing plants in containers—
pots, tubs, and boxes of all kinds—
lets you have flowers wherever you want
without having to create permanent
garden beds. And you can move containers
to have blooms at all times along walks,
on patios and porches, indoors and out.
An added attraction: no weeding!

Container Garden Design

You can grow almost everything in containers—flowers, ferns, shrubs, even fruits and vegetables. To take full advantage of the diversity container plants offer, you need to give some thought to design. In container gardening, good design involves choosing containers and plants that are appropriate for the locations in which you want to place them, as well as spacing and grouping containers effectively in each spot. The techniques of planting in containers are explained on pages 66–67.

Containers

The containers you put plants in are a visible part of your gardening scheme; don't limit your thinking to standard small clay and plastic pots suitable for one geranium apiece. Good appearance is not just a matter of the color and material of a container. It also should look—and be—big enough and strong enough for the height and spread of the flowers you plant in it.

A container that is too small not only looks dinky but will crowd the roots, restricting growth and limiting the blooms.

It may not hold enough soil to have the weight to resist being blown over on a gusty day. And thin container walls may crack as the soil expands and contracts with temperature changes, or when you move the plant.

Choose large, tall containers for big, showy plants *(below left)*. And the bigger the pot, the thicker its walls should be. Conversely, choose shallow bowl-like pots for low-growing, spreading flowers *(below right)*. Use a variety of sizes and, with pots, a variety of colors and surfaces: glazed, unglazed, plain, sculptured. Drainage holes in the bottom of a container are an important feature; if there are none, you may be able to put gravel in the bottom (see Watering and Drainage, page 66).

Don't restrict yourself to pottery containers or conventional window boxes. Unfinished or weathered wood tubs and boxes fit into many natural settings. Or you can keep them painted for a trim, new look that matches a fence or railing or the style of an entranceway. Hanging baskets or baskets large enough to sit on a wall, deck, or patio are also attractive. Fill them with plants in unobtrusive pots, which will protect the basket material from stains and rot.

Choose a container of appropriate size and character for the plants. Ceramic pots are only one possibility; wooden tubs and boxes, and baskets are others.

Broad, shallow containers are best for low-growing, spreading flowers. Group containers for variety in plant sizes and colorful mixes of blooms and leaves.

Choosing and Combining Plants

By all means choose the flowers and other plants that please you most—you will be living with them. But also select plants appropriate for the location. Pots of daffodils, for example, can provide delightful accents along a walk *(right)*, while a shallow bowl of lobelia would look better on top of a low wall. Following are some ideas for choosing and using container plants. Suggestions for various kinds of specialized container gardens are given on page 68.

▶ Add a couple of tall plants to a pot holding a shorter variety, to create a pleasing vertical layering and help balance the plants and the container. Dracaena is a classic tall choice, or you might try salvia, geraniums, tall marigolds, or zinnias, depending on the size of the container you want to use.

▶ Let trailing plants spill over the rim of their container to soften the edges or give a luxuriant feel to a hanging basket. Good trailing plants are ivy geranium, alyssum, vinca, and lobelia.

▶ Create a focal point among a group of containers by using one large plant in its own large container.

▶ Put simple plants in ornate pots, such as those with richly sculptured surfaces or vivid glazes. Often a single variety works well. Obviously, the corresponding design principle is to put busy plants and complicated arrangements in simple pots. In both cases, the contrast directs attention to the plants.

▶ Mix leaf colors. Dusty miller is a favorite for adding color, as are coleus and sweet potato vine. You can put colored-leaf plants in a container with flowering plants, or use three or four varieties in a single container. Place the latter with a group of flowering plants in containers for an effective accent.

▶ Mix leaf textures. Dusty miller, asparagus fern, and cupflower all provide textural variety. So do herbs and small grasses. Don't limit yourself just to flowering plants.

▶ Plant shrubs and evergreens in containers that you can place as movable borders along a walk, driveway, or terrace edge. Keep them trimmed to a height appropriate to the size of the container.

▶ Plant perennials. Most people choose annuals for containers, but in areas where winters are mild, you can plant perennials in containers and set the containers into the ground over the winter. Ask your local garden center if this is possible in your area. If you want to bring a container plant indoors for the winter, be sure it has a very sunny spot, or provide an electric grow bulb or fluorescent tube. In the early spring, prune back the plant and fertilize it.

Accent a walkway or direct the eye with repetitions of identical container plants, like these daffodils. Brightly colored plants can be spaced at greater distances than more delicate blossoms and still be effective.

Planting in Containers

Growing plants in containers is easy, but it's not enough just to buy a plant and dump it into a pot. You need to use the right soil, provide proper watering and drainage, and feed the plants. All of these things differ a bit from what you normally do for cultivating plants in the ground.

Soil and Planting

Plant flowering and leafy plants in a specially blended potting soil, not garden soil. (See the opposite page for growing shrubs in containers.) Garden soil won't work, because plant roots need air as well as water.

Plain garden soil in a container can get so saturated with water that there is no air and the roots "drown." Potting soils are light enough to retain air even when soaked. Use a "soil-less" mix composed of peat moss, perlite, and vermiculite. Or mix peat moss or compost about half and half with regular potting soil. Feel the mix: It should be soft and light to the touch. Place plants in the container soil at the same depth as you would put them in the ground.

After you have planted in a container, keep it in the shade for a couple of days until the plants recover from the shock of being transplanted.

Don't be limited to putting containers aboveground. To place flowers into difficult growing spots, for example where there are drainage problems, dig a hole and bury a pot there. Treat it like your other containers, but don't water it quite as often.

Watering and Drainage

Water your plants frequently. When all sides of a container are exposed to the air, far more moisture evaporates than from the soil around a plant in the ground. To check a container plant, stick your finger about an inch into the soil. If it feels dry, water until the water flows out the bottom of the container. Water the soil, not the leaves of the plants. In midsummer, containers often require watering every day. For ways to cut down on watering time, see the sidebar on page 68.

Watering is important, but it is just as important not to overwater your plants. The best way to avoid this is to make sure every container has good drainage so that plant roots will not sit in excess water. If a container has no drain holes, drill or cut some in the bottom if possible. To avoid stains on a deck or patio, place the plant container on 1/4- or 1/2-inch pieces of tile or other spacers in a larger, shallow container or tray. Excess water runout from the plant will drain into the lower container and evaporate.

If it is not possible to make holes in a solid container, place about 2 inches of gravel in the bottom of the pot and cover it with landscape fabric—available at garden centers—before putting in the potting soil. Use 3 inches of gravel in a very large or deep container. Be careful not to overwater when using a gravel base.

Plant in a light potting soil, not garden dirt, so that roots will get air as well as moisture. Containers must have drain holes or gravel in the bottom to avoid drowning the plants.

Fertilizing

Frequent watering tends to drain nutrients from the soil. For luxurious growth, use a soluble fertilizer, one you dissolve in water in order to apply it. But mix it at half strength—half as much fertilizer, or twice as much water, as called for in the instructions—and apply it at twice the suggested frequency. Make sure the fertilizer you use is labeled for use in container gardening.

If you can't schedule regular feeding for your container plants, use slow-release fertilizer tablets or beads. They are more expensive, but if you add them to the soil according to the directions when you plant the container, they should last all growing season. This is especially important if you are using a soilless potting mix, because unlike soil it has no nutrients to feed the plants. Of course, the plant will still require regular watering, both for its own moisture needs and to release the fertilizer in the tablets.

Other Care

To have more blooms, "deadhead" the plant by removing dead flower heads immediately. This essentially fools the plant into thinking it still has to bloom.

If plants start looking "leggy" (tall without many leaves), nip the tops off. This will encourage them to grow bushier.

Growing Shrubs in Containers

Many decorative shrubs can be grown in large containers, but they have somewhat different planting and care requirements than container-grown flowering plants, ferns, and decorative foliage plants.

Among the shrubs that do well in containers are barberry, bluebeard, camellia, clematis, small cotoneaster, escallonia, euonymus, false cypress, firethorn, flowering currant, forsythia, honeysuckle, jasmine, some lavenders, lilac, Mexican orange, passionflower, prunus, rhododendron, rockrose, spirea, and wisteria. Boxwood, privet, and other hedge shrubs also do well. Your nursery or garden center can give you good advice on what to choose.

Planting Shrubs

Shrubs generally grow larger than most other plants, so you need a sizable container—say, one 2-1/2 feet wide by 1-1/2 feet deep for a shrub that will grow 4 to 5 feet tall and spread 3 to 4 feet wide. Drainage holes in the bottom are essential.

Place about 2 inches of coarse gravel, broken clay pots, or similar drainage material in the bottom of the container. Then add a layer of potting soil. You need enough so the base of the stem will be level with the top of the container when the shrub is placed in it. To prepare a soilless potting mix for shrubs, use 3 parts peat moss to 1 part sharp or builder's sand, plus 4 tablespoons of all-purpose fertilizer per bushel of mix. A good soil-based mix is 2 parts soil plus 1 part compost or leaf mold plus 1 part sharp sand or perlite. Another is equal parts of soil, sand, and peat moss.

Make sure the root ball is moist and the root system healthy for planting. Trim away any dead or damaged roots. Set the shrub in the center of the container and fill around it with your potting soil. Firm the soil with your hands as you work until it is about 1/2 inch below the top of the container. Then water thoroughly, wait for it to drain, and water once again.

Caring for Container Shrubs

Water the shrub well whenever the soil surface dries out. About a year after planting, start feeding the plant with liquid fertilizer monthly or when growth is poor or the leaves become discolored.

Prune the shrub's top growth to shape it and keep to size as desired. Do this in late autumn or early in the spring, before sap begins to flow for new growth. Every four to six years, remove the shrub and prune it by stripping about 4 inches of root ends and soil from the root ball. Scrub the container and replant the shrub with fresh soil mix.

How to Cut Down on Container Watering

About the only drawback to container gardens is the need to water them frequently. Here are some ways to cut down on your watering time:

Plant drought-tolerant plants such as moss roses, herbs, marigolds, cupflower, and sedum. But even these need regular watering while they're getting established.

Use big containers, which hold water longer. You can also use double pots, one inside the other, to insulate the soil and slow the evaporation process.

Line porous pots with asphalt. Paint the inside of clay, wood, or concrete containers with asphalt roofing sealer. Paint clay and concrete pots up to the soil line; paint wood containers up to the top edge.

Cover the soil with 1–2 inches of mulch to slow evaporation. Use leaf mold or shredded bark as mulch.

Add a water-absorbing polymer to the soil. These products, available at garden centers, absorb tremendous amounts of water and then gradually release it.

Use drip irrigation for timed release of water to each container. See pages 73–75.

Cluster containers in sunny spots so the plants will shade one another and block the wind. Choosing drought-resistant flowers like these marigolds and using large pots also conserves water.

Specialized Gardening

Container gardening makes it easy to create specialized gardens for a particular growing location, or a distinct purpose or appeal. Here are some possibilities and plant choices.

▶ **Shade or Partial Shade**
Impatiens, coleus, lobelia, browallia, begonia (tuberous and wax), mimulus, torenia, German ivy, Swedish ivy.

▶ **Low Maintenance**
Moss roses, cupflower, Dahlberg daisy, marigolds, salvia, celosia, ivy geranium, impatiens, dusty miller.

▶ **Long Blooming**
Petunias, marigolds, moss roses, Dahlberg daisy, cupflower, impatiens, sweet alyssum, salvia, bachelor's buttons, zinnias, geraniums. Pick off dead blooms immediately for continued blooming.

▶ **Good Scents**
Heliotrope, sweet alyssum, nicotiana, mignonette, lavender.

▶ **Attractive to Hummingbirds**
Fuchsia, red salvia, petunias.

▶ **Herbs**
All types.
You can plant herbs that have similar soil or sunlight/shade requirements in the same container.

Growing
Ground Covers

*Here's the easiest, most effective way
to change your landscaping. Ground covers
comprise a range of plants that will grow
in all kinds of yards, from sun baked
to deeply shaded, and all kinds of terrain:
flat, steeply sloped, even rocky. And they
will stop erosion, too.*

Ground Cover Versatility

Ground covers include virtually every kind of plant there is. Simply put: If a plant spreads as it grows, it can probably be used as a ground cover. The most typical ground covers are low-growing foliage plants, either deciduous or evergreen. But many other plants work well, too, including small, spreading shrubs; ornamental grasses; certain varieties of succulents; and a number of hardy perennial flowers.

Using Ground Covers

Because there are so many species to choose from, you can plant ground covers in a wide variety of situations, from harsh, direct sun to the deepest shade, and on level, rolling, steeply sloping, or rocky terrain. Here are some ways to use ground covers:

▶ Control erosion. Varieties such as ice plant provide an attractive covering while keeping soil from washing away on slopes or in rock gardens. Crown vetch (photo, page 69) is another good choice for a slope, where it will provide attractive texture and color as well as stop erosion.

▶ Reduce weeds. The density of most mature ground covers keeps weeds in check. However, you may occasionally need to do some spot hand-weeding, because you can't use a hoe or tiller.

▶ Retain moisture. The close cover reduces moisture loss from soil, so you can water less often. That's often a great help in droughts.

▶ Cover problem areas. If you can't get grass to grow under a tree, try a ground cover such as the shade-loving barrenwort. If nothing survives in a sun-drenched spot, use the sun-loving artemesia. Many species actually thrive in tough growing conditions.

▶ Make transitions. Ground covers are a perfect way to make a transition between lawn and garden *(below left),* two separate gardens, or between other plants.

▶ Replace a lawn. Used in place of grass, ground covers reduce yard maintenance chores such as weekly mowing.

▶ Beautify the landscape. Whether you plant them alone or in masses *(below right),* this may be the best use for ground covers. The choice of flowers is virtually unlimited.

Transition planting places a ground cover between two different areas, such as grass and tall flowers. This delicate purple ground cover is vinca, also called periwinkle or trailing myrtle.

Mass-planted ground covers can create a spectacular carpet of color when they bloom. These are several varieties of phlox, one of the most popular flowering ground covers.

Some Limitations

Ground covers do have limitations. They can't withstand repeated trampling, so you shouldn't plant them in areas of heavy foot traffic—where children play, for example.

Some ground covers—particularly a fast-growing, invasive type such as crown vetch—can choke out other plants in a garden, even a lawn, if they're not closely watched and maintained.

Ground covers can be expensive. Depending on the variety you choose, ground covers can cost from $3 to $10 per square foot, compared to about 15 cents a square foot for sod. But you can take cuttings and root them to fill in bare spots after a year or two.

Brilliant color, such as these yellow lantana flowers, creates a vivid accent when used individually or when placed among other, green ground covers.

Choosing Ground Covers

Some of the most popular and versatile ground covers are listed on page 72. But which ones will be best for your yard?

The basic factors in choosing a ground cover are how it will be used, discussed above, and the exposure it will have: sun, shade, or both. There are other factors that will influence your choice, too. They include the following:

▶ Hardiness. Find a variety that is suited to the climate in your area.

▶ Soil type. Most ground covers require healthy soil. If you can't provide this, look for a variety, such as daylilies or pachysandra, which can tolerate poor soil.

▶ Maintenance. Once established and spread, ground covers need little attention. Some, such as astilbe, must be thinned and transplanted as they mature and become crowded. Others, such as crown vetch, need to be mowed or trimmed once a year.

▶ Growth habit. Some ground covers, such as hostas, grow in fairly neat clumps; others, like wintercreeper, send out runners in all directions. Most grow and spread slowly—that's what you want. Avoid those that fill in quickly unless that's what you need: to stop erosion, for example.

▶ Flowering habit. Most ground covers produce small flowers, some year-round and others just once each growing season. Flower colors are typically white, pink, or purple, although some, such as lantana *(left)*, produce red, yellow, or orange flowers.

Buying and Planting Ground Covers

Ground covers are sold in individual pots at most garden centers and nurseries. Ground covers are also sold by mail order. If you buy this way, get assurance—backed by a guarantee—that the plants are hardy enough for your locale.

Plant ground covers the same way as a perennial flower: Prepare the soil and add nutrients, depending on the ground cover's needs (the label should specify them). If you plan to do a major planting, have your soil analyzed by a local nursery or agricultural extension office.

Dig a hole large enough to accommodate the plant and the dirt surrounding the roots. Remove the pot—if the plant is root bound, loosen the roots—and set the plant in the hole at the same depth it was growing in the pot.

Spacing between plants varies with the type. Don't try to rush filling-in by planting too close, even if the area looks sparse at first. Follow the spacing recommended by the supplier to give the plants room to mature properly.

Once they are planted, add an organic mulch and water the plants frequently until they become well established. You'll need to weed during this growing period, since the plants will still be somewhat small and vulnerable.

Plants for Ground Covers

Here are some of the many possible choices of ground covers. Tell the nursery or supplier that you want a variety suitable for planting as a ground cover. Make sure that the plant will be hardy enough to survive typical winters in your area and is a variety that will grow in the shade or sun conditions where you will plant it. Also be sure to ask about soil requirements and planting instructions.

NAME	LEAVES, BLOSSOMS	CONDITIONS
Ajuga/Bugleweed	Green leaves; pink or blue flowers	Sun or shade
Bishop's weed	Pale green leaves, white edges; white flowers	Sun or shade
Chrysanthemum pacificum	Green, white-edged leaves; yellow flowers	Sun
Cotoneaster/Bearberry	Evergreen leaves; bright red fruits	Sun, moist soil
Crown vetch	Pink flowers; compound leaves	Sunny slopes
Euonymus/Wintercreeper	Evergreen leaves, dark purple in fall	Sun
American/European ginger	Vivid green leaves; maroon flowers	Shade or partial shade
Goldenstar/Green-and-gold	Bright green leaves; yellow-gold flowers	Sun
Hosta, many varieties	Green, blue-green leaves, some with white, creamy yellow edges; white, lilac flowers	Shade or partial shade
Ivy, English, various	Evergreen, variegated green-white leaves	Sun or deep shade
Juniper/Creeping juniper	Evergreen, bluish-green needles	Sun
Lantana, trailing	Toothed, crinkled green leaves; rosy lilac flowers; blue-black fruits	Sun
Lily of the valley	Green leaves; white, pink flowers	Sun or shade
Lilyturf	Dark evergreen leaves; blue-violet, white flowers; blue fruits	Sun or shade
Livingston daisy/Ice plant	Bright green leaves; buff, pink, rose, yellow flowers	Sun
Mazus reptans	Green leaves; violet flowers	Shade, moist soil
Moss or mountain pink/Phlox	Evergreen leaves; red, white, pink, or blue flowers	Sun or partial shade
Pachysandra	Evergreen foliage; creamy white flowers	Shade
Pearlwort	Deep emerald-green, mosslike leaves; white flowers	Sun or shade
Periwinkle/Vinca	Evergreen leaves; purple, lilac-blue, white, pink flowers	Sun or shade
St. John's-wort	Light-green leaves; large gold flowers	Sun or partial shade
Strawberry, wild	Evergreen leaves, bluish-white underneath; white flowers; red fruits	Partial shade
Sweet woodruff	Green, fragrant leaves; tiny white flowers	Partial shade
Verbena, trailing	Dark-green and gray-green leaves; purple, red, rose-pink flowers	Sun

Drip Watering
System

Don't be a slave to your garden hose. Bring automation to your most important gardening chore—watering. An easy-to-install drip system will deliver the water your plants need, when they need it, and exactly where they need it. What do you have to do? Sit and relax!

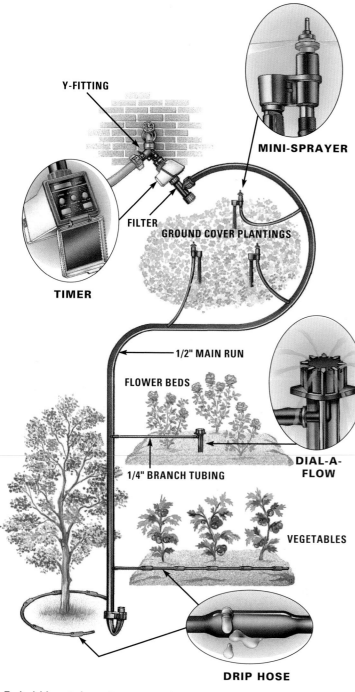

Y-FITTING

MINI-SPRAYER

FILTER

GROUND COVER PLANTINGS

TIMER

1/2" MAIN RUN

FLOWER BEDS

DIAL-A-FLOW

1/4" BRANCH TUBING

VEGETABLES

DRIP HOSE

Typical drip watering system components.

Anatomy of a Drip Watering System

A drip watering system for slow, controlled garden watering is not the same as a permanently installed underground sprinkling system such as is used for lawns. The drip system is a simple configuration that uses flexible plastic tubing and easy-to-connect sprayers and control devices. You can design a system to accommodate any kind of garden or landscaping and install it yourself. And you can afford it: A modest home system will cost about $150, including a timer.

The diagram at the left shows how you might set up a typical system. A Y-fitting screwed onto your outdoor hose faucet lets you connect both a hose and the main line of the drip watering system: a length of 1/2-inch diameter plastic tube. This carries water to the garden, where 1/4-inch diameter branch lines distribute the water to various emitters such as spray heads. The plastic tubing is flexible, so you can run it anywhere you want, and it is black, so it virtually disappears from view as it lies on the soil. You do not bury it. That not only saves work, but lets you reconfigure the system without difficulty.

At the beginning of the main line, you can install a battery-operated timer that you can program to turn the water on and off. The timer is optional—you could just turn the water on and off manually—but it is what makes the system automatic, so you don't even have to be at home to sit and relax while your garden waters itself.

A filter is installed after the timer to help keep the water emitters downstream in the system clean. This is an important component; don't leave it out.

If your household water system has high pressure (55 psi or higher; ask your plumber or utility company) you should include a pressure regulator at this point in the main line. Excessive pressure might force fittings to come apart in the system. Also, many plumbing codes require a backflow preventer at the beginning of the line, so that water cannot be siphoned back into the household water system. It's a good thing to have, even if your local code does not call for it. Both of these devices are inexpensive.

Three kinds of water emitters are shown in the diagram at left. Mini-sprayers, or mini-sprinklers, are just what you need to water grouped plants like perennial flowers or ground cover plantings. These sprayers can be mounted at any required height on plastic stakes. "Dial-a-Flow" emitters are adjustable to many flow settings so you can tune them to the plants' needs. Flowers and shrubs require a greater or more diverse flow than others. Like mini-sprayers, these emitters mount on plastic stakes that you shove into the ground. There are dozens of other special-purpose emitters also available, but these two and a drip hose will handle most home gardening needs.

A drip hose has small emitters built into it. It is smaller—1/4-inch diameter—than ordinary fabric soaker hoses, and does not spray the water out as a perforated sprinkler hose does. It is far more efficient than either of those hoses and is especially good for watering trees, hedges, and rows of vegetables.

Designing a System

You can install a drip watering system in any climate. If you live in an area with harsh winters, you can easily drain the system and leave it empty until spring. Just disconnect the faucet fittings and timer and take them indoors during the cold weather.

To design your system, sketch a simple map of the area you want to water. Draw a main supply run and the branches from the supply to individual areas. Next, time how long it takes to fill a 5-gallon pail from the outside faucet where you would connect the main run of the system. Divide the number of gallons the pail holds by the number of minutes it took to fill it, then multiply by 60. The answer is the gallons per hour (gph) available from that faucet. Your planned system can't exceed that many gph or the emitters at the end of the line won't receive any water. Add up their flow ratings to see. If you need more water you can set up an additional system to operate at a different time of day by adding another line from one more faucet or by installing another Y-fitting.

You can get tubing and fittings for a drip watering system at many home and garden centers as well as by mail order. Two sources of catalogs and information available by telephone are Dripworks (800-522-3747) and Rain Bird (800-435-5672). The catalogs from suppliers have hundreds of parts that are for very special applications and commercial use. Don't be intimidated by them. You can build a system as complicated as you wish, but it's best to start simple and add specialty conveniences later. A drip watering system can easily be altered in a matter of minutes.

Connecting a System

The parts of the system that join to the hose faucet have standard hose-thread connectors. The tubing has self-sealing push-in fittings; some are shown at right. To connect 1/4-inch tubing to the main line, use a special 1/4-inch punch *(top left)* to make a hole in the 1/2-inch tubing. Then insert a connector in the hole and slip the small tubing over the end. Use a tee connector *(top right)* to run a branch line to two emitters. To hook up an emitter, simply slip the branch line tubing over the connector stub.

There are also 1/2-inch 90-degree and tee connectors if you need them *(middle left and right)*. However, because the tubing is flexible you can bend it to go anywhere you need, so you may not need fittings except to connect the smaller branch lines. You can keep the tubing in position by pushing U-shaped wire stakes into the ground. The tubing, which comes in coils, will gradually relax from coiling as it is exposed to the sun.

To close off the end of the 1/2-inch main line, use an end fitting—a two-hole loop that slides over the end of the tube and kinks it *(bottom)*. To protect the system from freezing temperatures, remove an emitter from the lowest spot, slip off the end fitting, and let the water drain out.

Watering System Fittings

1/4-in. punch

1/4-in. tee fitting

1/2-in. 90-degree fitting

1/2-in. tee fitting

End fitting

Trees, Shrubs & Hedges

Planting Trees

Trees are enduring landscaping enhancements. Take the time to choose the best varieties and locations for trees in your yard, and plant them right—you may spend a lifetime together.

78

Pruning Trees

From first planting through maturity, you can encourage and control a tree's development with pruning. Done properly, pruning enhances the health as well as the appearance of the tree.

84

Planting a Hedge

For privacy or beauty, or both, a hedge is a natural way to mark a border or define a landscaping area. Plant and care for it the right way and you'll be rewarded with rich, healthy growth.

92

Foundation Plantings

Plant flowers and shrubs to blend your house, walk, and drive with the beauty of your yard and garden. They can hide the foundation, soften edges and corners, and provide color and grace.

97

Mulching Your Garden

Mulch is the smart gardener's best friend. It stops weeds, conserves water, and saves hours of work. Choose organic, mineral, or manufactured mulch to keep your gardening easy.

101

Planting *Trees*

A tree is both an immediate asset to your home and an investment in the future. Plant it right and you'll have a friend for life. Here's how to choose and plant a tree, and give it that all-important good start.

Choosing a Tree

Whether you want a tree as a gracious feature in your yard, such as the flowering dogwood on the opposite page, or to provide shade in a particular area—or both—your first concerns will be choosing an appropriate species, evaluating the soil, selecting the particular tree you will plant, and transporting the tree safely to your yard.

Choosing a Species

The two key factors in selecting a species of tree for your yard are climate and soil. Climatic factors include length of days, sunshine, temperature extremes, and rainfall. Some trees are hardier than others; they can withstand colder, drier, or wetter weather or other rigorous conditions better. Other local factors also make a difference. Some species are disease prone, some can't tolerate smog, and still others can't survive droughts.

To help you choose the best species for your yard, rely on the experience of plant professionals at local nurseries or the horticultural experts at your county agricultural extension office. Also call the local botanical garden or try the agricultural or forestry department of a university in your region. You're sure to find an expert or two happy to provide information and advice.

Evaluating the Soil

Soil is the source of the nutrients and water a tree must have. Heavy clay soils and low, swampy areas can hold too much water, which can cut off the oxygen supply to the roots and drown the tree. Sandy soil, on the other hand, can drain too fast and allow the roots to dry out, especially in windy areas.

To test the soil drainage, dig an 18-inch deep hole and fill it with water. If the water seeps away overnight, the drainage is all right. Otherwise, you can improve it by sloping the surface of the soil so excess rainwater runs off.

To improve nutrient-poor clay and sandy soil, turn up the earth around the planting site and mix in composted wood chips and compost. Limit the mix to about 1/2 new material and 1/2 original soil, especially where you will dig the planting hole, so the tree will use the enriched fill as a transition zone. If you make the immediate soil too different from the rest, the roots may ignore the outlying soil and grow in circles in the planting hole, stunting the tree's growth.

Selecting a Tree

As you visualize the size and shape of the tree you want, keep in mind how it will fit into your yard. Remember, a 6-foot spindly sapling can grow into an 80-foot oak. Find out what the mature size will be so you won't plant it too close to the house. List the characteristics you want most from your tree—size, shape, growth speed, shading, fall color—and discuss them with the experts you consult. They'll help you pick the best species for your yard.

Unless you're an experienced gardener, buy your tree from a local nursery that will guarantee it for at least the first growing season. Prices will range from ten to several hundred dollars, depending on the size and species you choose. Trees are measured by trunk diameter or height. Most come ready to plant in one of three ways: balled-and-burlapped, with bare roots, or in a container.

Balled-and-burlapped—B & B or "bagged"—trees (pages 80–81) are dug from the ground with their roots left encased in an earthen ball. This ball is held tightly together with burlap and twine or wire. When you select one of these trees, make sure the ball is still tight and intact and the tree trunk doesn't wobble in it. A loose ball or wobbly trunk signals mishandling and extra stress put on the tree. Be sure to lift the tree by the ball, not the trunk. You can plant a B & B tree at any time the weather permits during the growing season.

Bare-root trees (page 82) are dug in the fall or early spring while they are dormant and are kept that way until you buy them. They cost less than the other types, but they are also the most vulnerable to injury from even a slight drying of their exposed roots. You must keep the roots moist and plant a bare-root tree right away in the spring before it begins to grow.

Container-grown trees (page 82) can be planted anytime during the growing season. These trees have grown in a container for one to four years. The soil should hold together when you remove the container, so you can plant them with the roots intact. Avoid trees with large circling roots. They indicate a "root bound" condition that can make it difficult to straighten the roots when you plant the tree.

Transporting a Tree

A tree of a size suitable for planting can be badly damaged if handled improperly. Be especially careful to protect your tree when transporting it from the nursery or garden center to the spot where you will plant it. Here are some important points:

Keep bare roots moist and covered at all times. Exposure to sun and wind will dry them out very quickly.

Ask the supplier to bind paper around the leaves with twine, to keep them from blowing and whipping in the wind as you drive.

If you put the tree in the back of your car, cushion the edge of the car frame under the trunk of the tree. And secure the vehicle's hatchback or trunk lid so it can't bounce down against the bark or branches of the tree.

If you use a trailer or van, make sure the tree will not bounce or roll around. Fasten it with ropes just above the root ball, but don't tie them directly against the bark. Wrap the trunk with thick cloth first.

If you have far to go, lay the tree on its side so the trunk and branches won't be wind-whipped. But support or tie the trunk to keep branches from being crushed against the trailer bed.

Protect your back—a balled-and-burlapped tree is quite heavy. Get a helper to lift and move the tree with you. Loop short lengths of rope through the wire or twine that surrounds the ball so you both can lift it without bending over.

Don't carry a tree any farther than necessary. Use a wheelbarrow or hand truck instead. Or lift the ball onto a heavy-duty plastic tarp, or even a child's plastic sled or wagon, and pull it across the lawn. A helper can steady the tree as it is moved.

Planting a Bagged Tree

The steps for planting a bagged or balled-and-burlapped tree are described below and shown on the opposite page. The differences in planting a bare-root tree or a container-grown tree are shown on page 82.

Prepare the Hole

Dig a hole at your planting site. If you improve the surrounding soil (see Evaluating the Soil, page 79), dig the hole at the same time and mix compost with the earth taken from the hole as well.

The size of the hole helps establish the tree in its new site. Make it 1 to 2 feet wider than the ball of the tree, and 4 to 6 inches deeper *(Figure 1)*. Dig the hole wider and deeper in poorer soil, so the tree has better initial growing conditions.

Position the Tree

Put some fill dirt in the hole and tamp it down with your foot. You want enough in the bottom of the hole so the top of the ball is at ground level or slightly above *(Figure 2)*. It will settle somewhat when you water it in Step 4. If you have not previously composted the fill, make a 50-50 mix of soil with compost and wood chips. You can also mix in a balanced (20-20-20) fertilizer with the fill soil or, better yet, use a special slow-release type to help nourish the tree through the initial stress period. Experts differ on first-year fertilizing; ask at the nursery where you buy the tree or consult your county extension agent.

Set the Position

With the tree centered in the hole, look at it from two or three different viewpoints to check that it is standing straight. Then fill the hole about three-quarters full all around. Tamp the soil with a 4x4 *(Figure 3),* but don't ram-pack it. Cut away and remove the burlap and twine or wire around the exposed portion of the ball and trunk.

Water and Fill

Fill the hole with water up to the top *(Figure 4)*. This will settle the soil and remove air pockets. Don't tamp, just let the wet soil settle from its own weight. As the water sinks into the soil, the ball of the tree may settle a bit lower; that is all right. Don't try to raise it. When the water has drained completely into the soil, add enriched fill dirt up to the surface level.

Mound and Mulch

Mound up fill soil at the surface to make a ridge 2 to 3 inches high all around the circumference of the planting hole *(Figure 5)*. If the soil in your yard drains poorly, omit the ridge.

Lay a 3- to 6-inch deep bed of mulch (noncomposted bark chips are good) around the tree to help retain soil moisture and discourage weeds. Keep the mulch a few inches away from the trunk. Then water thoroughly. If you wish, tag the tree as shown on page 82.

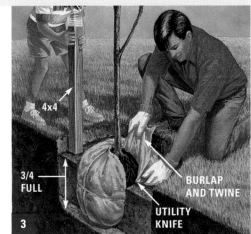

Prepare a planting hole larger and slightly deeper than the tree ball. Make the sides vertical and roughen them with your shovel.

Position the tree on foot-tamped soil so that the top of the ball is at, or slightly higher than, its previous ground level.

Set the position of the tree by filling the hole about 3/4 full. Tamp the soil lightly with a 4x4 and cut away the exposed burlap and twine.

Water, filling the hole to the top to settle the soil. When the water has drained away, fill with dirt to the top.

Mound the fill edges if the surrounding soil drains well. Add 3–6 in. of mulch, keeping it away from the trunk.

All-Weather ID Tag

Nurseries identify saplings with commercially produced tags. You can make tags that will always stay readable, at little or no cost. Cut them out of a frozen dinner tray or foil pie pan.

Place each tag on a soft surface and inscribe it using a ballpoint pen. Press firmly to impress the letters into the soft metal. Attach the tag loosely to your tree, or to anything else that needs weatherproof, permanent identification.

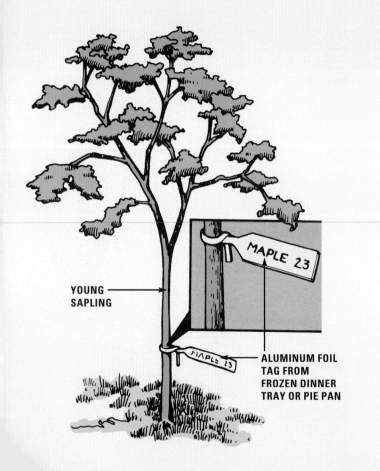

YOUNG SAPLING

MAPLE 23

ALUMINUM FOIL TAG FROM FROZEN DINNER TRAY OR PIE PAN

Bare-root Tree

Handle a bare-root tree with care, and keep the roots covered with a moist cloth while you prepare a hole as explained in the procedures shown on page 81 for planting a bagged tree. Make the hole big enough so you can straighten and spread the roots as you fill in around them *(below)*. Compress the soil with your hands as you work, pulling up on the trunk to keep it from settling too low. When the hole is 3/4 full, water and fill and finish as for a B & B tree.

Spread the roots of a bare-root tree evenly and backfill, working the soil around the roots with your hands. Other steps are the same as for a bagged-and-burlapped tree.

Container-grown Tree

With a container-grown tree, begin as for planting a B & B tree. However, cut away the container before putting the tree in the hole *(below)*. Be careful not to break up the dirt ball. Use a knife to cut encircling roots by making four 1-inch deep slices down the sides and across the bottom. Try to straighten the roots to get them to grow outward. Then fill, water, mound, and mulch as described previously.

CONTAINER

1" DEEP CUTS

Cut away the container before putting a container-grown tree in its hole. Score 1 in. deep grooves on four sides and across the bottom with a knife to cut encircling roots. Plant as with other trees.

Caring for a New Tree

How much water a tree needs depends on the soil and the rainfall in your region. Sandy soils dry out faster and need more water than heavy clay soils. In general, let the soil dry to a depth of about 4 inches before watering. Then, when you set out the hose, let the water run slowly and soak deeply into the soil to promote deeper root growth. The denser the soil, the longer it takes to soak the soil to a sufficient depth.

Fertilization can make your tree grow faster, but you only need to fertilize it every two to three years. Buy tree fertilizer and apply it after the leaves have fallen or before spring growth begins.

Except for removing damaged limbs, prune your tree only when it is dormant. You can prune and shape a bare-root tree immediately (see Pruning Trees, pages 84–91).

Staking isn't usually necessary unless regular high winds threaten to blow your tree over. You may need to stake bare-root trees, because they're poorly anchored during their first year. Loop the ties around the trunk with a soft, loose material that will neither rub the bark off nor block the flow of water and nutrients just under the bark.

Finally, ask local experts about special problems your tree species might have. Thin-barked trees like apple and maple trees "sunburn" in cold winters. Evergreens can dry out during winter if they aren't watered just before freeze-up. Follow the experts' advice in dealing with such problems.

Siting Trees for Shade

For maximum protection from the hot afternoon sun, plant shade trees about 15 feet south and 20 feet west of where you want the shade to fall.

Fast-growing trees, like gum and willow, will give you considerable shade in a very few years, but they contain weak wood that may break off in high winds or heavy snows, making them bad choices for planting close to a house. Slower growing, stronger trees such as oak, maple, or walnut are better candidates for those locations.

Pruning *Trees*

Trees are graceful landscape features that also provide shade and protection for other plants. Proper pruning stimulates healthy tree growth over the years and helps develop an attractive appearance. But improper pruning can ruin the look of a tree and adversely affect its health, or even kill it. Here's what you need to know to prune trees correctly.

The Parts of a Tree

To understand pruning instructions, it helps to know what the various parts of a tree are called. The underground root system supplies water and nutrients to the tree. Pruning deals with the aboveground parts of a tree, labeled in the diagram *(right)*.

The trunk, or leader, extends the tree to its highest point. Cutting it off stops tree growth. If a competing branch forms, creating a double leader, it is usually best to cut it off, leaving the main leader to develop in the center of the tree.

Scaffold branches are the major limbs that grow out of the trunk and establish the spread and structure of the leafy crown. Branches that grow out of the trunk at an angle of about 30° or less are deep-crotch or weak-crotch limbs. They generally should be removed, because with the weight of mature leaf growth the crotch is very susceptible to splitting.

Cross branches grow back at an angle toward the trunk rather than outward. They interfere with the growth of normal branches and they frequently die, leaving unsightly and dangerous dead wood.

Suckers are sprouts that grow out of the trunk near the ground, or upward from the tree roots. Water sprouts most often emerge from the sides of branches. Both should be pruned off at their first appearance. Stubs—unproductive branch ends left by careless pruning—should also be removed by cutting them back to the trunk or the branch from which they grew.

Deciduous trees grow from buds that develop at the ends of branches *(diagram inset)*. Terminal buds form at the very tips of twigs and continue the outward or upward growth of the branch. Lateral buds form on the sides of a twig. They develop into leaves and eventually into branches. Dormant or latent buds are lateral buds that have not yet produced any growth and may not do so for many years. They may start to grow only after other branches have been injured and the tree needs to reestablish the equilibrium between the leaf area—crown size—and the size of the root system.

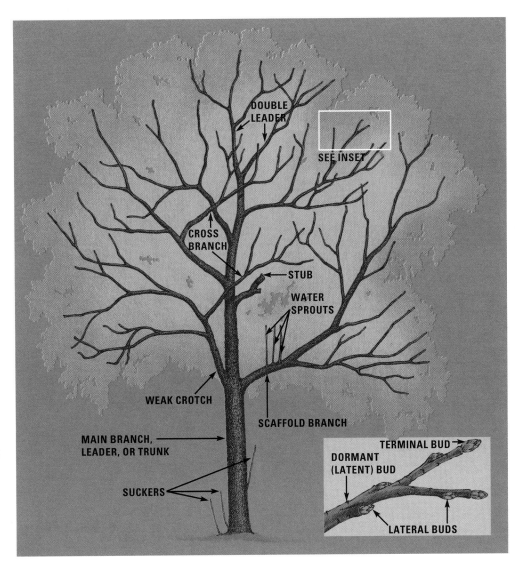

DOUBLE LEADER

SEE INSET

CROSS BRANCH

STUB

WATER SPROUTS

WEAK CROTCH

SCAFFOLD BRANCH

MAIN BRANCH, LEADER, OR TRUNK

SUCKERS

TERMINAL BUD

DORMANT (LATENT) BUD

LATERAL BUDS

Why Prune?

Pruning is much more than a corrective measure. Properly done, pruning strengthens rather than weakens a tree. In fact, it is one of the best things you can do for any tree. There are many important reasons for pruning, including the following:

▶ To ensure good growth when transplanting a tree or planting a new one. Pruning both the roots and the young branches helps the tree get a healthy start.

▶ To control tree shape or form. This is one of the major reasons for pruning during the first years of growth. Later, after the tree has reached maturity, you can't alter its shape or form significantly.

▶ To produce a better appearance. This is something you can do with pruning at all stages in the growth of a tree.

▶ To keep a tree healthy. Like cutting hair and selective surgery, pruning can stimulate growth as well as remove damaged or diseased parts of a tree.

▶ To rejuvenate a tree that is showing signs of neglect or age.

▶ To help the tree produce more and better blossoms or fruit. In fact, without pruning a tree will produce less each year.

▶ To remove branches that endanger property or interfere with overhead wires or nearby structures. A well cared for tree seldom needs this kind of "defensive" or safety pruning, but it is often necessary with a tree whose growth has not been controlled.

When to Prune

A common mistake is to neglect a tree for several years and then, in a flurry of hard, tiring work prune it too severely. Instead, doing just a bit of pruning each year can control growth and appearance and keep trees healthy with a minimum of effort.

You can prune away dead and dying branches anytime during the year, and you can remove weak branches, water sprouts, and suckers anytime during the summer months. The best time to prune living branches is when the tree is dormant—late in winter—when the temperature is in the low 20s F (about –5°C or lower), or early in the spring before the sap begins to flow and new growth begins. That way, wounds can heal without "weeping" or bleeding sap, and without the risk of fungus infection, which is encouraged by heat and humidity. Also, it's much easier to prune when the leaves are gone. You can see the branches clearly, and they are less likely to get hung up as they fall when cut.

Start Young

When you first plant a tree, prune away broken or girdling roots back to the healthy wood; both can restrict growth. Also remove broken or damaged branches, which may be diseased. This will keep any infection from spreading to the good wood.

When you transplant a tree, many roots are severed, which destroys the healthy balance in size between the roots and the crown—the top of the tree. To restore the balance so the tree will survive, a good rule of thumb is to prune it back by one-fourth *(below).* For example, if the planted tree is 4 feet tall, cut away about 12 inches from the branches. Then, during the early years, prune to encourage good growth, as explained on the following pages.

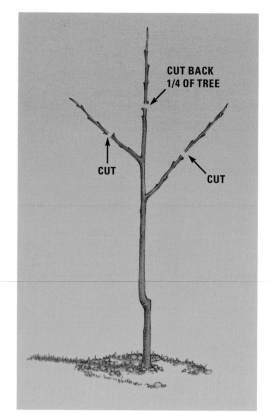

Pruning a new or transplanted tree.

What to Prune

When you examine trees to see what needs pruning, look for the following:

Dead or dying branches. Dead branches are brittle, with no growth or perhaps dead leaves from the previous season. Dying branches have yellowing or brownish, wilting leaves. Cut all such branches back to another healthy branch or to the trunk.

Branch stubs. Remove all stubs by cutting them back to the nearest fork or healthy branch, or the trunk.

Branches growing too close together. Thin out the density to let in the air, light, and rain necessary for the leaves on the inside and lower portions of the plant to grow properly. Thinning also reduces the area where snow or ice can build up and break limbs.

Rubbing branches. Remove any branch that rubs against another. Rubbing can create an open wound where insects can enter and disease can start.

Suckers and water sprouts. These growths are unattractive and weaken the tree.

Dangerous branches. Prune to protect people and property. Eliminate branches that are, or may be, on their way to interfering with power lines; weak branches that overhang play areas, houses, or anyplace frequented by people; and low branches that make the tree climbable, attracting children.

Weak-crotch limbs. Remove branches that have weak or narrow-angle crotches, those that grow at less than 30° from the trunk *(below)*. Weak-crotch limbs are the most likely to tear away, damaging the bark and nearby branches.

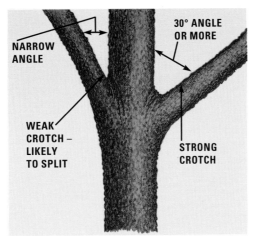

Cut off weak branches, those that have crotch angles of about 30° or less with the main trunk. They are prime candidates for splitting under loads.

The Ideal Tree

With proper pruning during the early years of a tree's growth you can help it to grow straight, with a crown of well-balanced shape and density on all sides.

The ideal development of a tree with a single central leader is shown below. It has a strong, tall-growing main leader or trunk, and scaffold limbs spaced along and around the trunk with no two of them directly above and shading another, lower branch. The key to arriving at this configuration is to examine the tree during the dormant season each year, when there are no leaves, so you can easily see what branches to prune away.

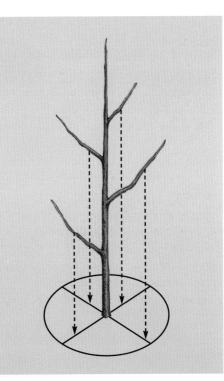

The ideal tree configuration does not have scaffold branches directly above one another.

Pruning Tools

There are two basic kinds of tools you need for pruning, shears and saws. But you need the right kind. Wire cutters or tin snips are not right for cutting twigs and branches. Similarly, a carpenter's saw is for cutting boards, not branches; a chain saw is for cutting down trees or performing major surgery. Neither is a proper tool for tree and shrub pruning in your yard. The tools you do need for pruning are shown below. You can start with a modest investment in shears, a pruning saw, and perhaps a bow saw, and rent the others if you wish.

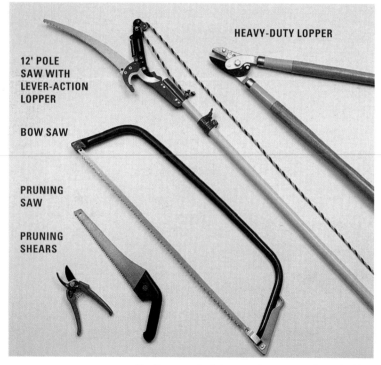

12' POLE SAW WITH LEVER-ACTION LOPPER

BOW SAW

HEAVY-DUTY LOPPER

PRUNING SAW

PRUNING SHEARS

Use the proper tools to prune trees correctly, and with the least amount of work.

Shears for Pruning

For pruning small trees and the buds on branches (page 90), the single most important piece of equipment is a pair of good-quality pruning shears, or an equivalent scissors-type hand pruner. This tool makes it possible to cut branches up to 1/2 inch thick very close to the trunk. Position the thin blade of the shears on the trunk side to keep the resulting stub as short as possible.

For larger branches, you need heavy-duty lopping shears, often simply called a lopper. The long handles give you the leverage needed to let the strong jaws cut through branches up to about 2 inches in diameter; the maximum size depends on the size of the blade or jaw opening.

Saws for Pruning

Branches that are too large for lopping shears have to be sawed off. But never use a conventional shop saw. It requires much more effort, the teeth clog quickly, and it will do a poor job. A pruning saw has larger, self-cleaning teeth, and the blade may be Teflon coated to overcome friction or binding from sap. Depending on the branch size, you may be able to use a pruning saw with a straight or curved blade; there are both rigid and folding models. A curved blade is best for smaller branches, because the saw cuts on the pull stroke. Large, straight-blade, rigid tree saws are used for larger cuts. Avoid saws with teeth on both the top and bottom edges of the blade. For the largest branches, a bow saw is best. Usually you will be cutting with the saw close to the trunk or in other spots where surrounding branches won't interfere.

To deal with high branches, you have two choices: climb a good-quality step or extension ladder, or use a pole saw. If you use a ladder, have someone on the ground to anchor it as you work, and don't carry the saw up with you. Pull the saw up on a rope after you are in position.

If you choose to stay on the ground, use either a pole saw or a pole-pruner, which has a lever-action lopper as well as a slightly curved blade. The blade can be set at various angles to give the best attack; use it for large branches. The lopper is operated by a pull cord or a rod. Use it for small branches that the saw would just rip away, tearing the bark in the process. Poles may be wood or aluminum. A telescoping pole lets you reach more branches than a one-piece pole.

When dealing with large trees and thick branches, hire a professional. No tree is worth risking injury or your life. For the pruning work you do yourself, exercise extreme caution when using saws, poles, or ladders near any overhead power lines. Also check to make sure that any branch you cut, or that may be ripped off when another branch is cut, won't fall onto a power line. Call the utility company if there is any question about whether it is safe for you to do the work yourself.

Sawing Off Branches

Branches too thick for shears or a lopper must be sawed off. Proper sawing technique will prevent damage to the bark and the bark ridge at the base of the branch, and will leave a clean, slightly angled cut, which produces the smallest wound. It will also avoid long stubs, which are avenues for insect infestation and rot. The right and wrong ways of cutting off a branch are shown below. The saw must be sharp, to get a clean, smooth cut that will heal quickly.

Always cut a branch back to its origin in a fork, a larger branch, or the trunk. Make the cut next to, but not into, the branch bark ridges, which are located on the upper side of the point of origin. Cut at an angle to expose a minimum amount of surface. To avoid splintering or tearing when a cut has gone partway through, support the outer end of the branch with a prop from below, if possible, or tie it up with a rope.

Large, heavy branches require a three-cut technique *(below)*. Before starting, tie off the branch just beyond the cutting point to prevent the end from kicking or swinging dangerously when the cut is complete. Then make a first cut about 12 inches out from the origin. From the underside, cut about one-third of the way through the branch, stopping before the saw binds. Make the second cut from the top, about an inch farther out. Cut all the way through. Finally, make the third cut at the branch origin to remove the 12-inch stub.

Working Tip

Do not apply tree paint or wound dressing where you have cut off a branch. Extensive forestry research has determined that these treatments do not stop decay or prevent rot. It is best to let the tree's natural processes heal the wound.

BRANCH BARK RIDGES

WRONG: TOO CLOSE TO BARK RIDGE AND EXPOSES TOO MUCH SURFACE AREA

RIGHT: MINIMAL STUMP, NO BARK DAMAGE, CUT AT AN ANGLE TO MINIMIZE WOUND SIZE

WRONG: TOO MUCH STUMP LEFT—UGLY AND CAN LEAD TO EXTENSIVE TREE DAMAGE

Removing branches the right way *(left)* and the wrong way *(right)*.

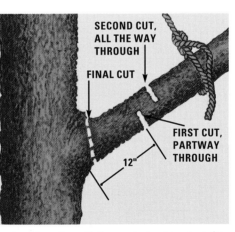

SECOND CUT, ALL THE WAY THROUGH

FINAL CUT

FIRST CUT, PARTWAY THROUGH

12"

Saw large branches with three cuts, two to remove the branch and a third to remove the stub. If possible, tie off the branch before cutting.

Controlling Branch Growth

Branch growth determines the shape of a tree. Controlling branch growth depends on how you trim the buds at the end of each deciduous or coniferous branch.

Pruning Deciduous Branches

The diagram below shows how to encourage three kinds of growth: increasing length (A), branching to all sides (B), and branching to one side (C).

To let a branch grow longer, never trim off the terminal or end bud. As long as this leader bud is intact, the major development of the branch will be in length. When it is trimmed off, the next closest lateral buds inherit its strength and growth. To stop a branch from growing toward a wall, or over a roof or sidewalk, trim off the terminal bud.

If you want to increase the fullness of growth in a tree, remove the terminal buds from some branches, to stimulate the growth of side branches. The lateral buds will develop branches on all sides, with the major amount of growth in the branch closest to where the terminal bud was removed. As these side branches grow, remove those you don't want and control the development of the others by how you trim their buds.

To stimulate growth to just one side, remove the terminal bud and the lateral buds where you do not want growth. All the growing energy in the branch will go into the buds that remain.

Whenever you trim a branch back to a lateral bud, cut to within about 1/4 inch of the bud. Always make the cut at an angle, to minimize wound size for quicker healing.

Pruning Coniferous Branches

Conifers—cone-bearing plants such as pine, juniper, and spruce—need pruning and often shearing as well. Prune conifers only to remove dead or broken branches, or limbs that are interfering with buildings, power lines, other trees, and similar situations.

Shear conifers in the late spring or very early summer just after the new growth, called "candles," is completed. This growth is at the branch ends and usually is a lighter shade of green than the previous growth *(below)*. Trim off about one-third of the new growth for slow, controlled growth. Trim up to two-thirds of the candle length to confine the plant's growth to its existing space. Cut when the new growth is soft; if it has hardened, new buds won't form. Use sharp shears and work just after the tree has been watered, to help avoid needle burn, which occurs when a too-dry conifer is trimmed.

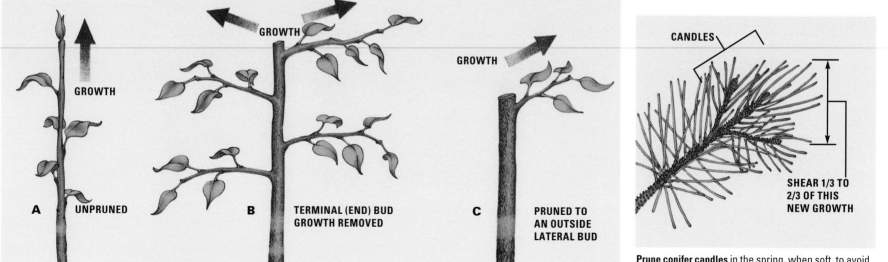

GROWTH

A UNPRUNED

GROWTH

B TERMINAL (END) BUD GROWTH REMOVED

GROWTH

C PRUNED TO AN OUTSIDE LATERAL BUD

CANDLES

SHEAR 1/3 TO 2/3 OF THIS NEW GROWTH

Pruning a branch for growth: (A) in length, (B) for branching on all sides, (C) for branching on one side.

Prune conifer candles in the spring, when soft, to avoid damage. Trim a small amount to slow growth, or more to confine growth to the present space.

Controlling Trunk Growth

When a tree is young, you can prune the main leader or leaders to influence the growth of the trunk. Most shade trees are central-leader trees; others, such as flowering varieties and many fruit trees, are or can be pruned to develop as open-center trees.

To train a central-leader tree, prune back the top in the first year. Over the next few years, prune away some branches to let others develop as scaffold branches. These should be well spaced, each growing out in a different direction. The ideal development of a central-leader tree is shown on page 87.

If a young tree develops a competing leader, or forks from the main trunk *(below left)*, you can do some surgery so it will straighten out significantly in its subsequent growth. Cut away one leader and provide support for the remaining leader *(below)*. As the tree grows, prune the developing branches to encourage scaffold growth that will balance the offset from the main trunk.

To encourage the growth of spreading branches in an open-center tree, prune its leader to keep the height of the tree low. This is the same method as that described at the right for pruning fruit trees.

Special Techniques

Some plants need to be pruned differently than ordinary trees. These plants include fruit trees and shrubs.

Pruning Fruit Trees

Fruit-bearing trees won't always have a strong central leader, as preferred for most other trees. Instead, prune fruit trees to encourage strong scaffold branches. Keep the branch structure fairly open so light and air can reach all parts. This prevents diseases and preserves the fruiting ability of lower limbs. Keeping the crown of the tree low makes it easier to prune and spray, and to harvest the fruit.

Various types of fruit trees have different requirements. Do some research at a nursery or in the library before starting to prune.

Pruning Shrubs

Deciduous shrubs should have branches of all sizes and ages throughout the plant. To keep them healthy, cut away any inward-facing, crossing, or rubbing branches. Remove oversized or lopsided branches that sag toward branches below. Prune some of the older branches back to their origins every few years, to increase flowering and allow new growth. Cut old woody stems down to the soil level.

When an old shrub has grown out of control, cut it back to within 6 inches of the ground. It will send out new shoots and you can raise a new shrub from the old rootstock.

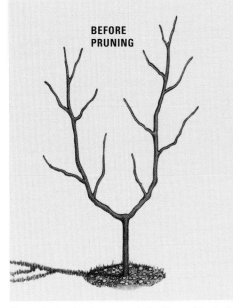

Competing leaders in a young forked tree will retard growth and may produce a major weak crotch in its structure. Remove one leader at the main trunk.

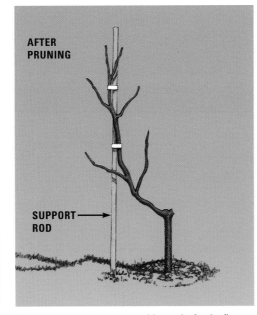

Support the remaining leader with a stake for the first year or two. Correct the shape by pruning emerging branches for good balance as the tree develops.

Planting
a Hedge

*A hedge provides an organic boundary
that encloses your yard, blocks the wind,
and gives privacy. It will blend with other
plants and change with the seasons,
but it takes time. Even a fast-growing hedge
can take three years to grow shoulder high,
so it's important to make a good start now
in order to have a healthy hedge later.
Here's how.*

Planning for a Hedge

A great number of shrub varieties can be planted in a row to grow into a hedge. Among the dozens of species available, you're sure to find several that will thrive in your yard. You need to visit some nurseries and seek out some knowledgeable salespeople, preferably trained horticulturists, for their advice. But first think about what you want, so you'll be prepared to answer the following questions:

▶ Approximately how many hours of direct sunlight will your hedge get each day during the summer months?

▶ How high a hedge do you want? Some species top out at less than 2 feet, but others can grow to over 10 feet. Since taller also means wider, is your yard large enough to accommodate a 3- or 4-foot wide hedge?

▶ Do you want leafy deciduous plants, broad-leaved evergreens, or needled conifers? An evergreen or coniferous hedge stays dense and green year-round. Deciduous species generally grow faster, however, and some provide berries for birds or rich-hued leaves or colorful blossoms.

▶ Do you want a formal hedge *(below left)* or an informal one *(below right)?* Some species are better suited for one than the other.

▶ Are there any special growing conditions? Will the hedge be in a low area that remains soggy after a rain? Will it have to endure constant exhaust fumes and winter road salt along a busy street?

▶ What kind of soil do you have? You'll need a soil test to answer this. Send a sample of your soil to a laboratory, usually at a university or agricultural extension agency; a local nursery can tell you where in your area. You'll get an analysis, plus recommendations for dealing with any problems—for example, whether you should amend the soil with peat moss or fertilizer.

With the above information in hand you can go shopping—see page 96. But you should also be aware of what work you'll have to do. Procedures for planting a hedge are explained on the next two pages.

Formal hedges are tightly shaped by careful and frequent pruning or shearing. This handsome greenery is a row of arborvitae.

Informal hedges, like this row of abelia, are pruned less strictly or even not at all, allowing the natural shape to develop freely.

Dig a trench using stakes and string as a guide. Locate it well within your property line. Pile sod and dirt on tarps or sheets of cardboard to make cleanup easier.

Planting Hedges

Before you can plant a hedge you must prepare a "hedge patch" by removing the sod and digging a trench. You may need to amend the soil you took from the trench to encourage hedge growth; you'll use it as backfill around the roots of the plants. The procedures for planting bare-root and container-grown plants are slightly different. Here's what to do with each type.

Digging a Trench

To prepare for planting bare-root stock, dig a trench about 18 inches wide and 12 inches deep. For container-grown plants make it twice as wide and about as deep as the containers. Use stakes and a string as a guide *(left)*, and make sure the trench is far enough inside your property so that the mature hedge won't encroach on your neighbor's yard. Pile the sod and dirt on a tarp or large sheets of cardboard or scrap panels so you can work with it later and clean up easily.

If you're planting a long hedge, save yourself some hard labor by renting a power sod cutter. You can use the sod elsewhere in your yard if you keep it moist and put it in place within a day (see Laying Sod, pages 28–31). Otherwise, turn it upside down in the completed trench; it will decompose and nourish the hedge.

Preparing the Backfill

When the trench is complete, amend the backfill dirt as recommended by the soil testing lab or the experts at the nursery where you bought the hedge plants. You may need to add manure, peat moss, fertilizer, or other ingredients to the backfill *(below)*. Mix everything thoroughly: unmixed pockets of manure or fertilizer can damage the roots. Even if you don't have to add anything, break up all large clumps and get rid of stones, dead roots, dog bones, and similar unwanted items.

Prepare the backfill by mixing in peat moss, manure, or fertilizer as recommended in your soil test. Mix thoroughly, break up all clumps, and remove foreign matter.

Setting Bare-root Plants

Put the plants in the trench one by one, aligning them against a string stretched down the center. For each plant, form a cone of soil in the bottom of the trench and fan the bare roots out over the cone *(below)*. The cone must be high enough so that the plant is at its original depth. A visible soil line around the stem will show how deep to plant it. When the height is right, spread backfill up to about half the depth of the trench. After all the plants are placed this way, thoroughly soak the trench to settle the soil, then backfill completely and water again. If you make the entire trench area an inch or two lower than the surrounding soil, it will act as a basin to make watering more effective.

Set bare-root plants with their roots fanned over a cone of soil in the trench *(inset)*. Backfill to half the trench depth, water, backfill completely, and water again.

Setting Container-grown Plants

Remove a plant from its container, keeping the ball of roots and soil intact. It may be easiest to slit the sides of the container with a utility knife to do this. Cut away any girdling, dead, or damaged roots and loosen the roots a bit by working the tip of a trowel down the sides of the root ball *(below)*. This will help them spread into the surrounding soil. Set the plant in the trench, using backfill soil to put the top of the container soil at the intended top of the trench. Water thoroughly when the trench is about half full of backfill, and then again after the final filling, as described for bare-root plants.

Remove container-grown plants and loosen their roots before planting, but do not lose the soil around the roots. Backfill and water as for bare-root plants.

Caring for a Hedge

After planting and thoroughly watering the hedge area you may want to lay down mulch to help keep the soil cool and moist and discourage weeds. Use an organic mulch (see Mulching Your Garden, pages 101–107), not decorative stones, which reflect sunlight and may damage the plants.

Water and feed the hedge as recommended by your nursery or supplier. When it has grown enough to be pruned, trim the growth so that the hedge is wider at the base than at the top *(below)*. That way sunlight will reach the lower branches and the hedge will grow dense with healthy leaves. Shaping the bottom narrower than the top will produce a crown of leaves with bare spindly stems below. The suggestions given for pruning shrubs on page 91 also apply to hedges.

Prune a hedge so the base is wider than the top, to let light reach all the leaves. A tall hedge, like this laurel, needs a wide base; be sure to plan for that in planting.

Popular Hedge Plants

SPECIES	CONDITIONS
Deciduous	
Barberry	Sun; shade
Beech	Sun; partial shade
Buckthorn	Sun; partial shade
Flowering plum	Sun
Flowering quince	Sun; partial shade
Forsythia	Sun; partial shade
Fuchsia	Sun; partial shade
Hawthorn	Sun; partial shade
Hornbeam	Sun; partial shade
Mock orange	Sun
Privet	Sun
Rose	Sun
Siberian pea tree	Sun
Willow	Sun
Evergreen	
Arborvitae	Sun
Boxwood	Sun; partial shade
Bush cherry	Sun
Camellia	Partial shade
Cotoneaster	Sun; partial shade
Escallonia	Sun
Euonymus	Sun; partial shade
False cypress	Sun
Firethorn	Sun
Hemlock	Sun; partial shade
Holly	Sun; partial shade
Honeysuckle	Sun; partial shade
Japanese pittosporum	Sun; partial shade
Leyland cypress	Sun; partial shade
Mahonia/Oregon grape	Partial shade
Prunus	Sun
Yew	Sun; shade

Shopping for Hedges

When you are ready to buy hedge plants, you will find most of them come packaged in one of two ways. However they are offered, you need to inspect them carefully when buying stock for your yard.

Plant Packaging

You can buy hedge shrubs as either bare-root or container-grown plants. The bare-root kind are by far the cheapest. And because they don't come set in several pounds of soil, they're easy to transport and plant. But bare-root plants are small—usually only one year old when you buy them—so you'll need to be patient waiting for significant growth. They should be planted when they're dormant—early spring in most places, or winter in warmer climates.

Container-grown plants are sometimes larger than bare-root plants and may be up to three years old. They will cost more and will be significantly heavier to transport, but they can be planted at any time of year.

You may also find large hedge plants sold with their root balls wrapped in burlap. These will be very heavy and the most expensive of all. Save work and a great deal of money by buying one of the other forms.

When comparing the prices of hedge plants, remember that different species are spaced at different intervals, usually 1 to 3 feet. So for a 60-foot hedge you may need as few as twenty plants or as many as sixty. Remember too that you may save money by buying in the fall, when nurseries are anxious to clear their inventories. But look things over carefully. Weak, sickly, or potbound plants are not a bargain.

Look Carefully

Although you can find hedge plants in the garden sections of home centers and in mail-order catalogs, you are best off buying from a local nursery. Deal with a nursery that guarantees to replace any plants that die after planting for at least three months; many offer a year's guarantee. Some also offer quantity discounts; be sure to ask.

Inspect the plants before you take them home. Bare-root plants are usually dormant when sold, but there are signs of life to look for. Healthy roots are thick, plump, and supple. Roots that are shriveled or brittle have dried out and may have died. Avoid plants with split or sun-scorched bark on the stem. And the more buds on the stems or branches, the better.

Inspect the leaves of container-grown plants. Trouble signs are fairly obvious: black spots, yellowing, ragged edges, or holes created by hungry insects.

Plant the shrubs as soon as possible after you buy them. In the meantime, store them in a cool shady place. It's best to pack the roots of bare-root plants in damp peat moss and then soak them in a bucket of water overnight before planting.

Foundation *Plantings*

The plants you use next to the house are the key to integrating your home with its surroundings. Here's how to choose and place foundation plantings to bring out the best in your home—and hide the worst!

Create a Master Plan

Foundation plantings give scale and balance as they integrate your home with its surroundings. They direct attention, prevent soil erosion, and attract birds. You'll need to have a plan before you begin.

Start by making a scaled drawing of your house on 1/4-inch grid paper, one square equaling 1 foot. Include any existing trees and other major features. Make multiple copies so you can sketch various schemes as you consider the following points:

▶ What do you want to hide, and what do you want to draw attention to? For example, a window can be shielded for privacy or shade, or left with a clear view of a garden.

▶ What do you want to see from inside, both as a view and immediately outside the window? Evergreens? Flowering bushes? An ornamental shrub? Vines?

▶ How large do you want the plants to be? Generally, deciduous plants that lose their leaves naturally grow about as wide as they are tall. Coniferous and evergreen plants tend to grow either vertically or horizontally. Keep the mature plant size in mind when considering what to use in various spots.

▶ How much time can you spend on maintenance? Some plants require little care, but others need frequent feeding and pruning.

▶ What plants do well in your area? Ask nurseries, garden clubs, and fellow gardeners.

▶ What colors and textures do you want? There is an enormous range. Choose blossoms and greenery that compliment your house. Mix sizes and shapes of coniferous and deciduous plants for variety.

Foundation Planting Principles

When you begin to work on master plan sketches to lay out what plants you will place in various locations, visualize the effect when seen from the street, sidewalk, driveway, or other points of view. It may help to have some color photographs of your house from various angles. In addition, there are certain principles or guidelines for choosing and placing foundation plantings effectively. The key points are labeled in the illustrations on the opposite page and on page 100. Here's what they mean.

Pull attention away from the driveway. Locate mass plantings around the house and walkway leading to the entrance. Avoid placing plants along the driveway. Use progressively larger plants nearer the house, as suggested below, so the visual effect develops in scale.

Draw attention to the entrance. Flank the walkway with low-growing plants, such as hostas, to serve as guides that lead visitors to the front door.

Highlight the front door. Surround the entry with taller plants, such as arborvitae, or vines like Boston ivy, to draw the eye upward and focus attention on the porch and front door. Be careful in your choices: Some vines will damage siding and bricks over time.

Create smooth transitions at corners. Wrap plantings around the corner of the house to visually link the side yard to the front yard.

Do this with a series of plants of the same type or same general color along the lawn edge. Use a tall shrub, such as peegee hydrangea or winged euonymus, behind them to soften the hard-edged look of the corner of the house.

Control your views. Use tall shrubs or vines to screen windows for privacy. Place low-growing shrubs beneath windows where you want to keep the view open. To shade a window without blocking the view, plant a tree a short distance from the house and to one side, in the direction of the predominant angle of the sun (see Planting Trees, pages 78–83).

Hide unattractive features. Plant full shrubs such as viburnum, and ground covers, like pachysandra, or ferns to hide an exposed foundation from view. (See Growing Ground Covers, pages 69–72.)

You can also use plantings to hide air conditioners, meters, and other less than attractive features. Be careful, however, not to block access to hose faucets or exterior electrical outlets. And anticipate plant size at maturity. Planting too close to the house can make painting difficult, or restrict the air circulation necessary to evaporate moisture from the foundation or house siding.

PULL ATTENTION AWAY
FROM THE DRIVEWAY

HIGHLIGHT THE
FRONT DOOR

DRAW ATTENTION TO
THE ENTRANCE

CREATE SMOOTH
TRANSITIONS AT
CORNERS

CONTROL YOUR
VIEWS

HIDE UNATTRACTIVE
FEATURES

**CHOOSE PLANTS WITH
SEASONAL INTEREST**

VARY PLANT TYPES

USE COLORS WISELY

Additional Principles of Foundation Planting

Foundation plantings should extend around the sides and the back of the house to make the landscaping as pleasant for you and guests in your yard as it is for passersby. Several of the principles already discussed apply all around the house too, so consider the following as you create your plan:

Choose plants with seasonal interest. Consider how various plants will look during each season of the year. Some shrubs, such as the red-twigged dogwood, have beautiful red branches in the winter; others, such as the yew, are attractive and green all year long. Still others, like the winged euonymus, have sculptural branches that become visible when the leaves drop. Many nurseries have catalogs that show you how various plants look, but remember that the photographs are taken at the peak of each plant.

Vary plant types. Mix deciduous and coniferous shrubs with ground covers, vines, and flowers to give a variety of texture that will add interest to the overall landscaping.

Use colors wisely. A colorful flower or plant draws attention. Be sure to place color where you want to focus attention. Whether you plant flowering shrubs or flowers, or choose plants with colorful spring, summer, or fall foliage, their colors should complement each other and the colors of your house.

Finally, remember that you don't have to make an investment all at once. Break your project into easily manageable phases of investment and work.

Mulching
Your Garden

Mulch is the smart gardener's magic carpet. Around foundation plantings, on flower beds, in vegetable gardens, it will save you time, conserve water, and stop weeds. What more could you ask?

Marvelous Mulch

Mulch is a fantastic landscaping material. It slashes water bills, improves the health and appearance of your plants, and saves your back from hours of weeding.

Serious vegetable gardeners have used and praised mulch for years, but they shouldn't be the only ones to enjoy its benefits. Whether you're creating new planting beds or rearranging old ones, whether you raise flowers in great number, want to landscape around your house, or simply want to grow some blooming plants or vegetables with a minimum of effort, mulch should be an integral part of your plan.

What Mulch Does

Mulch is any material spread atop the soil in planting beds. It may be organic, such as plant and tree materials, or inorganic, usually rock or stone. Whatever its size, shape, or form, mulch can do many things, including the following:

▶ Greatly reduce soil moisture loss. One-third of the water consumed around our homes is used on landscaping—and half of that is wasted through evaporation. Mulch acts somewhat like a one-way door: It allows water into the soil, but slows its departure through evaporation. Mulch also limits soil erosion and runoff.

▶ Eliminate or suppress weed growth. A 3- to 4-inch layer of mulch makes it difficult for weed seeds to work their way into the soil. And by blocking light, mulch makes it harder for seeds that do sneak into the soil to germinate and grow. If a weed does struggle through—thistle and quack grass are tough customers—it will be easier to pull, because the soil will be loose and moist. This means you can get by with few or no chemicals and weed killers.

▶ Protect soil and plants from temperature extremes. Mulch acts like insulation; it keeps the ground cool on hot days and warm on cold ones. It helps protect roots and plants by moderating traumatic day-night, freeze-thaw cycles.

▶ Promote vigorous growth in young plants, newly planted trees, and shrubs. These all have shallow root systems, totally dependent on rain or manual watering for moisture. Mulch holds that moisture in the soil for their use.

▶ Enrich the soil. Organic mulches add valuable nutrients to the soil as they decompose. Earthworms are attracted to the cool, rich soil beneath. Soil that normally bakes to a hard crust stays loose and moist.

▶ Provide a protective buffer. Mulch forms a border to keep your mower and string trimmer at a distance, and absorbs the damage when they accidentally come across that border.

▶ Improve the appearance of the landscape. Mulch adds color and texture to your planting beds. It prevents mud from splashing your house and plants during rains, and provides a clean "carpet" for you to walk on as you tend your garden. It also helps to visually fill in the space while young plants grow to maturity to round out a planting bed.

Organic Mulch

There is no perfect mulch. When selecting one, consider how it will look vs. how it will perform; how long it will last vs. how hard it is to maintain. Compare the features of organic mulches, discussed here, with those of rock and stone (opposite page) and choose what is best for your needs.

Shredded and chipped tree and bark products. These materials *(below)* are the most popular mulches. Cedar, redwood, and hardwoods like oak or maple last longer and are less likely to promote mold than pine and other softwoods. Shredded mulches interweave into a large mass, making them less likely to blow or float away. This makes them ideal for use on sloped hillsides or in areas where water splashes from roof overhangs.

Chipped or shredded bark and other tree products provide an excellent mulch around ornamental bushes and shrubs, with or without a weed barrier.

Grass clippings, shredded leaves, and leaf mold. These are home-grown mulches that do everything a good mulch should do, but use them with care. They break down rapidly, so don't use a weed barrier (see page 104) beneath them. Spread grass clippings in thin layers and beware of clippings that contain heavy doses of lawn fertilizer or weed killer, which may harm your plants or change the balance of your soil. Grass and leaves may smell as they decompose if they are in dense layers. Try them first in a spot well separated from your house or patio and use dry material.

Peanut, cottonseed, and cocoa bean hulls. The hulls of seeds and similar plant products make excellent mulches, especially in flower beds. Cocoa bean hulls *(below)* smell sweet and chocolaty after a rain. That may make them irresistible, or something to avoid.

Bean and seed hulls and other finely ground materials make excellent mulches for annual and perennial flower beds. A weed barrier is not ordinarily used under mulch in a flower bed.

Straw, hay, and pine needles. For inexpensive, easily renewed mulches, these are good choices. Be sure to use weed-free hay or straw that was cut before it went to seed. Pine needles tend to make the soil more acidic, which is fine for plants like azaleas and philodendrons, but not for others. If you're not sure, ask at a local nursery or garden center.

Compost. You can buy compost, but you can also get it for nothing: create a compost pile to dispose of leaves, clippings, and even household vegetable waste. Used as a mulch, compost provides protection and slowly feeds nutrients to the soil. Many gardeners place wood chips or other mulches on top of a thin layer of compost.

Rock and Stone Mulch

Crushed rock or stone suitable for use as mulch ranges from plain gravel to volcanic rock to multicolored stone *(right)*. These materials are generally 50 to 70 percent more expensive than organic mulches, but they can add color, texture, and variety to the landscape around your house.

Use rocks or stones with caution. They are heavy and permanent, and need to be used in the right places. They can complement the stone or brickwork of your home, especially when used next to the foundation, but may be hard-edged and out of character with landscaping that is intended to soften the lines of your house, driveway, and sidewalk.

You need to judge visual appropriateness. Rock makes a great pathway or border along a driveway. It can also define a space around trees and shrubs. But you should consider the following potential disadvantages.

▷ Rock can overheat plants and damage tender stems and leaves. It can act as a heat sink and literally bake some shrubs, especially low-growing ones like junipers. This is an important consideration with sun-drenched planting beds.

▷ Rock will prevent the growth of ground cover plants that spread by dropping runners that take root in the soil.

▷ Rock can crowd out or damage the stems of plants as they grow. Organic mulches easily move aside to accommodate the growing trunk of a tree or shrub, but a layer of rock stubbornly tends to stay put.

▷ A fabric or plastic weed barrier *(next page)* must always be used with rock. Otherwise, weed seeds will easily wash down into the soil and take root.

▷ Rocks that migrate from the planting bed into your grass present a danger when they are thrown by a lawnmower.

Washed gravel, crushed rock, and stone provide a permanent mulch in established planting beds. Always use a fabric or plastic weed barrier underneath stone.

Weed Barriers

Whether or not to use a weed barrier under mulch is a much-argued question among serious gardeners. Weed barriers *(below right)* are plastics or fabrics laid over the soil before the mulch is spread, to further suppress weeds and limit water evaporation. Some landscapers choose not to use a weed barrier. Among those who do use barriers, some prefer fabric and others plastic materials.

One problem is that over the years, dust, dirt, and decaying matter build up on top of a weed barrier, forming a thin bed in which weed seeds can grow. Hardy weeds can eventually take root and grow right through fabrics. Another objection is that weed barriers, particularly plastics, prevent the nutrients in decomposing mulches from working their way into the soil. They also take away flexibility: If you want to add or remove plants, you need to deal with the weed barrier beneath.

Nevertheless, weed barriers have much to offer. A simple rule of thumb for using weed barriers might be that the more permanent the planting bed, the more you should consider using them. Therefore, avoid using them in annual flower gardens. Strongly consider using them in ornamental or perennial planting beds, and with mature trees or shrubs—in areas where you don't want to spend any time pulling weeds.

Here are some features of the two major types of weed barriers, fabric and plastic.

Fabric Barriers

Gardening or landscape fabrics—geotextiles —cost about ten to fifteen cents per square foot and are available in a variety of materials and construction. A nonwoven fabric has a texture somewhat like felt. A woven fabric barrier has a loose plastic weave on one face for strength and a fuzzy textile-fiber surface on the other to wick moisture down into the soil. All fabric barriers allow moisture, air, and varying amounts of nutrients to work their way into the soil, yet help prevent weeds from taking root or sprouting. However, because fabrics are penetrable, even the best of them can't stop all weeds.

You can safely lay fabrics right up to the plant stems without affecting the health of a plant, and you can cover them with either organic mulch or rock. Because they cling to the soil, fabric barriers are a much better choice than plastic for use on steep hills and rolling terrain.

When you use a fabric barrier, make certain to cover it with a 3- to 4-inch layer of mulch, to help prevent weed seeds from reaching it. Mulch will also keep the fabric from deteriorating by blocking the sun's ultraviolet rays.

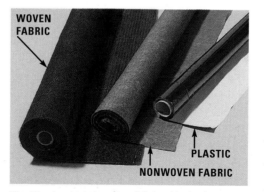

Weed barriers include woven fabric with plastic on one side, fibers on the other; nonwoven, feltlike fabric; and plastic, either all black or all white on one side, and black on the other.

Plastic Barriers

Plastic weed barriers cost about five cents a square foot and are impenetrable to weeds. But they reject rain, air, and nutrients with equal efficiency, which means the plastic must be perforated to let these elements through. And that provides a place for weeds to enter and germinate.

If you are going to use plastic, use 6-mil thick black or black/white rather than clear plastic; it does a better job of keeping sunlight from reaching weed seeds and will last longer when exposed to the sun. Also, bear in mind:

▶ Black plastic absorbs and holds heat, which can damage a plant and its root system. It can also promote shallow or weak root growth.

▶ Never use plastic under loose or organic mulch in an area where you walk; it will produce a dangerous, slippery surface.

▶ If you do use plastic, you must cut a 1- or 2-foot diameter hole around each plant so it can receive plenty of moisture. Cover any plastic completely; sunlight will quickly deteriorate it.

There are situations where plastic is a good idea. If you have a wet basement, slope the soil away from the house, then cover it with plastic and rock to direct water away from the foundation. Black plastic is also a good choice for rock gardens or gardens containing well-established trees and shrubs. Where you want to use light-colored or white decorative stones, use black/white plastic underneath with the white side up.

Principles of Mulching a Garden Bed

There is no one-and-only way to prepare and mulch a planting bed, but this diagram shows the most important principles of mulching any kind of flower or vegetable planting bed.

Make sure the bed slopes away from the foundation of a house, for good drainage. When planting, improve the soil in the planting hole by adding peat moss and nutrients as recommended by the plant supplier. Lay down a weed barrier; fabrics can touch the plant stems, but keep plastic 1 to 2 feet away. Cover the barrier with 3 to 4 inches of mulch, but use less around the base of the plants. To avoid insect and moisture problems make sure no mulch touches the siding of your house.

Detailed instructions for mulching a planting bed in this way are given on pages 106–107.

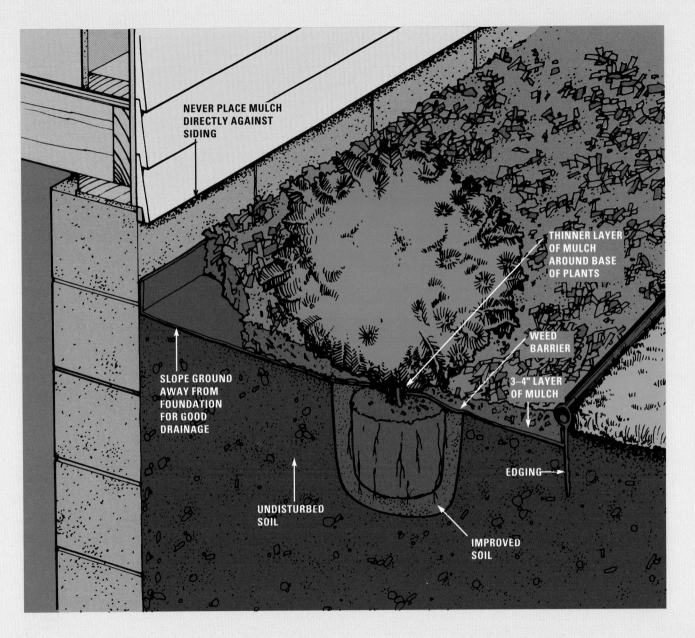

NEVER PLACE MULCH DIRECTLY AGAINST SIDING

THINNER LAYER OF MULCH AROUND BASE OF PLANTS

WEED BARRIER

SLOPE GROUND AWAY FROM FOUNDATION FOR GOOD DRAINAGE

3–4" LAYER OF MULCH

EDGING

UNDISTURBED SOIL

IMPROVED SOIL

Mulching a Planting Bed

It's not difficult to prepare and mulch a planting bed. If you are planting lots of small perennials, you may want to prepare the bed as described here, lay down a weed barrier first, and make slits in it in order to dig holes and plant the flowers; then spread mulch and finish up as described. However, the steps illustrated here are much better for putting in larger plants and shrubs, where all the digging and jostling involved can damage the barrier and leave soil on top of it.

Prepare the Bed

Remove the sod and add black dirt if needed as you loosen the soil. If the bed is next to your house, slope it away from the foundation by at least 1/4 inch per foot. Pull up every weed you see, roots and all. Because weed seeds can lie dormant for years before springing to life, consider sprinkling a preemergent herbicide over the area to kill most seeds before they germinate. Then install edging to contain the mulch. You can use plastic, wood, modular concrete pieces, or even large stones.

Dig holes and place the plants *(Photo 1)* according to their planting directions. Be sure to position the plants in terms of how much space they will require when fully grown. Fill around the plants with dirt, then soak thoroughly to eliminate air pockets around the roots. Clean the bed a final time and rake it smooth.

Install a Weed Barrier

Lay your fabric or plastic weed barrier loosely over the plants and cut through it at each plant position. Cut an X in the material *(Photo 2)* so you can slip it down around the plant and cut off the excess close to the plant stems. If fabric touches the stems, that's all right. If you use plastic, cut out a 1- to 2-foot diameter circle around each plant so that plenty of moisture can reach the roots.

MULCHING A PLANTING BED

FABRIC WEED BARRIER

UTILITY KNIFE

OVERLAP EDGING

OVERLAP SEAMS 6"

Prepare the bed by weeding, sloping, and loosening the soil. Add black dirt or nutrients if needed and install a border edging. Leave enough space between plants to allow for their mature size.

Install a weed barrier loosely over the plants. Use fabric or plastic as appropriate. Cut an X through fabric; cut out a 1- to 2-ft. circle in plastic so adequate moisture can reach the soil.

Overlap barrier seams at least 6 in. wherever two pieces must be joined. Don't use an adhesive, which could damage plants; the weight of the mulch or rock will hold the edges in place.

Overlap Barrier Seams

Wherever you need to use more than one piece of barrier material, overlap the seams by at least 6 inches *(Photo 3)*. Do this with both fabric and plastic barriers. Do not use adhesive in the seams. The weight of the mulch or rock will keep the seams closed, and most adhesives contain substances that can damage plants. Let the fabric extend well beyond the edges of the bed; you'll trim it off neatly later.

Spread Mulch or Rock

Add a layer of mulch or rock, whichever you have chosen, over the barrier *(Photo 4)*. Make the layer 3 to 4 inches deep between plants, but only 2 to 3 inches deep under plants and around the trunks and bases of shrubs. Don't skimp, or weed seeds are more likely to slip in and water is more likely to evaporate. Keep mulch from touching the siding of your house; it can cause rot or give insects access to the siding.

Trim the Weed Barrier

As a final step, trim the weed barrier neatly along the inside of the edging you placed around the borders of the bed *(Photo 5)*. Check annually to make certain the weed barrier remains totally covered by mulch; direct sunlight will cause it to deteriorate.

Maintaining Mulch

Mulches and rock eliminate most maintenance chores, but they present a few of their own. In the fall, leaves must be removed from the planting beds. Shredded materials, because they interweave, are resistant to being raked from the bed; wood chips or hulls tend to get raked up with the leaves. A blower is an effective way to clean rock beds.

When you mow your lawn, direct grass clippings away from mulched beds, especially those with an underlying weed barrier. Grass clippings rapidly decompose and form a weed-planting bed on top of weed barriers; that's a real chore to correct if you have used rock mulch.

In the spring you can renew the depth and color of organic mulch by top-dressing your beds with 1/2 inch of fresh material. Occasionally during the growing season, fluff up the mulch with a pitchfork to reestablish air circulation.

Some mulches, particularly straw, sawdust, and wood shavings, can rob the soil of nitrogen as they decompose. If your plants appear yellow or stunted, you may need to add high-nitrogen fertilizer.

Over time you'll get a feel for how much weeding and watering your planting bed requires. When you do water mulched plants, stick the end of the hose down under the mulch and slowly, but thoroughly, soak the soil. Or lay the hose from a drip watering system under the mulch to water the bed thoroughly (see pages 73–75).

4 WOOD CHIP MULCH SPREAD 3–4" THICK

Spread mulch or rock on top of the weed barrier. It should be 3–4 in. deep between plants, but only 2–3 in. deep under the foliage and next to the trunks of shrubs.

5

Trim the weed barrier neatly along the inside of the border edging as the finishing step. Keep the barrier covered with mulch or rock to prevent deterioration.

Walks & Walls

Laying a Flagstone Footpath

A flagstone walkway will add the charm of natural colors and varied shapes to your yard or garden. Laying flagstones in a bed of sand is easy and gives you complete freedom in design.

110

Brick Accents for Walkways

For a distinctive-looking sidewalk, edge it with brick pavers. It's quick and easy, and far more attractive than concrete. You can edge planting beds the same way.

114

Building Landscaping Walls

Use landscaping walls to create terraces and raised planting beds. Straight or curved walls are easy to build using modular, decorative concrete blocks that don't need mortar.

120

Building Dry Stone Walls

Natural materials harmonize beautifully with natural surroundings. A mortar-free wall of natural stone is a structure you can erect at your own pace; built well, it can last a lifetime.

128

Building a Timber Retaining Wall

For holding earth in place, a wall of landscaping timbers is both strong and good looking. All you really need to build it are a shovel, a saw, spikes, a sledgehammer, and a strong back.

136

Laying a
Flagstone Footpath

A walkway with the natural colors and varied shapes of flagstones can be a beautiful feature of a garden or a handsome complement to a house. There's a hard way and an easy way to lay a flagstone footpath. Here's the easy way.

Getting Started

Your two initial concerns in laying a flagstone footpath will be to choose the right method of construction and to select the materials you will use.

Two Methods

There are two principal methods of laying flagstones. For a one-person, homeowner project, one method is to lay flagstones in a bed of mortar on top of a concrete slab. But that is expensive, time consuming, and very hard work. Although such a walk can survive many disasters, like any concrete slab it's destined to crack sooner or later. Making repairs can be a big job.

Another method is much simpler: you lay the flagstones in a bed of sand. It is far cheaper and much less work. The actual steps are shown on pages 112–113.

The sand-bed method gives you great flexibility in what you choose to do. You can easily curve the path as you wish. You can use fairly uniform stones for a somewhat formal effect, or various sizes and shapes for a gracious, informal look. You don't have to build forms, lay down gravel, or mix concrete and mortar. The biggest maintenance problem will be a stone that sinks or perhaps one that gets pushed up by a frost heave. It's a simple matter to pry up the stone, add or remove some sand as necessary, and set the stone back in place.

Materials and Costs

You will need landscape fabric, sand, and flagstones. The cost of these materials varies greatly from region to region and among suppliers in any given region, so it pays to do some comparison shopping. The walk illustrated in this project cost about $225 for a 3-foot by 25-foot section. You can use that to estimate what a longer or wider walk might cost. The figures given below indicate the proportionate expense of various items, but the actual prices you will pay will probably be somewhat different. And tool rental—for a sod cutter or soil tamper, for example—will be additional.

Landscape fabric. Underneath your walk you'll need a layer of good-quality landscape fabric. A 3-foot by 25-foot roll costs about $15 at home centers. Do not use plastic sheeting. Although it will keep weeds from popping up between stones, plastic will not let water flow down into the soil. Instead, it will flow between and under the stones, washing away the sand.

Sand. You'll need enough sand to make it impractical to try to haul it yourself. One cubic yard of washed sand—delivered—costs about $50, but the price varies greatly among suppliers. To minimize delivery fees, you may want to buy both the sand and the stone from the same source. Check the Yellow Pages under "Landscape Equipment and Supplies" and "Stone, Natural."

Flagstones. The generic term "flagstone" covers dozens of stone types—look at what's available before ordering. A ton of 1-1/2 inch thick yellow flagstone is about $150, but again the cost will vary widely, depending on where you live and the type of stone you choose. Suppliers can tell you roughly how many square feet of coverage you'll get from a ton of a given type of stone. Thinner flagstone will give you more coverage for your money, but the thinner the stone, the more likely it is to crack and the less likely to stay put. Stones less than 1 inch thick are easily cracked or kicked out of place.

The Sand-bed Method

Laying flagstones in sand involves work: you'll have to move lots of soil, sand, and stone, but not nearly as much as a concrete walk would require. The great virtue of the sand-bed method is simplicity. You dig a shallow trench, add sand, fit the stones together like a puzzle, and fill the cracks with sand. The individual steps are explained at the right. Following are some tips:

▶ If you want a path with straight rather than irregular edges, choose stones that have one straight edge and lay them first, using their straight edges to form the outside lines of the path. Then fill in between them with other pieces to complete the path.

▶ Step back occasionally and take a look at the pattern you're creating, before it's too late to make rearrangements easily. Try to avoid clusters of stones that are similar sizes, shapes, or colors. A great part of the appeal of a flagstone walk is its variety.

▶ Cutting some kinds of stone accurately is difficult; with other kinds it's almost impossible. If you must cut, try this—wearing safety glasses and work gloves. Score a straight line on the back side of the stone with a hammer and cold chisel. Turn the stone over, place a 2x4 or metal pipe under the scored line, and strike the waste side with a hammer.

▶ To break up a stone that is too big to look good in your path, set it in place on the sand and strike it with a sledgehammer—it will break into several pieces with matching edges. This works better with some types of stone than others, of course. Again, wear safety glasses.

Working Tip

Lay one or two large stones rather than several small ones wherever the path meets a set of steps, a sidewalk, or a driveway.

Laying the Footpath

The procedures for laying a flagstone footpath are shown on the opposite page. Here's what to do at each step.

Dig a Trench

Lay out a pair of garden hoses to mark the edges of your path *(Photo 1)*. Remove the sod and dig down about 4 inches. If you can use the sod elsewhere in the yard, skim it off using a flat spade or—much easier—rent a gas-powered sod cutter to lift it neatly. If you don't have a wheelbarrow, pile the dirt on a tarp, plastic sheeting, or even large sheets of cardboard to make lawn cleanup easy. Lay a 2x4 across the trench and check the depth with a measuring tape or ruler.

Lay Landscape Fabric

Roll out landscape fabric to cover the bottom of the trench *(Photo 2)*. If the fabric is a bit too wide, you can cut it with a utility knife or just fold over the excess. To go around curves, pleat the fabric and fold it onto itself. If you find it necessary to cut the fabric into separate pieces to make a bend or turn a corner, overlap their edges about 6 inches. Adhesive is not necessary; the weight of the sand will hold the overlap in place.

Spread the Sand

Shovel sand on top of the landscape fabric all along the trench *(Photo 3)* and level it with a garden rake. Use the tines of the rake to distribute the sand; turn the rake over and use the back edge to smooth the surface. Bring the sand about even with the surrounding soil, then tamp the sand to

compact it. A 6-inch scrap of 2x6 nailed to the end of a 6- or 8-foot 4x4 makes a good tamping tool. Hold the 4x4 upright and pound the sand with the 2x6. For a big path, consider renting a gas-powered tamper to do the work quickly and easily.

Lay the Stones

Put each stone in place and settle it by twisting it back and forth slightly as you apply downward pressure *(Photo 4)*. Check the evenness of the path frequently by laying a 2x4 on edge across the stones. You can adjust the level of a stone easily by adding or removing sand. If an edge is a bit high, step firmly on it, or lay a 2x4 flat across it and tap with a hammer. Don't pound forcefully with a sledgehammer, and never pound directly on a stone with a hammer of any size unless you intend to break it.

Fill the Cracks

Sweep sand over the path to fill the cracks between the stones *(Photo 5)*. Settle and solidify the sand by soaking the path with a light spray of water. Don't use a heavy stream that will wash the sand out of the cracks. When the sand has settled, sweep on some more and water again. You may need to add sand a few times in the first weeks, especially after a heavy rain. After that, your flagstone footpath will need only an occasional sweeping or a light surface hosing to keep it clean.

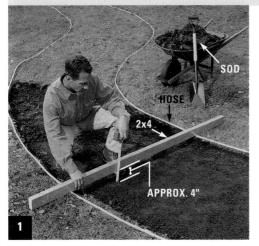

Dig a trench about 4 in. deep between two garden hoses laid out to mark the path edges. Measure the depth from the bottom of a 2x4 as shown. Remove sod carefully if you can use it elsewhere.

Lay landscape fabric on the bottom of the trench. To minimize cutting, fold over a too-wide edge, and pleat the fabric to conform to the curves. Where necessary, cut with a utility knife and overlap edges about 6 in.

Spread the sand on top of the landscape fabric. Shovel and rake the sand into a smooth, uniform layer even with the surrounding soil. Then compact it into a firm bed with a homemade or rented tamper.

Finishing Tip

Apply a clear masonry sealer to deepen the color of the stones in your path. Try this on a piece of scrap stone first to judge the effect and to see if it makes a smooth surface slippery when wet.

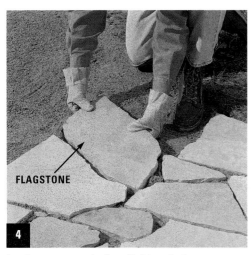

Lay the stones one at a time. Twist each stone as you press it downward to settle it. Lay a 2x4 across several stones to check that their surfaces are even with one another. Step back frequently and inspect the mix of sizes, shapes, and colors.

Fill the cracks by sweeping sand back and forth over the surface of the path. Work in sections. Soak with a light spray of water to settle the sand, then sweep on more and spray again. Repeat during the first weeks until no more settling occurs.

Brick Accents
for Walkways

In a weekend, you can turn your plain concrete sidewalk into an inviting, eye-catching path to your door. The way to do it is with an accent border of easy-to-lay paver bricks. You can use the same technique to edge a driveway or garden beds, too.

What You Need

You can lay a brick accent border with a few common tools, possibly a couple of rental items, and readily available materials. The tools you probably already have include a flat-nosed spade, a metal garden rake, a 3-pound hand sledge, a wheelbarrow, and a stiff-bristled broom. You'll also need a 3- to 4-foot length of 2x10 to make a smoothing tool called a screed.

The two rental items you'll need are a tamping tool to compact the dirt and possibly a masonry or "wet" saw, if you need to cut pavers to fit around tight curves or into angled corners.

The necessary materials are shown in the diagram below right. They are: brick pavers, plastic edging, Class V (5) rock (the light, reddish-colored crushed rock often used along road shoulders), construction sand, and some 10-inch spikes to hold the edging in place. You'll also need a bag of silica sand to fill the gaps between the bricks. Check the Yellow Pages under "Landscape Contractors" for dealers who carry these materials.

The amount of pavers, edging, rock, and sand to buy will depend on the length of your sidewalk and the width of the accent strip. Your dealer will be able to help you figure the quantities you'll need.

It's best to have the materials delivered. If you try to haul them yourself, you'll need a heavy-duty trailer and a vehicle that can pull it, and you'll have to make more than one trip because of the weight of the materials. The cost in trailer rental and the effort involved can make the dealer's delivery charge seem quite reasonable.

What You Need to Do

Adding brick borders to an average front yard sidewalk can be done in a weekend if the weather is good. All you have to do is lay out the design, dig out for the bricks, edging, sand, and rock, and put them in place. Of course, that all calls for some work. The brick border diagram *(below)* will help you see just what you need to do.

First, you must strip back the sod and dig out the dirt beneath so you can put down a 2-inch layer of crushed rock and cover it with a 1-inch layer of sand. That requires a good deal of bending, lifting, and shoveling. Although you'll reuse some of the dirt, a lot will be left over, because you will have to dig down about 6 inches along the entire length and width of each accent strip. You'll also

have sod left over from the area occupied by the bricks. If possible, use the dirt and sod elsewhere in your yard or let neighbors have it. Otherwise you may have a disposal problem. Replant sod immediately.

Once the rock and sand base is ready, you place the bricks, adjust them for even spacing, and cut any that must be fitted in tight curves or difficult corners. Then you install plastic edging along the outside ends of the bricks and drive spikes to hold the edging in place. Finally, you replace the sod up to the edge of each accent strip.

That may sound like a lot. But if you take it step by step as explained on the following pages, you can do it efficiently and with no wasted time or effort. The handsome result will be well worth everything you put into it.

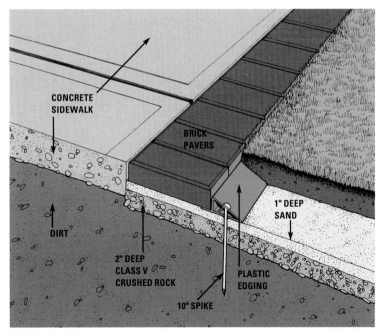

Brick border diagram

CONCRETE SIDEWALK

BRICK PAVERS

1" DEEP SAND

DIRT

2" DEEP CLASS V CRUSHED ROCK

10" SPIKE

PLASTIC EDGING

Building the Base

The several steps involved in adding brick accents to your sidewalk can be divided into two major phases. The first phase, building a proper base for the edging, has six steps, which are explained below and illustrated on the opposite page. The five steps in the second phase, laying the border, are explained on pages 118–119.

Lay Out the Design

To see what the border will look like, lay some of the pavers along the edge of the sidewalk *(Photo 1)*. Do a strip 6 to 8 feet long, just enough to let you see the effect. Look carefully at the design and the spacing and make any adjustments before you start digging. Placing the bricks as shown, with their ends against the sidewalk, gives a clearly visible border and makes it easy to work along most curves without having to cut any pavers. Laying the bricks with their long sides parallel to the sidewalk not only results in a skimpy-looking border but creates large gaps on curves unless you cut the ends of both bricks to fit (cutting just one brick produces erratic spacing of the seams along a curved border).

Strip Back the Sod

Remove the pavers in your sample layout and strip back the sod all along both edges of the sidewalk. Use a flat-nosed spade *(Photo 2)* to cut back about two blade lengths, or about twice the width of the accent strip. To avoid damaging the sod, keep the shovel blade as flush as possible with the sidewalk surface. If the blade points up, you'll rip through the sod instead of

making a clean cut just below the roots. If the blade angles down, you'll dig too far into the dirt instead of cutting the sod away.

Fold the cut sod back on itself and avoid walking on it. The less additional stress, the easier it will be for the sod to take root again once you lay it back in place and trim it to fit against the brick edging.

Dig a Shallow Trench

Dig out the dirt for the full width of the uncovered area to a depth of 5-1/2 to 6 inches *(Photo 3)*. Try to stay within these depth measurements. If you dig too deep, you'll have to use more crushed rock or sand to get the pavers even with the sidewalk surface. If you dig out less than 5-1/2 inches, the pavers will stick up above the edge of the sidewalk, which can be a real hazard. A flush surface is not only safer, it also makes it easier to clear away snow or sweep the sidewalk, and mow the lawn. Exposed paver edges and corners chip easily, too.

Tamp the Dirt

Before adding the new base material, tamp the dirt in the bottom of the trench to provide a solid foundation *(Photo 4)*. Tamping will compact the soil, so measure frequently and add or remove dirt to keep the tamped level 5-1/2 to 6 inches below the surface of the sidewalk. A rented tamping tool with an 8- or 10-pound plate will do a better job than a homemade substitute, but either way this is tiring work. Don't try to do it all at once—take a break now and then, so your muscles won't protest so much later.

Spread the Rock

You need a layer of crushed rock about 2 inches deep in the trench on each side of the sidewalk. The depth will vary with the bottom of the trench, but you want to end up with the surface of the rock layer uniformly 3 inches below the surface of the sidewalk, to allow for the sand and pavers that go on top.

Begin by dumping rock into each trench and raking it out in a rough layer. Then use a screed to smooth it to the right depth *(Photo 5)*. Make a screed by cutting a long 3-inch notch out of a piece of 2x10, leaving a wide "paddle" at one end. The paddle should be the full width of the 2x10 and as long as the trench is wide. The long, narrow part of the screed will serve as a handle.

To use the screed, rest the handle on the surface of the sidewalk with the paddle extending down into the trench and pull it toward you, leveling off the rock. Add rock to fill any low spots so that you get an even surface. Do this in the trench along each edge of the sidewalk.

Add a Layer of Sand

Pour construction sand on top of the rock and spread it in a layer that is uniformly 1 inch thick *(Photo 6)*. To do this, tack a 1-inch strip onto the underside of the handle of the screed, so that the paddle is raised that much above the surface of the rock layer. (In the photo, the added strip is green, for visibility.) Screed the sand in each trench just as you did the rock. When you are finished, the top of the sand will be 2 inches below the surface of the sidewalk, just the thickness of the brick pavers.

Lay out the design along one edge of the sidewalk for a distance of 6 to 8 feet. Now is the time to decide on any changes or adjustments, before you start digging.

Strip back the sod about twice the width of your pattern. Use a flat-nosed spade, flush with the sidewalk. Lay the sod back on itself.

Dig a shallow trench, 5-1/2 to 6 in. deep, the full width of the uncovered area on both sides of the walk. Keep some dirt to fill in under the sod later.

Tamp the dirt in the trench to make a solid foundation. A heavy, metal-plate tamper is best. Make sure the trench is still 5-1/2 to 6 in. deep after tamping.

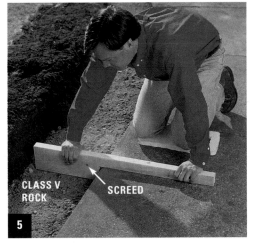

Spread the rock in the trench and screed it to a uniform depth 3 in. below the sidewalk surface. Cut the screed from a 2x10 as described in the text.

Add a layer of sand on top of the rock bed. Tack a 1-in. strip on the screed handle so the sand will be 1 in. deep and 2 in. below the sidewalk surface.

Laying the Border

The first phase of your brick accent project was the most labor intensive. The five steps in this second phase are easier—and a good deal more satisfying, because they finish the job. Each step explained below is illustrated on the opposite page.

Lay the Pavers

Set the pavers in place on top of the sand bed according to your design *(Photo 1)*. Butt their ends up against the edge of the sidewalk, and fit their sides together as tightly as possible. Use a 3-pound hand sledge to tap each paver slightly into the sand; a regular hammer isn't heavy enough. Tap with the sledge handle, not the head, to keep from chipping or cracking the pavers.

If your sidewalk has a curve, there will be gaps between the outer ends of adjacent bricks along the edge of the outside curve, and gaps at the inner ends of the bricks along the inside curve of the sidewalk edge. Unless these gaps are quite wide, you'll be able to fill them later with silica sand.

If you have really wide gaps on an inside or outside curve, you may need to cut the pavers to fit with a masonry wet saw. If you are not familiar with using a wet saw, be sure to ask for instruction when you rent one. For a wide gap, measure the angle and cut half that much from each paver. You don't have to be precise; sand will fill in where needed.

Install the Plastic Edging

The wedge-shaped plastic edging keeps the pavers tight against the sidewalk *(Photo 2)*. The flat end of the wedge fits against the ends of the pavers, and a small lip slips under them (see diagram, page 115). To fit the edging along curves, use a hacksaw to cut V notches along the pointed edge of the wedge. This will work for both inside and outside curves. How close you need to space the notches will depend on the radius of the curve, but every 10 or 12 inches should be enough in most cases. Notches are visible in the edging photos on the opposite page.

Secure the Edging

The plastic edging won't stay in place by itself, so you must fasten it with 10-inch spikes driven into the ground *(Photo 3)*. Some edging has predrilled holes for spikes. If yours does not, you can use a 3-pound sledge to drive the spikes right through the plastic; you won't need to drill holes first. Put a spike through each predrilled hole. In edging without holes, space the spikes about every 12 to 18 inches.

Don't omit this step; your bricks will shift and work loose over time if you do.

Fill the Gaps

Brush silica sand over the pavers, the sidewalk edge, and the plastic edging to fill the gaps *(Photo 4)*. Use a stiff-bristled broom and work back and forth to get sand into all the cracks: between the pavers, between the pavers and the sidewalk, and also between the pavers and the edging. Because it is extremely fine, silica sand will fill cracks that are too narrow for the construction sand you used under the pavers. In addition, silica sand has a light color that makes it an attractive accent in the brick edging.

Replace the Sod

As the final step, you'll have to lay the folded sod back into place and trim the excess with a utility knife so it fits neatly against the brick edging *(Photo 5)*. Before doing that, however, use some of the excavated dirt to fill in behind the plastic edging and under the sod. If you don't add dirt, the sod strip will be lower than the rest of the lawn and water will pool each time it rains or when you water the grass.

To make sure the sod takes root again, keep it watered for at least two weeks once you have laid it back in place and trimmed it. Also, check the sand fill in the cracks after the first two or three rains or lawn waterings, and sweep in some more if any gaps appear.

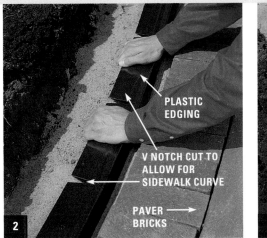

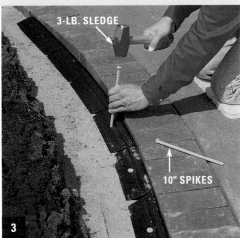

Lay the pavers as close together as possible on the sand. Tap them in place with the handle of a 3-lb. maul. You may have to cut some to fit tight curves.

Install the plastic edging with its flat edge against the paver bricks. A narrow lip goes under the bricks. Notch the edging to bend it to conform to curves.

Secure the edging with 10-in. spikes driven into the ground with the sledge. Space spikes every 12 to 18 in. if the edging does not have predrilled holes.

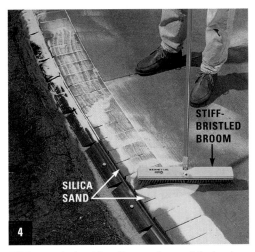

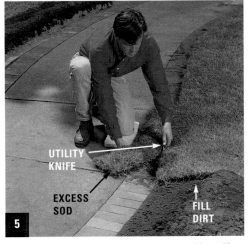

Fill the gaps by brushing silica sand over all the border edges with a stiff-bristled broom. Construction sand is too coarse to go into some gaps.

Replace the sod and trim away the excess with a utility knife. Add dirt behind the edging and under the sod to keep it level. Water the sod.

Building
Landscaping Walls

Use mortar-free, easy-to-stack concrete blocks to build walls for raised planting beds, terraces, and other landscaping features. The blocks are attractive and long lasting, and best of all, they keep the dirt in place.

Landscaping your yard can add significantly to the beauty and value of your home. But projects such as creating raised planting beds or terracing a sloping lawn can seem impossibly large. They don't have to be, because there is an easy way to build the walls you need to hold the soil in place.

The solution is to use concrete blocks that are ready-made for installation. Various manufacturers make wall systems with blocks that stack like children's interlocking toy blocks. The blocks in a given system are identical—except for the special-purpose blocks—and they fit tightly enough so you don't need mortar to make them stay put.

Blocks in different systems vary somewhat in style and how they interlock, but the basic installation process for all types is the same. Ask the dealer who supplies the blocks for any special installation details.

In most regions, you can find decorative blocks through landscaping specialists (look in the Yellow Pages). Because the blocks are heavy, they are almost always made locally by concrete companies. This means your choice might be limited to only one or two types.

Decorative blocks are not cheap. Whatever the block size, figure a minimum of $10 per square foot of exposed wall face. That's twice as much as or more than landscape timbers, but concrete blocks go together faster and easier, they last indefinitely, and they look better, too.

The instructions on the following pages show you how to build the two-level wall system shown on the opposite page. You could build just one wall, of course, perhaps to hold back a sloping bank instead of creating a planting bed. You might want to divide a sloping lawn into terraced sections. Or you might want to create attractive borders around trees, bushes, and other yard features. Whatever your landscaping aim, the procedures will be the same as illustrated in this project.

Block Wall Construction

In whatever system of decorative stacking blocks you use, the blocks will be the same size and shape. A typical size is 4 x 18 x 12 inches. One long side—the exposure face—is usually curved or faceted and may have a decorative texture. The back is flat and so are the ends, which are usually angled toward the back. This permits laying adjacent blocks in a straight line, or angling them to form a curve. The end angle determines how tight a curve you can build. Check on this limit when choosing blocks.

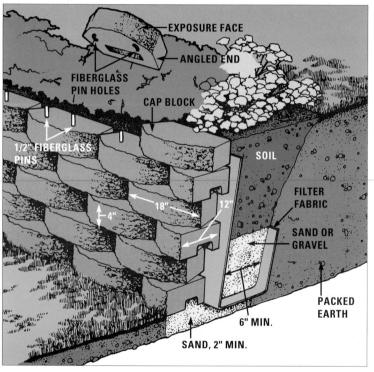

Stacking-block wall construction

In some systems, blocks are interlocked by matching ridges and grooves or knobs and holes on their tops and bottoms. The blocks used in this project have holes for fiberglass pins. They are flat on the top and have a recess in the bottom to reduce weight and help the block sit better on the row, or course, below. All block wall systems have cap blocks with solid top surfaces that are used for the course at the top of the wall.

Height Limitations

The diagram of stacking-block wall construction *(left)* shows the kinds of blocks used in this project, but it applies to all systems. The construction illustrated is fine for walls up to 3 feet high. However, if you try to hold back more than about 3 feet of soil, the pressure could distort or rupture the wall, especially after heavy rains. Although stacking blocks can be used for higher walls, you need a different design, better drainage, and perhaps larger blocks. In many areas you must have plans for a tall wall approved by your building department and have the wall inspected. To avoid that, if you have a tall slope to deal with, divide the overall height into two or more levels, each no more than 3 feet high, and set the upper wall(s) back to terrace the slope.

Wall Base and Top

The bottom course of blocks in the wall is set on a bed of sand at least 2 inches deep over a base of hard-packed soil. If the soil is soft, there should be 4 to 6 inches of gravel under the sand. The upper rows are set so

that the end joints between blocks are staggered from course to course. That means you must start every other course with a half-block to get the required offset. The top course is laid with cap blocks, which provide a finished surface.

Backfilling

In order for the wall to be built, the soil behind it has to be dug away. After the wall is up, it is backfilled as shown in the diagram. A layer of filter fabric prevents water from washing soil through the wall. The soil backfill should have a layer of sand or gravel 6 to 12 inches deep underneath it, for good support and drainage. Notice that the filter fabric runs under and up behind this layer of support material.

Figuring Materials

When you plan your wall, sketch its design and mark its height and length. Multiply them together to calculate the area of the face. Do that for each wall if you are going to build more than one. From the face area, your dealer can help you order the correct number of blocks and the necessary amounts of other materials. Unless you have a substantial truck and strong helpers, don't think of hauling the materials yourself. Blocks weigh 30 to 90 pounds each, so have them delivered.

Preparing the Site

Before you can start construction, you must lay out the wall, mark its height, and dig a base trench.

Lay Out the Wall

Lay out the line of your wall. If it is to curve, use a garden hose or heavy rope, which is easy to adjust to the shape you want. For stepped terrace walls, lay out the line of each wall *(right)*. Adjust for the best-looking contours—you are marking lines for digging.

Measure and Mark the Height

For a wall that starts against your house, measure the height on the side of the house and mark a level line to indicate the new soil line behind the wall *(below right)*.

If the new soil line will cover any wood siding, cut back the siding and cover the house foundation with plastic so that water can't leak through the wall. If the siding cannot be cut back, get some professional advice before you cover it in order to avoid moisture problems.

Dig a Base Trench

Skim off the sod and dig a trench along your layout line *(far right)*. If the soil packs hard, dig the trench 2 inches deep. In soft soil, dig about 6 inches deep and fill with gravel up to 2 inches below the surface. In either case, make the trench 6 inches wider than the blocks, leaving enough space behind the wall to backfill with sand or gravel for good drainage. Make the dirt trench fairly level. Then fill with at least 2 inches of sand up to the existing soil level so the entire face of the bottom course of blocks will be aboveground.

Lay out the line of your wall or walls with garden hose or heavy rope. Either one makes it easy to shape and adjust curves.

Tools You Need

Measuring tape

Level

Shovel

Wheelbarrow

Hammer

Small sledgehammer

Framing square

String line

Circular saw with masonry blade

LEVEL LINE

Measure the intended height of the block wall and mark a level line on the side of the house. Extend the line until it encounters the slope.

Dig a base trench for each wall. Make it at least 6 in. wider than the blocks and 2 in. deep over hard soil. Go 6 in. deep in soft soil to allow for 4 in. of gravel fill.

Setting the First Course

The first or base course is the most important row in your wall. The blocks must be absolutely level, and properly spaced, because everything else sits on top of them. To do this, you must set and adjust each block carefully.

Set the First Block

Position a full-size block at the end of the wall next to the house. Get it square to the house, with its front edge on the line of your wall. Pound it into the sand with a small sledgehammer and a short 2x4 *(below)*. Don't pound directly on the concrete block; it may crack into two pieces.

Level the Block

All blocks in the first course must be level, both side to side and front to back. You cannot be too careful in getting them set right. Place a bubble level on the first block in one direction *(below)*. If the block is not level, tap on the high corner with the hammer and 2x4 to adjust it, or lift the block and add sand under the low corner. Place the level in the other direction and tap the block as necessary to make it level that way. Then go back and check the first adjustment.

Set the Remaining Blocks

Put the second block in place and level it just as you did the first one. Stretch a string line over the tops of the blocks to keep the row straight as you lay additional blocks *(below)*. Where the wall begins to curve, angle each block as necessary but keep its front corner aligned with the preceding block.

When you adjust a block, place the level so it rests on the adjoining blocks as well, to make sure their surfaces are all on the same plane. Remember, whenever you make an adjustment in one direction it can throw off the level in the other direction. Cross-check each time you make a change. Every bit of care you take with the first course makes laying the remaining courses easier.

Set the first block square with the house and pound it into the 2-in. sand bed. Pound on a 2x4, never directly on the block, to avoid cracking it.

LEVEL BOTH DIRECTIONS

Level the block from side to side and back to front. Tap down high corners or fill under low corners. Double-check the level both ways.

Set the rest of the first course level with the first block. Use a string line to keep the course straight. Be exact; this course is the base of the entire wall.

Cutting Blocks

You will need to cut blocks in order to stagger the joints at the ends of the wall. You can cut stacking blocks in half with a circular saw and a masonry blade, or you can rent a wet or dry masonry saw. Whichever kind you use, do not fail to wear safety goggles, a dust mask, and hearing protection, as well as heavy work gloves.

Mark a line across the middle of the block on both the top and bottom, then cut along the line as deeply as possible on each side *(below)*. You will need to make two or three passes, setting the blade deeper each time. Do not force the saw, and above all do not twist it—the blade can shatter. After cutting, lay the block over a 2x4 and whack it with your sledgehammer to break it into two pieces.

Setting Additional Courses

Use an ordinary hammer to tap fiberglass pins into the holes in the top of the first course of blocks, then begin setting the blocks of the second course *(below)*. Start with a half-block and follow it with full-length blocks until you get to the other end, where you may need another half-block. The holes in the bottom of each block are offset from those in the top so that each course sets back just a bit from the front edge of the course below it. This gives the wall a slight backward slant that increases its resistance to the pressure of the soil behind it.

If the far end of your wall runs into a slope, the first course will reach a point where it is almost buried and you will need to step up the sand base to support the block that runs farther at the end of the second course *(below)*. Simply dig out the soil as you did for the base trench, add sand, and then lay the second-course block in place. Do the same where each upper course extends beyond the end of the one below.

Step up and continue the sand base under the second course when the first course becomes buried. Do the same to support the ends of higher courses.

Cut blocks with a masonry blade in a circular saw, or rent a masonry saw. Wear eye, breathing, and ear protection. Score both sides deeply, then break the block over a 2x4.

Tap fiberglass pins into the holes of the first course, then set second course blocks on the pins. Start with a half-block so joints will be staggered between courses.

Building Curves

A curved wall often blends more gracefully with the contours of a yard than a straight wall. As explained earlier, blocks with angled ends allow you to easily lay them in curves.

That is true for the lowest courses, but two problems arise when you lay higher courses. First, as you add each row, the curve sharpens. That's because retaining wall systems don't rise straight up but are built with offset courses that produce a slight slant backward, for stability. As a result, the curve tightens as the wall gets taller and the blocks no longer center exactly over the joints beneath. To maintain your pattern, you will have to cut some blocks narrower.

Second, curves cause the spacing between the fiberglass pins to change, so they no longer fit the block above. Even in a low wall, you'll have to nudge the blocks a bit to make the pins fit *(below left)*. If you can't get one pin aligned, simply leave it out. That won't appreciably affect the strength of the wall.

Always ask the block dealer about specific curve-building details for the system you choose for your wall.

Setting the Top Course

Once you have the base course laid, the upper courses go quite quickly, especially because you don't have to mix and spread mortar. Before you know it, you're ready to put the final course in place.

Use special cap blocks at the top of the wall, laying them in place to interlock with the course below *(below right)*. Whatever stacking-block system you use, there are no holes, grooves, or ridges on the top surfaces of cap blocks. They are smooth and flat for the best appearance and weather resistance.

Angle blocks to lay out curves. Trim blocks narrower to fit the tighter curve as the wall gets higher. Push and tap to get blocks onto their pins as the alignment shifts.

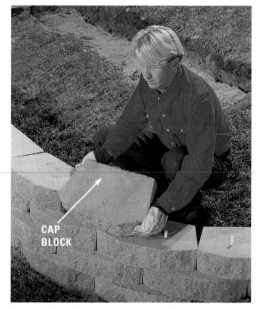

CAP BLOCK

Set cap blocks for the top course to give the wall a smooth, finished top surface. Set them firmly on their pins so they can't be dislodged.

Finishing the Wall

The final step in building your decorative block wall is to fill in soil behind it. The key concerns in doing this properly are preventing soil from washing through the wall when it rains, and providing proper drainage. If water builds up behind the wall, it can slowly undermine the base layer under the bottom course, and it increases hydrostatic pressure against the wall. Either or both can cause the wall to fail.

To prevent soil wash-through, place filter fabric behind the wall *(below left)*. As shown in the diagram on page 122, the fabric should start above the joint between the cap blocks and the course below, run down the back of the wall, across the exposed bottom of the trench, and up the slope behind the wall at least 12 inches. With the fabric in place, fill the bottom 12 inches with sand or gravel, so water drains easily, and fill the remainder with soil.

Building a Second Wall

The steps for building a second block wall are the same as for the first. However, if the two walls intersect, as in the photo on page 121, it is important to start the second wall at just the right level so its bottom course will rest on the top course of the first wall where they come together.

To make sure this will happen, set an extra block on top of the first wall and use a straight board and a level to extend a line back to where the second wall will begin *(below)*. Mark the line at the bottom edge of the straight board. This shows you where the top surface of the bottom course of blocks should be in the second wall. Adjust the depth of the trench and the sand fill to position the first block there. Lay the rest of the first course level with this block and it will be properly aligned when it meets the first wall.

FILTER FABRIC

Finish the wall by placing filter fabric behind it to prevent soil from washing through. Fill first with 12 in. of sand or gravel for drainage, then with excavated soil.

Mark a level line from a block on top of the first wall to guide you in laying the bottom course of a second wall. That way they will be aligned where they intersect.

Building
Dry Stone Walls

Natural stone is the perfect choice for a wall
that harmonizes with the beauty of an informal garden
or a rolling, sloping yard. Building the wall is strenuous
but rewarding work, and you can take your time with
this project.

Throughout the world, stone walls have stood for centuries. From garden and crop terraces in Asia, to moats and enclosures in Europe, to the boundary fences in North America built by settlers clearing fields for farming, few things have endured so long or so well as natural stone walls built without mortar, concrete footings, or other modern modifications and additions.

You probably will not be concerned about building for the ages when you improve the landscaping of your home, but you will be concerned with beauty. And you may well need to deal with practical matters, too, such as shoring up a steep slope, making terraces, or creating raised garden beds. There are many kinds of walls that can do these things, but none fits in with the surroundings as gracefully as a wall built of natural stone.

Building a stone wall is a rewarding project in many ways. There is the satisfaction of turning a pile of rocks into something beautiful, useful, and enduring. There is the challenge of fitting together a giant, three-dimensional puzzle. There may even be a sense of pride in carrying on a human building tradition at least as old as civilization itself.

Whatever the reasons you choose to build a wall, it's a big project, so you should do your best to make it enjoyable and satisfying. To begin, you need to understand how to plan and build a wall efficiently and correctly. That's what the information on the following pages will tell you, first in an overview of materials and wall construction, and then by explaining specifically what to do.

You also need to be realistic about how long it may take to build the wall. Don't overwhelm yourself by trying to do too much too fast. It's possible to turn any project into drudgery by overdoing it. Two hours of wall building is pleasant exercise; six hours is an ordeal. To keep the work enjoyable, approach your wall as a summer hobby, to be plugged away at on weekend afternoons, not a project to be completed in a single weekend. It takes nature millions of years to produce rocks; you can afford to take your time arranging them into a pleasing garden wall.

Planning the Wall

When you begin to plan a stone wall project, you first must decide what kind of wall you need. There are two kinds of dry stone walls, retaining and freestanding, and they have some differences in construction. A retaining wall has one exposed face and the other face against soil that it helps to hold in place—an existing slope or bank, or soil that has been put in place, for instance for a planting bed. Retaining wall design and construction are shown on the opposite page and the techniques for building a wall are explained on the following pages.

A freestanding wall is exposed on both sides. It is the kind of wall you might build to mark the boundaries of your property, or to separate two distinct areas from each other. Its construction is shown in the sidebar on page 134. Most of the building techniques for a freestanding wall are the same as for a retaining wall.

To provide a transition between two levels, you may want to include steps in your stone wall. The construction of both rectangular and circular steps is explained on page 135.

If you want a straight wall, you can mark its line with stakes and a string. For a wall with curves, lay it out with a garden hose or heavy rope. In either case, measure the overall length in feet. Multiply this by the planned height of the wall—4 feet is the maximum safe height—and then by the intended width of the base (same as height). The result is the approximate number of cubic feet in your wall; divide by 27 to get the number of cubic yards, which you need to know for ordering stone.

Stones for a Retaining Wall

The basic materials for a retaining wall are lots and lots of rocks. You may be able to find what you need and haul it yourself, or you may decide to purchase it, but in either case there are different types to look for to make the job a success.

Finding Rocks

Gravel pits, quarries, farms, and construction sites are good sources of low-cost or no-cost rock. But don't assume what you find is simply there for the taking; ask.

Getting rocks home is the hard part, because a wall takes so much material. A wall 3 feet high and 35 feet long needs almost 8 cubic yards or 10 tons of rock. Even if you have a full-size pickup truck, you'll need to make many, many trips.

For your wall-building project, rocks fall into two categories: angular (like shale, sandstone, marble, or slate) and rounded (usually granite). Angular rocks have a definite grain, somewhat like wood, so natural forces break them into irregular blocks with flat sides and sharp, squarish edges. These flat surfaces make the rocks easier to fit together. They're also easier to split, because they usually break along predictable lines.

Rounded rocks are much harder and have a less definite grain. They come in all shapes but tend to have humped surfaces. Fitting them together takes a lot more trial and error.

In most regions, you just take what you can get. Still, there are a few things to keep in mind while you fill your truck or trailer:
▶ You'll need a mix of sizes, everything from baseball size on up. But don't play Hercules. If it's too big, leave it alone.

▶ The flatter a rock's surfaces are, the better. Block-shaped rocks are valuable; those with one or two flattish sides are good; round rocks are almost worthless.
▶ Long rocks, which you will use as "tiestones," are treasures. The more you have, the stronger your wall.
▶ Wedge-shaped rocks are handy for chinking—filling in small gaps and holes.

Buying Rocks

If rocks are scarce in your area, or if you have no way to transport them, you can buy a load (or loads) and have it dumped in your yard. Begin by looking under "Stone" in the Yellow Pages or by calling a landscaping supplier. In small towns, look in the local paper for ads by excavation contractors, gravel dealers, and farmers.

Don't just phone in an order. Buying stone gives you a choice of types and colors. Go and look things over before you buy. Prices will vary widely, depending on what you get and whom you get it from. A farmer may deliver a load of fieldstone for little more than the cost of transportation. A few tons of richly colored granite from a landscaping supplier could cost $1,000, but perhaps half that from an excavation contractor.

You'll also need 3/4-inch gravel or rock aggregate as a base for your wall. To find the number of cubic feet, multiply wall length by width (same as height) in feet by 0.5 (6-inch depth).

When the stone and gravel are delivered, have them dumped as close to your work site as possible. Choose a spot on the same level or uphill of the wall, so you don't have to push wheelbarrow loads up a slope.

Tools You Need

Shovel

Garden rake

Wheelbarrow

Sledgehammer

2- 3-lb. blacksmith's hammer or hand sledge

4x4 by 8-foot post for tamping

4-ft. level

Safety goggles

Heavy work gloves

Dry Stone Retaining Wall Construction

A dry wall is built without mortar to hold the structure together. Instead, the stones are carefully fitted into place and held there by gravity. When well put together, a dry stone will outlast a mortared wall for two reasons: It can flex slightly, moving with the ground beneath it instead of cracking as a stiff mortared wall would. And it won't fall apart as mortar wears away, which all mortar eventually does. The basic construction of a dry stone retaining wall is diagrammed below; a comparison of good and bad stone-setting techniques is shown in the diagram below right. Here are the important points:

Foundation and base. A trench filled with a 6-inch deep layer of 3/4-inch aggregate (gravel, crushed stone) forms a foundation that provides drainage and absorbs some movement of the soil below. The largest rocks are set on the gravel as the first or base course of the wall. The base should be as wide as the wall will be tall; 3 feet wide for a 3-foot height, for example.

Coursing. Although stones are irregular in size and shape, it is important to lay them in roughly even horizontal courses. To do this, lay rocks flat, not on edge, avoiding peaks and chinking (filling in) valleys and holes with small stones. It is also important to lay stones "one over two, two over one." That is, one stone spans the gap between two stones in the course below, and two stones in the upper course meet above one stone below, just like a bricklayer lays bricks. Without this pattern, vertical runs that weaken the wall are sure to occur.

Tiestones. Long rocks laid perpendicular to the face of the wall, running front to back, are called "tiestones." There must be one tiestone at least every 4 feet on each course to help hold the structure together. The more tiestones, the stronger the wall.

Slant and height. All rocks on the face of the wall must slant down toward the inside of the wall, as indicated in the diagram at the left. Those that don't will eventually fall out. To hold all the earth behind it, the wall must lean back into the slope behind it. The front face should slant back 2 inches or more for every foot of height; the back of the wall can slant into the slope even more. Do not build a wall more than 4 feet high. The higher the

wall, the more potential for injury should it collapse. Special construction techniques are required for tall walls.

Backfill. The slope behind the wall must be dug away at least 6 inches more than the wall thickness to allow access for setting stones. Backfill is tamped in place as each course is laid. The back of the wall is covered with landscape fabric before the fill is added. The fabric prevents soil from working its way into the wall and forcing stones apart.

Capstones. The top course should be large, tight-fitting capstones to provide stability and to block rain and snow. If they won't stay in place, they must be set in mortar.

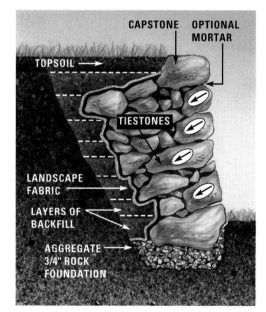

Dry stone retaining wall construction

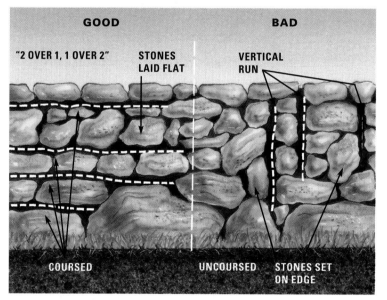

Good and bad stone setting

Building the Wall

The techniques described on these two pages show you how to build a safe, long-lasting wall. The basic procedure is to lay a course, backfill; lay another course, backfill; and so on to the top. If the wall is not more than 15 feet long, do the whole length every course. Divide a longer wall into 8- to 12-foot sections. Lay up about a third of the wall height in one section before going on to the next. This will let you connect the sections without having vertical runs.

Prepare a Foundation

Following the line of your wall layout, cut back the slope and dig a trench 1 foot deep and as wide as the wall will be tall. Pile the topsoil and subsoil separately nearby; you'll need them for backfill. Pour 6 inches of 3/4-inch stones in the trench as a foundation.

Prepare a foundation by digging a trench as wide as the wall height and 1 foot deep. Fill it with 6 inches of 3/4-in. gravel or crushed stone.

Lay the First Course

Choose your largest rocks for the first or base course, especially those that are too big and heavy to lift onto an upper course. Place them on the gravel bed, aligning them along the outer edge of the trench. Let some run lengthwise along the trench, others crosswise toward the back of the trench, like tiestones. Fill in with other large rocks behind this first row where necessary to provide a full-width base for the wall. The back edge can be quite irregular, because it will be covered with fill.

Lay the first course using the largest rocks. Place them against the front of the trench; use others behind. The rear edge can be irregular; it will be covered.

Backfill the First Course

Lay out landscape fabric along the entire length of the course and tuck it behind and slightly under the back sides of the rear stones. If you are working in sections and cannot leave enough for the entire length of the wall, cut the fabric off about 12 inches beyond the end of the first section. Overlap the fabric for the next section at least that much when you put it in place.

Fold the fabric forward over the rocks and shovel in backfill behind them. Then tamp all the fill soil with the end of a tall 4x4 post. Raise and drop the post, letting its weight do the pounding.

Backfill the first course after tucking landscape fabric under and behind the stones. Use excavated subsoil; tamp thoroughly with a 4x4 or other tamper.

Lay the Next Course

Fold the landscape fabric back against the slope, exposing the rocks in the base course, and set the second course on top of them. Follow the principle of placing one stone over the gap between two, and placing two stones so the gap between them is in the middle of a single stone below. Be sure to include tiestones at least every 4 feet in this course, but don't place them directly over similar front-to-back stones in the first course. When the course is in place, fold the landscape fabric forward, backfill, and tamp the soil. Continue this pattern, completing one course before starting the next. The photo below shows the third course in progress before the second has been finished only for illustrating the procedure.

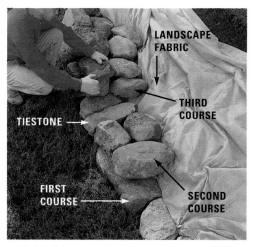

Lay the next course on the principle of "one over two, two over one" so joints between rocks are staggered from course to course. Include tiestones.

Chink the Gaps

Drive smaller chinking stones into the face of the wall to fill gaps between the large rocks. Do this after three or four courses have been laid, not every other course. Use a heavy 2- or 3-pound hammer such as a blacksmith's hammer or a hand sledge. Drive chinking in firmly, but don't dislodge the stones you have already set. Wear gloves and safety glasses to protect your eyes from flying stone chips.

Chink the gaps by pounding small stones into them with a heavy hammer. Wear safety glasses; don't dislodge large rocks already in place.

Lay Capstones

The final course of capstones should bring the top of the wall to a height roughly the same as the embankment behind. Use a 4-foot level to check from the top of the stone back to the unexcavated part of the bank. When the height is right, tuck the landscape fabric behind the capstones, but not below their joint with the course below. Backfill and add topsoil.

If you have chosen good capstones and set the lower courses well, they should stay in place without trouble. If some do not fit well or work loose later, hold them in place with some package-mix mortar.

Lay capstones as the top course. Use large flat rocks and get them roughly level with the existing ground. Then backfill with subsoil and topsoil.

A Freestanding Dry Stone Wall

A freestanding dry stone wall is similar to a retaining wall, but there are some important differences. With a freestanding wall you must be much more careful about fitting the stones. A retaining wall leans against a solid mound of earth. A freestanding wall leans in on itself, so the two faces must slant into each other and lock together.

The key to a strong freestanding wall is building it with a V slant. Each course must be highest at the face on each side, with a gradual depression toward the middle. With the stones sloping down toward the middle, gravity holds each one in place and the entire wall together. Tiestones from the face of the wall to the center are very important.

For stability, the base of a freestanding wall should be as wide as the wall is tall. Both faces should slant inward from bottom to top, at least 2 inches for each foot of height. Nonprofessionals should build a freestanding wall no higher than 3 feet.

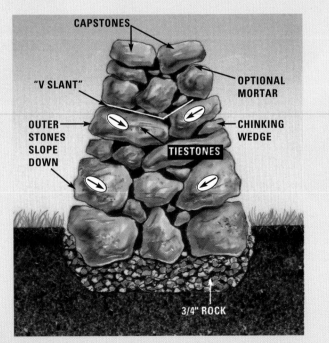

A freestanding dry stone wall

Labels: CAPSTONES, "V SLANT", OPTIONAL MORTAR, OUTER STONES SLOPE DOWN, CHINKING WEDGE, TIESTONES, 3/4" ROCK

Helpful Hints

The techniques and procedures on the preceding pages are those used by experienced stoneworkers and landscape gardeners to construct dry stone walls in all kinds of climates. Here are some of their tips and special techniques for making the work easier or dealing with difficult spots.

▶ If you haul in or move dirt to create or enlarge a slope, it will be loose. Soak it thoroughly two or three times with a hose, or leave it uncovered in the rain, so it settles before you build against it.

▶ Big tree roots can slowly tear a wall apart. Cut back any that threaten to reach your wall. Don't just cut them at the rear edge of the wall; go back farther if possible.

▶ Building with stone is like putting together a jigsaw puzzle. So begin by spreading out the rocks just as you would the pieces of a puzzle.

▶ Choose rocks for the face of the wall carefully—they are what will be seen. If you have different colors, mix them into a patchwork. For a neat, controlled look, lay stones with their flattest sides facing out; for a more natural, rustic look, leave the rounded, irregular sides exposed.

▶ Put the best wide, flat stones aside to be used as capstones.

▶ Use the biggest stones for the first course. Nestle extra-big stones down into the gravel foundation so they don't stick up so much above their neighbors.

▶ Don't try to be a lifting hero; that's a sure way to strain or injure your back muscles. If there are some big or heavy stones to be used in upper courses, roll or slide them up a plank to put them in place.

▶ Fitting stones together is mostly trial and error. Cut down on both by mentally measuring the shape and size of the stone you need first. Then hunt for the perfect fit; you may even want to use a tape measure. Spreading out the rocks before you begin makes hunting easier.

▶ Stone cutting is hard work, and doing it well is difficult. Avoid it if possible. If you must knock off troublesome crags or knobs, use a heavy hammer and a cold chisel. Above all, wear eye protection and keep others out of the flying-chip zone.

Building Dry Stone Steps

Where a stone wall separates two levels of landscape, rectangular or round steps can be included in the wall at a convenient point. Here are some pointers for building them.

Choose heavy flat, squarish stones for the steps. If you do not have the right kind, or enough for all the steps, it might be worthwhile to buy cut stones from a supplier. Stones with flat sides and squared edges are much easier to build into a safe, comfortable set of steps.

Cut into the slope to form steps in the soil, then put down a gravel or rubble base (cross section, top right). Because each step is just barely held in place by the weight of the stones above, it is important to have good drainage, to prevent washout.

Choose stones of nearly the same thickness so that the rise—the vertical distance from one step to the next—does not change significantly. The rise should be between 3 and 7 inches, no higher. The depth of each step, from front to back, should be at least 8 inches; 10 inches or more is better.

The very top step should be flush with the soil on the upper level and should be made continuous with the capstones on the wall, as shown below.

A nice touch is to lay a flagstone walkway leading to and from the steps (see Laying a Flagstone Footpath, pages 110–113).

Cross section of dry stone steps. Each step must overlap the one below for at least one-fourth of its total depth. A base of gravel or stone rubble is essential for good drainage so the steps will stay in place.

Rectangular dry stone steps. This is the easiest design to build and is equally suitable in straight and curved walls. Framed by the wall structure, the steps provide convenient access to the upper level.

Rounded dry stone steps. This half-circle pattern requires careful layout planning and is more work to construct. But it breaks the regularity of a straight wall and gives a feeling of greater depth.

Building a
Timber Retaining Wall

If you want to hold back a bank or keep a slope from slipping, a retaining wall is what you need. Big timbers and elbow grease can do the job cheaper and easier than working with poured or block concrete. The color and texture of timbers look more natural, too.

A retaining wall can beautify your landscaping as well as help to control it. While its primary purpose may be to hold a slope in place and stop erosion, or to turn an impossible-to-mow hill into level terraces or a usable garden space, a well-designed wall will also add visual interest to a yard.

You can build a retaining wall in many ways, with many different materials. If you want something that is both attractive and moderately priced, wood timbers are an excellent choice.

There's no arguing the fact that retaining walls built from modular concrete blocks, stone, or poured concrete will outlive those built from wood. Even the best constructed timber walls rarely last more than 25 years; moisture, fungus, decay, and weather slowly but surely take their toll, especially in regions where there are definite seasons—snowy, rainy, hot and dry—throughout the year.

But wood timbers have their own advantages, including lower cost in almost all cases; greater flexibility in designing a wall to fit the terrain; quicker construction, with no mixing of concrete or mortar; and better appearance—many homes and yards cry out for the soft, mellow look of wood rather than the hard-edged appearance of masonry.

Timbers and spikes for a wood wall cost about half as much per square foot as modular block. It is easier to build and securely anchor a timber wall than any masonry counterpart. And since installing a single 8-foot long timber immediately creates 4 square feet of wall, timber walls can be built faster than one-at-a-time block or stone walls, especially when it comes to constructing long, straight sections.

The following pages show you how to plan and construct a timber wall the right way—so it will be both strong and attractive.

Timber Retaining Wall

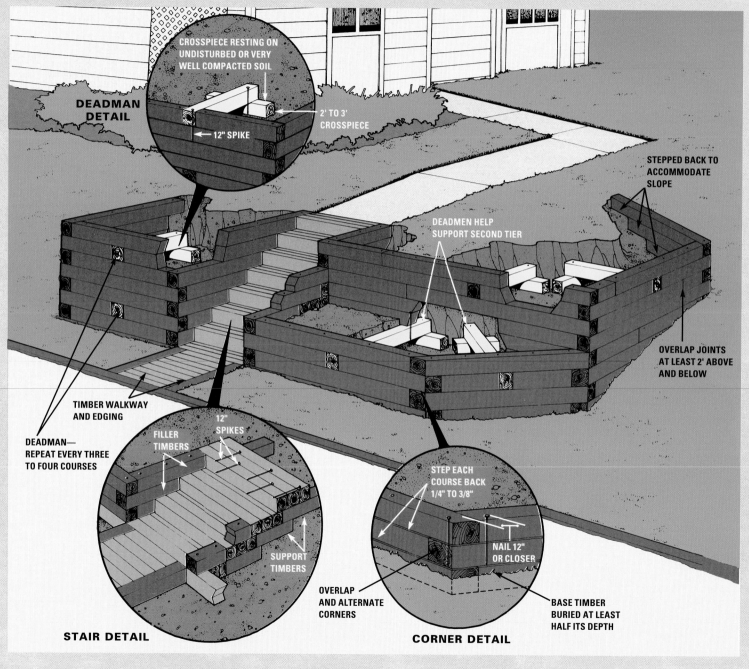

CROSSPIECE RESTING ON UNDISTURBED OR VERY WELL COMPACTED SOIL

DEADMAN DETAIL

2' TO 3' CROSSPIECE

12" SPIKE

STEPPED BACK TO ACCOMMODATE SLOPE

DEADMEN HELP SUPPORT SECOND TIER

OVERLAP JOINTS AT LEAST 2' ABOVE AND BELOW

TIMBER WALKWAY AND EDGING

DEADMAN— REPEAT EVERY THREE TO FOUR COURSES

FILLER TIMBERS

12" SPIKES

SUPPORT TIMBERS

STEP EACH COURSE BACK 1/4" TO 3/8"

NAIL 12" OR CLOSER

OVERLAP AND ALTERNATE CORNERS

BASE TIMBER BURIED AT LEAST HALF ITS DEPTH

STAIR DETAIL

CORNER DETAIL

Construction and Tools

Before starting on as big a project as a retaining wall, you need to understand how it is built and what you will need to put it together.

Timber Wall Construction

The diagram on the opposite page shows all of the construction features you might need in building a timber retaining wall. These include both square and angled corners, two-tiered construction on one side, stairs, and concealed anchors called "deadmen." Depending on the terrain and the length of the wall you build, it might not have an angled corner or stairs, but every timber wall must have deadmen to stabilize it and help resist the pressure of the soil behind the wall.

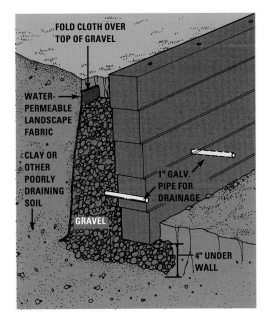

Backfill in poorly draining soil

FOLD CLOTH OVER TOP OF GRAVEL

WATER-PERMEABLE LANDSCAPE FABRIC

CLAY OR OTHER POORLY DRAINING SOIL

1" GALV. PIPE FOR DRAINAGE

GRAVEL

4" UNDER WALL

The wall is built by piling timbers on top of one another and securing them with long spikes. Choosing the right size timbers and cutting them to length are discussed on page 141. Actual construction procedures are explained and illustrated on pages 142–145.

Instead of 12-inch spikes, timbers can be fastened with lengths cut from 3/8-inch thick concrete reinforcing rods, called rebar. It's more work to cut the rebar, but that allows you to have fastening pins long enough to reach through three or four timbers at a time, instead of just two.

As shown in the corner detail *(opposite)* each course of timbers is set back 1/4 to 3/8 inch from the face of the course below. The timbers overlap in alternate courses at the corner, much the same way as in a log cabin. Corners are secured with a spike driven through the overlapping ends; timbers that butt into the overlapped pieces are spiked within 12 inches of the corner.

Where the timbers run into the slope, they are extended to step back up the hill, as shown at the right end of the wall (see the plans, opposite). The various wall sections are anchored by deadmen buried in the soil. Basic deadman construction is shown in the plan detail and is explained further on page 144, along with information about placement and spacing.

The steps in the stair are one timber high and at least three timbers deep. This gives a safe, comfortable rise and a safe depth when each step is overlapped a half-timber depth by the step above. The pieces in each step are spiked together from behind, so no fasteners are exposed. The overall height of the slope determines how many steps are required. Notice in the stair detail in the construction plans that support timbers must be placed under the ends of each step, and then fill timbers are added above them to form the sides of the stair.

Proper drainage is important so that the timbers are not always in contact with wet soil. If the soil is clay or some other poorly draining consistency, there should be gravel under and behind the wall as shown in the diagram *(left)*. Landscape fabric separates the gravel from the wall, and 1-inch "weep" pipes extending through the wall let water drain out of the gravel layer.

Tools

Your basic "tool" will be strong muscles—there is lots of digging to do, and timbers weigh 40 to 80 pounds apiece. A willing helper is a second valuable "tool." The other tools you'll need are listed at the right.

Tools You Need

4-foot level and 8-inch torpedo level

3-pound hand sledge-hammer

8- or 10-pound sledge-hammer

Tape measure

Drill with long-shaft bit

Shovels

Wheelbarrow

Saw (see page 141)

Gloves for all handling

Eye protection and face mask when sawing, hammering, or drilling

Designing the Wall

Before you can order any materials, and certainly before you start digging, you need to know how long, how tall, and what shape your timber wall is going to be.

Estimating outdoor spaces by eye is difficult, because you can't really separate individual features from the larger context of the yard and house. What looks like a "small" hill can easily turn out to be 5 feet high; a "little" embankment may actually be 20 feet long when you measure it.

So start by using a tape measure, a level, and a straight 2x4 to size up the area involved. First, determine the overall height as shown in the photo *(below)*. Place one end of the

2x4 on the highest point of the land to be retained directly by the wall, and extend the other end until it is over the point where the base of the wall will sit. Get the 2x4 level—tape the level on top if it tends to wobble off—and measure the distance from the bottom of the 2x4 to the ground.

You can determine two things from this height measurement. One is whether you can build a single wall or whether you need to divide it into two sections, one stepped well back from the other for safe construction, as on the right side of the stairs in the plans on page 138. The other information you can determine is how many timbers you need to reach that height. Simply divide the height measurement by the vertical or face dimension of the timbers you plan to use (see opposite page) and take into account that the bottom timber will be half-buried in the ground.

You also need to know how long the various sections of your wall will be. Since each section will be a straight line, making measurements will be easy, but first you need to work out the shape or configuration of the wall. Make sketches on graph paper to try various designs that will fit the slope and contours of the land. Remember that you can do some cutting and filling to change a slope somewhat, but moving soil is the heaviest, dirtiest part of the project.

As you design, keep the following guidelines in mind:

▶ Limit the height of your timber wall to 4 feet or less. If you need to hold back a 7-foot embankment, split the wall into two or three stepped-back terraces. If you don't have room for terracing and your wall must exceed 4 feet, hire an engineer to design the wall; some communities require this.

▶ Break up long stretches—those more than 16 feet—with angles, jogs, and corners; these add strength as well as visual interest.

▶ Work in 8- and 4-foot increments, which correspond to full and half timber lengths. You'll do less cutting and make better use of your materials.

▶ Match the wall to the hill. You may be in love with a retaining wall design you've seen in a magazine or in someone's yard, but unless you plan realistically you may wind up hauling in, or digging out, literally tons of dirt.

▶ Think about extras. You can incorporate stairs, benches, light posts, and planting areas into your design.

When you have a final design, drive stakes at the base level of each corner of the various sections. Measure the distances between them and add them together. Working from this overall length and the height, you can figure pretty closely how many timbers you will need. If you want to really refine your estimate, draw out each wall section with the length and height of each timber marked in scale and make a count from that.

Determine the height of your retaining wall using a 4-ft. level, straight 2x4, and tape measure. Divide a height of more than 4 ft. into two terraced sections.

Timbers for the Wall

Selecting high-quality timbers is the key to sturdy, long-lived walls. You'll be burying wood in dirt, so you must use pressure-treated timbers. These have had chemical preservatives forced into them by a pressurizing process. The pounds of preservative retained by each cubic foot of timber is represented by a number, usually .25, .40, or .60. The most widely available timbers are treated to a .40 concentration, which should be stamped or labeled on the timber.

Timbers may be stained brown or green during or after treatment to give them a more pleasing, uniform color. All timbers, stained or unstained, will eventually weather to a mellow gray.

Common timber cross-section dimensions are 4x4 , 4x6, 5x6, and 6x6 inches; most are 8 feet long. Unlike board lumber, where a 2x4 actually measures 1-1/2 x 3-1/2 inches at best, timber dimensions are much closer to the true size. However, there will probably be 1/4 to 1/2 inch variation in face and width size. Check on that before making up your final order so you don't come out short.

The project shown in this chapter was built of 5x6 timbers with the 6-inch face stacked vertically. You could use 6x6s for taller, longer walls, 4x6s for smaller projects.

Timbers may cost up to $15 per 8-foot length; 12 inch spikes will be 50 cents or so apiece. For large walls, buy "units" consisting of 25 to 30 timbers and have them delivered. The timbers in a unit were most likely sawn, treated, and stained at the same time and so will be fairly uniform in color and size.

Cutting Timbers

A timber retaining wall can call for a lot of sawing. The wall in the illustrated project required more than 90 square cuts and 35 angled cuts. There are three options for sawing timbers, explained here, but whichever you choose, keep the following points in mind:

Always wear gloves when handling the timbers. When sawing, also wear eye and ear protection and a dust mask. Do not fail to do this—preservative-soaked splinters and sawdust can cause severe irritation.

Neither end of a timber is necessarily perfectly square, so check before measuring and cutting.

Always support the timber off the ground, so the cutoff end will drop free and not pinch the saw.

After sawing, soak the freshly cut end of a timber in wood preservative. If possible, precut several timbers at a time and stand them in a 5-gallon pail with 6 inches of preservative in the bottom. Keep them there overnight or while you do other work for a few hours. Secure the timbers so they can't topple over while soaking.

Option 1
Circular saw and handsaw
This is slow, especially for cutting angles, but most homeowners have these tools. Mark all four sides of the timber with a pencil and square, making sure the lines meet. Set the saw to its greatest depth and saw along each line, turning the timber each time. Cut through the remaining nub in the center with a handsaw.

For 45° cuts, mark all four sides. Cut through two opposite sides with the saw base tilted at 45° and the remaining two sides with the blade set square.

Option 2
Chain saw
This is fast, great for angles, and can trim timbers even after they're installed. But if you haven't handled a chain saw before, don't try it here. Chain sawing can be dangerous, and it takes a real knack.

To make square or angled cuts, mark the top of the timber and the side that will face you, then keep the saw bar cutting along both lines simultaneously.

Option 3
Sixteen-inch circular saw
You can rent a circular saw with a 16-inch blade that can make square and angle cuts through 6x6 timbers in a single pass. It is bulky, but not as heavy or hard to control as it looks. You must have a sharp blade and a heavy-duty extension cord or the saw won't cut properly.

Circular saw and handsaw

Chain saw

Sixteen-inch circular saw

Building the Wall

The following techniques for building a timber retaining wall are illustrated in the photos on the opposite page.

Dig a Trench

Your wall must start straight and level, and stay that way to the top. If you have not already done so, drive stakes and connect them with strings to mark the front line of the wall *(Photo 1)*. Then use a round-nose spade to dig a trench, using the strings as a guide. Start at the lowest spot so you can step up timbers as necessary where their ends run into the slope. You need to bury at least half the depth of the lowest timber so the pressure of the earth behind the completed wall won't push it out of line. In clay soil, dig deeper so you can put down 4 inches of gravel for drainage (diagram, page 139).

It is essential to get the first row of timbers level, which means that the trench itself must be level. Check the bottom of the trench with a 4-foot level and a long, straight 2x4 (it's easier to handle than a timber). When it is within an inch of level, switch to a flat-nosed shovel to even it off into a level, flat bottom. Repeatedly drop a sledgehammer headfirst in the bottom of the trench to tamp the dirt or gravel.

Install the First Course

Place a timber in position in the trench and check it for level along its length with a 4-foot level *(Photo 2)* and across its width with an 8-inch torpedo level. If it isn't quite level, use a hand sledgehammer to tamp down the high end. Or stand on the timber and wiggle or jump on it to help settle it.

Continue leveling and laying as many first-row timbers as the terrain allows. Pack dirt along both sides to hold the leveled timbers in place and pack it into place with your foot. Don't pack dirt up to the top of the timber. The joint between the first two courses must be covered by landscape fabric you will install in the final step of construction (page 145).

Install Additional Courses

Lay the second course of timbers on top of the first row. Then follow with other courses in the same way. Make sure the ends alternate at the corners, and step back each course 1/4 to 3/8 of an inch *(Photo 3)*. This gives the wall a slight backward slant that improves its stability. Where two timbers butt together end to end, make sure the joint is at least 2 feet away from a joint in the course directly below or above. At intervals in the second course or third course from the bottom and in the second course from the top, install deadmen to anchor the wall. This technique is explained on page 144.

Fasten Each Course

As you put each course in place, fasten it with 12-inch spikes or longer pins (see Wall-building Tips, page 145). Drive spikes through overlapping ends at corners, and within 12 inches of an end that butts into another timber. Space other spikes about every 24 inches along the length of a timber. To prevent splitting, you must drill holes at timber ends *(Photo 4)*. Use a spade bit just slightly smaller than the spike shaft and 12 inches long. You can also drill holes for the mid-timber spikes—a good job for a helper. That's not absolutely necessary, but it makes driving spikes go faster. Use a hand sledge or a full-size sledgehammer, whichever you feel comfortable handling.

Step Up the Slope

Where the ends of the wall run into the soil, step up the slope by using progressively longer courses of timbers *(Photo 5)*. Tamp the soil well and make sure the timbers stay level as they run off the course below onto the soil. Notice that you do not do any back-filling as you go, except for the soil you used to hold the very first course in place. You will backfill the entire area in the final step, which is explained on page 145.

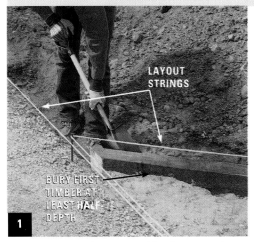

Dig a trench for the first course, following your stake-and-string outline. The trench bottom must be level and deep enough to bury the timber at least half its depth.

Install the first course timbers, getting each one level. Tap the high end with a sledge to make adjustments. Pack in some soil behind to hold the timber in place.

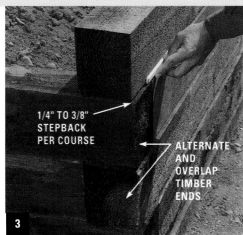

Install additional courses with a slight stepback in each course. Alternate overlapping ends at corners; place joints in adjacent courses at least 2 ft. apart.

Fasten each course by spiking it into the course below. Predrill through both timbers to prevent splitting at corners. Maintain the stepback between courses.

Step up the slope as the wall ends run into the soil by extending each course. Make sure the timbers remain level as they extend onto the ground.

Installing Deadmen

A deadman is a T-shaped anchor constructed by fastening a 2- or 3-foot crosspiece to a longer leg *(right top)*. The base end of the leg is fastened in the middle of a course in the wall and the crossbar rests on the soil behind the wall. When completely buried by the backfill, the deadman ties its section of the wall into the soil behind and prevents the wall from leaning, bulging, or being pushed out of position.

Almost all retaining walls require more than one deadman. As dirt settles, water builds up, or frozen soil expands, pressure increases against the back of a retaining wall. But since these forces also exert downward pressure, they lock the deadmen—and therefore the wall—in place. You must install deadmen in any wall that is three or more courses high or longer than 6 feet. Do not even think about leaving them out.

Install deadmen in the second or third course from the bottom and in the second course from the top. A rule of thumb many landscapers use is to install one deadman for every 16 square feet of wall face. For walls higher than 4 feet, hire an engineer to determine the placement of the deadmen.

There is less chance of a deadman settling later on if it is laid on undisturbed soil. This means the length of the main leg will vary, depending on the slope of the hill. Do some rough calculations, using a level and a 2x4, to determine how long a deadman leg should be. If you're terracing, make certain the upper deadmen in the first wall are long enough to support the bottom course of the next terrace back *(right bottom)*. Spike that course into the deadmen to further help tie things together.

Prebuild each deadman by drilling and spiking the crosspiece to the leg. This is a good way to use up ugly and short ends of timber. Position the free end on the wall and level the crosspiece into the dirt. It will take some trial and error. When the deadman is level, drill and spike the free end to the timber wall. Pile up and pack dirt around the crosspiece firmly with your foot.

Professional wall-builders rough-lay and position an entire course of timbers and deadmen before spiking them together. This allows them to make slight adjustments.

Along steep embankments or among mature trees, where it's impossible to install timber deadmen, you can use auger-type metal anchors, available at larger landscaping and home centers. These are "cork screwed" into the embankment, then bolted to the back of the retaining wall. They don't hold as well as timber deadmen, and any large rock will stop their installation, but sometimes they are the only alternative.

Make a deadman by spiking a long leg to a shorter crosspiece. The leg rests on the wall and extends far enough to put the crosspiece on firm, undisturbed soil.

Locate deadmen in the second or third course from the bottom and second course from the top. Extend the top deadmen in the lower wall to support a wall above.

Finishing the Wall

The top of your wall may be level or stepped, depending on the contour of the yard. Just make sure each section is tall enough so soil won't wash over the top during heavy rains.

When the final course has been spiked in place, fill in behind the wall with dirt. First line the back side of the wall with landscape fabric to prevent dirt from oozing through gaps between the timbers *(below)*.

If you need a truckload of dirt delivered, have it dumped on the uphill side of the wall, if possible, but not so close that the truck threatens the wall. Put in a layer of dirt about 12 inches deep and pack it firmly with your feet. Add another 12 inches, pack it, and repeat until you get to the top. Packing each layer firmly is important to minimize future settling that could create depressions that might hold water, or affect your plantings. If you set aside topsoil when you first excavated the slope, finish with that and plant it as you choose. Or cover the area with sod (see Laying Sod, pages 28–31).

In extremely clayey soils, you must provide drainage so that the timbers are not constantly wet and so that water pressure does not build up against the wall. Pile gravel directly against the retaining wall and separate it from the fill dirt with landscaping fabric (diagram, page 139). Drill holes in the second course about every 36 inches and drive in lengths of 1-inch galvanized pipe to let water "weep"—drain—out of the gravel.

LANDSCAPE FABRIC

Fill in behind the wall as the final step in construction. First install landscape fabric, then pack soil in 12-in. layers. Where drainage is poor, backfill with gravel.

Wall-building Tips

Here are some ways to make building a timber retaining wall easier and improve the finished appearance.

The largest spikes will only fasten two courses of 5- or 6-inch thick timbers together. To secure three or four courses at a time, cut lengths of 3/8- or 1/2-inch steel rod—called rebar—used in reinforced concrete construction. Drill holes to avoid splitting the wood; don't try to sharpen the ends of the rods.

If your drill bit is only long enough to go through one timber at a time, lay the timber in place and drill through so it marks the one below, then shift it aside and drill the lower timber. Use this technique to drill holes for long fastening pins, as above. Be sure each timber is set back from the face of the one below by the proper amount before drilling. And be sure to drill vertical holes. A helper watching the drill bit from the side can check the alignment so you get started right.

When driving spikes or rods into the very top course, stop just above the surface and use a short length of steel rod as a giant nail set to finish up. That will avoid sledge-head dents in the surface of the timber.

Preassemble sets of timbers for steps (plans, page 138), driving fasteners from the rear side so they won't show on the face. The ends will be hidden, so the pieces don't all have to be the same length. Be sure to soak the cut ends thoroughly with preservative, or coat them with roofing cement, because the end grain will be in direct contact with the soil.

If you will need weep pipes at the bottom of your wall, predrill holes for them in the second-course timbers before spiking the timbers in place. Be sure the holes angle down about 1/4 inch from the back of the timber to the face for proper drainage.

The exposed cut ends of deadmen and of timbers at the corners of the wall will be much lighter in color than the face of the wall. Stain them darker, so they don't stand out. End grain soaks up a lot of liquid, so you'll probably need to stain them more than once to get a close match. Be careful not to drip stain on the face of the wall.

Garden *Structures*

A Garden Arbor

This charming arbor can support vines or climbing flowers while serving as an entranceway to a garden or patio. You can add a gate, or install a seat to make a leisure-time haven.

148

A Post-and-Beam Pavilion

This handsome pavilion combines a paved patio with a natural-wood structure that provides shelter from sun or rain but allows cooling breezes to pass through freely.

156

A Graceful Wooden Bridge

Sure to be a unique landscaping feature, the main components of this bridge are curved beams you construct using a clever glue-and-screw technique. Final assembly is done on-site.

168

A Domed Gazebo

This very distinctive octagonal structure makes a wonderful retreat or picnic spot. The openwork dome is built with strips of a highly flexible composite wood and plastic material.

178

A Garden *Arbor*

This graceful, easy-to-build archway will complement any lawn or garden. You can add a gate to make a dramatic entranceway, or include a seat to create a shady place to relax.

Planning an Arbor

Arbors have been a feature in gardens around the world for centuries and can be a charming addition to a present-day garden. You can use an arbor as a decorative touch at any point in the expanse of a lawn, perhaps to set off a special area such as herb beds or a fish pond. For greater separation of two areas, add a gate, as in the photo at the right. You may also wish to plant hedges or flowering bushes on either side of the arbor, or add decorative fences. A third possibility is to create a pleasant nook in which to sit and enjoy nature or read. You can do this by building a seat inside with a latticed back that matches the sides of the arbor.

Whichever way you want to use an arbor, you can choose to keep it free of growth so its character and design can be fully seen, or you can let its latticed sides and openwork arched top become a support for roses, wisteria, or other climbing plants.

Easy to Build

The arbor described in these pages is modeled on a traditional English design. The curves and arches may look difficult at first, but don't be put off by their appearance. The arbor was designed with simplicity in mind. If you have a drill, a jigsaw, and a circular saw—and some experience in using them—you can build this arbor in two or three weekends. You'll need a few common hand tools, too. And instead of dragging the tools and materials into the garden, you can work in your garage or on your patio or other convenient spot, then move the finished unit to the spot where you want to place it permanently.

The construction plans on pages 150–151 show you how to build the basic arbor, and also how to make an optional gate. Plans for adding a seat to the arbor are on page 155. Along with the plans you'll find shopping lists of all the materials you'll need, and cutting lists that identify all the parts in the plans, the number required, and their sizes.

Project Expense

The cost of this arbor depends mainly on the wood you choose. The gate version, built from nearly knot-free cedar, will cost $250 or more. Lower-grade cedar might drop the cost by $50 to $70. You could save even more by using green pressure-treated lumber, but that's not a good idea. Dry, good-looking treated lumber is often hard to find and it's more likely to warp, check, or crack than cedar. Whatever grade of wood you use, including a seat will add about 25 percent more to the cost of the basic arbor.

You can include a gate when you build an arbor, or add it at any later time.

Arbor and Gate

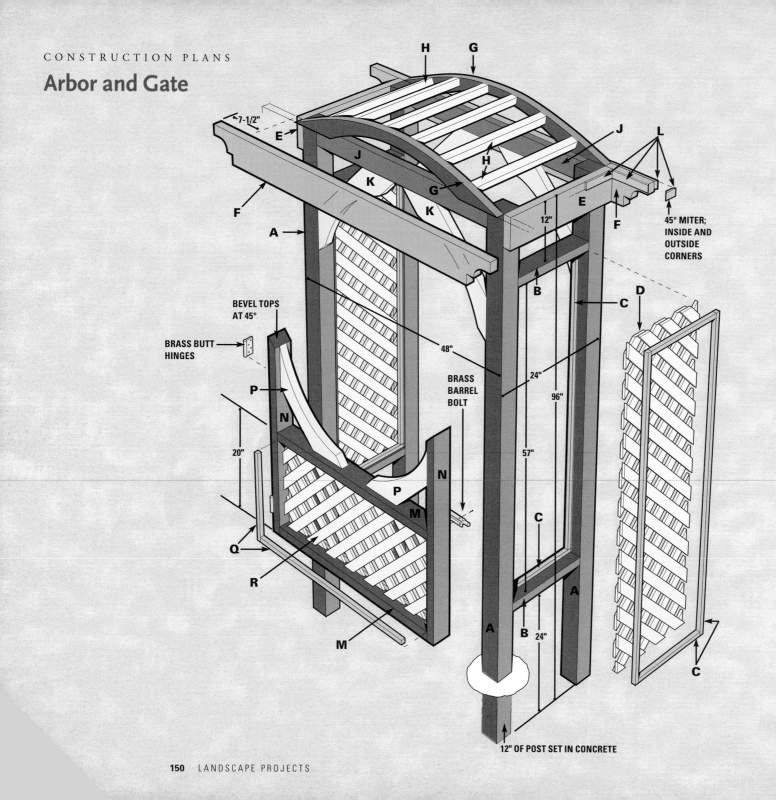

7-1/2"

E

F

J

K

K

G

A

H

G

H

J

L

E

F

12"

45° MITER;
INSIDE AND
OUTSIDE
CORNERS

B

C

D

BEVEL TOPS
AT 45°

BRASS BUTT
HINGES

P

N

48"

24"

96"

BRASS
BARREL
BOLT

20"

57"

P

N

M

C

A

Q

R

M

A

B

24"

C

12" OF POST SET IN CONCRETE

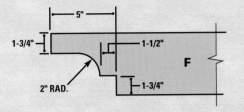

HEADER PATTERN

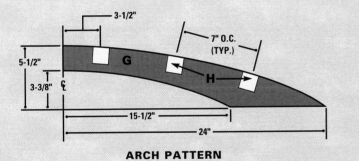

ARCH PATTERN

BRACKET PATTERN

Shopping List

For the archway:

Quantity	Item
4	4x4 x 8' cedar
3	2x4 x 8' cedar
4	2x6 x 8' cedar
2	1x4 x 8' cedar
1	4' x 8' lattice panel
3	8' pine doorstop
4 60-lb. bags	Concrete mix
1 gal.	Stain blocker
1 gal.	Paint

Also: 2-1/2" and 3-1/2" exterior screws;
4d and 8d galvanized casing nails;
exterior spackling compound.

For the gate:

Quantity	Item
2	2x4 x 8' cedar
1	2x6 x 6' cedar
2	Hinges
1	Barrel bolt

Cutting List

For the archway:

Key	Pcs.	Size and Description
A	4	4x4 x 8' posts
B	4	2x4 x 17" stretchers
C	16	Approx. 3/4" x 3/4" x various lengths; lattice mounting strips
D	2	16-3/4" x 56-3/4" lattice
E	2	2x6 x 24" rails
F	2	2x6 x 66" headers
G	2	2x6 x 48" arches
H	6	2x2 x 24" rungs
J	2	2x4 x 41" blocks
K	4*	2x6 x 27-3/4" brackets
L	12	Doorstop, various lengths; trim.

For the gate:

Key	Pcs.	Size and Description
M	2	2x4 x 37-1/4" gate rails
N	2	2x4 x 37-1/2" gate stiles
P	2	2x6 x 22-3/4" gate brackets
Q	8	Approx. 3/4" x 3/4" x various lengths; lattice mounting strips
R	1	16-3/4" x 37" gate lattice

* For an arbor with a seat (page 155),
cut only two brackets.

Cutting the Archway Parts

Mark and cut out the parts on the archway cutting list with the plans. Follow the instructions below to cut parts C, D, F, G, and H. Cut parts J and L after you've assembled the arbor, for an exact fit.

Strips, Rungs, and Lattice

Rip strips C from a 1x4 that is screwed to your sawhorses *(below)*. Mark off 3/4-inch widths across the board and saw along the inside of each line. Set up another 3/4-inch thick board alongside so the base of your circular saw won't tip and cut strips with slanted edges. Use this same method to rip the rungs (H) from 2x4s.

When cutting the lattice sections (D) with a circular saw, wear both safety goggles and gloves to protect against flying fragments.

Headers

Cut a piece for one header (F), then mark and cut the end notches and curves. After sanding, use it as a template to mark out a second, matching header.

Use a section of plastic pipe *(below)* or anything else with a 4-inch outside diameter to mark the decorative curves in the header ends. Then cut along the marked lines with a jigsaw. A jigsaw blade often bends one way or the other, especially when cutting curves, leaving a cut that is not quite vertical. To minimize this problem, move the saw at a slow, steady pace.

Even the cleanest jigsaw cuts will need to be smoothed with coarse-grit sandpaper. You can sand by hand, but a finishing sander will cut down on the drudgery. Use feather-light pressure and keep the pad moving back and forth across the workpiece.

Arches and Brackets

Mark the curves of one arbor arch (G), and one bracket (K) on pieces of stock. After cutting and sanding these pieces, use them as templates for the other arch and the other three brackets. The following technique will make it easy to mark both the arch and the bracket curves.

Clamp a stop block in position on the workpiece and measure and mark the straight-line distance to the point where the curve will end. Then set one end of a flexible strip of plastic doorstop or similar material against the block and bend the other end to the mark there *(below)*. Make sure the center of the strip arcs up to the required point on the workpiece, then trace the curve. Use this same method to mark all the curves, then cut them out with a jigsaw and coarse-sand them as you did the headers.

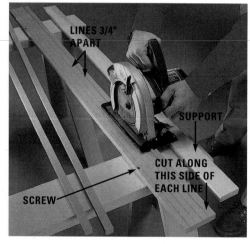

Rip lattice-mounting strips from a 1x4 secured to your work surface. Use a support board of the same thickness to keep the saw from tilting. Cut along the inside of each marked line.

Mark header curves with a 4-in. diameter plastic pipe coupler or other cylinder. This will give a 2-in. radius curve. Cut the header end details with a jigsaw.

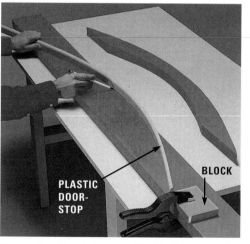

Mark arch and bracket curves with a flexible strip such as plastic doorstop. Set one end against a clamped-on block and bend the strip to form a curve of the required height and length.

Building the Arbor

Build the arbor in stages: First, assemble the latticed sides, then install headers, arches, and brackets to join the sides. When you complete the assembly (page 154), add trim and prime everything. Then set up the arbor in the garden.

Assemble the Sides

Mark each post (A) with the positions of the stretchers (B), then screw the stretchers to one post for each side *(Photo 1)*. Drive one screw at an angle through the center on one side of each stretcher, then drive two angled screws from the other side about one-third of the way from each edge. Screw the stretchers to the other post for each side in the same way.

Screw a rail (E) to the top on the outside of each frame. Make sure it is flush with the post tops and edges, and use a framing square to get it square with the posts.

Next, install the lattice sections (D). Nail a row of strips (C) to each post using a spacer to inset them from the inside edge of each post *(detail photo, far right)*. Use a 1/2-inch thick block as a spacer for 1-inch thick lattice, a 3/4-inch thick spacer block with 1/2-inch thick lattice. Set the lattice in place *(Photo 2)* and nail a second row of strips to hold it in place.

Install Headers, Arches, and Brackets

Joining the sides to one another is a bit delicate: the assembly is flimsy until you can attach some temporary X-braces.

Begin by setting the two side assemblies on edge and screwing a header (F) across them at the top *(Photo 3)*. Make sure the overall width of the arch is 4 feet, measured from the outside edges of the posts. Use a framing square to get the posts square with the header before driving any screws.

After fastening the header, use the framing square to double-check its alignment with the posts. Then screw temporary X-braces to the posts, below the bottom stretcher. With a helper—better yet, two helpers—gently turn the entire assembly over and attach the other header and screw on two more temporary X-braces *(Photo 4)*. Now complete the arbor as explained on the next page.

SPACER

Using a spacer

BUILDING THE ARBOR

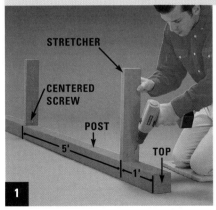

1

Screw the stretchers to one post for each side, then to the other post. Measure and mark their positions from the top end of each post. Space the screws as explained in the text.

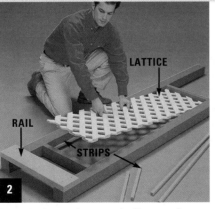

2

Set the lattice sections onto the first row of mounting strips. Then nail a second row of strips over the edges of the lattice to hold it in place.

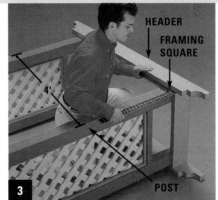

3

Square the posts with the headers before screwing them together. Drive one screw into each post and recheck with a framing square before driving a second screw.

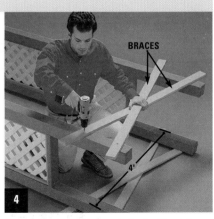

4

Screw temporary X-braces to the first face, then turn the arbor over with a helper. Add braces on this face after attaching the header square with the posts.

Completing the Arbor

Cut and install a block (J) against the back of the header that is on the ground. Screw the arch (G) to the top of the posts on the other, uppermost side. Then add the brackets (K) between these posts and the header. Double-check that all is square before screwing the brackets in place.

Turn the assembly over again. Install a block (J) on the header that is against the ground. Install the arch and brackets on the upper header and posts, as before.

Now add the rungs (H) between the arch pieces. Drive one screw through each arch into the end of each rung. To make this job easier, turn the arbor on one side, with a board on the ground to protect the header ends. Be sure to maintain even spacing between the rungs.

Add Trim and Prime

The trim (L) that wraps around the headers and rails is made from pine doorstop. Measure and cut each piece as you work, making outside and inside miters at the corners to ensure a tight fit and finished appearance. Don't try to cut the miters with a jigsaw or circular saw—the doorstop is too small for clean, accurate cuts. Use a power miter saw, or a miter box and a handsaw. Fasten the trim with the 4d galvanized nails.

Patch all nail, screw, and knot holes with exterior spackling compound, then sand and prime the arbor. Cedar is full of brownish pigments called tannins that will bleed through latex paints, so use an oil-based stain-blocking primer.

Set Up the Arbor

At your selected location, dig four holes about 16 inches in diameter and 1 foot deep. With a helper or two, set the arbor into the holes and adjust it to stand perfectly upright, or plumb. This is a trial-and-error process of digging one hole deeper or throwing dirt into another, as needed. When you get it right, lift the arbor out and firmly tamp the bottoms of the holes with a 2x4. Then mix up concrete according to the directions printed on the bag.

Replace the arbor and check one last time. Make sure the outside edges of the posts are 4 feet apart and that each post is plumb. If all is well, shovel concrete into the holes.

Finally, when the concrete has set, give your arbor two coats of exterior paint.

Building a Gate

A gate for your arbor is constructed of stiles (N) and rails (M), with lattice and brackets as shown in the construction plans. The methods of cutting and assembly are the same as explained for the basic archway.

Notice that the pattern for the gate brackets (P) is the same as for the archway brackets (K), but with one end cut off to make the gate brackets shorter. Notice too that while the archway brackets (K) are installed flush with the outside faces of the arbor posts, the gate brackets are centered in the thickness of the gate.

Cut the lattice mounting strips (Q) in the same way as the strips (C) for the archway sides. Install them in the same way, too, using a spacer block to inset the first set of strips from the back edge of the gate frame. Cut the gate lattice (R) from the leftover portion of the panel used for the side lattices. Remember to wear both eye protection and gloves when cutting the lattice.

When the gate is constructed, sanded, and primed, attach the hinges and barrel bolt. Hold the gate in position to mark and drill holes in the posts for the hinge screws and the barrel bolt. Drill the holes, but do not hang the gate at this time. It will be easier to move and "plant" the arbor in the ground without the gate attached.

Building a Seat

A seat will make your arbor a charming place from which to view your garden or house, to read or knit, or simply to relax. The additional materials you need and a cutting list are given with the seat plan *(below)*. When you build the archway, put brackets (K) on only one side under block J.

Rip the lattice mounting strips (T) in the same way as you did the archway strips (C). Mark the 2-inch radius curves in the front seat support (V) with a 4-inch diameter template and cut them with a jigsaw. Wear eye protection and gloves to cut the lattice (U).

Add the two stretchers (S) between the rear posts at the same heights as side stretchers (B). Install the seat supports (V, X), cutting off the inside lattice mounting strips (C) if necessary. Nail the inside lattice mounting strips (T) on the post, and the upper stretcher (S), using a spacer block to get the proper inset as before. Do not add the strip across the lower stretcher until after you have put in the seat blocks (W) with screws through the rear and front seat supports. Then add that strip, put the lattice in place, and install the second set of strips (T) to hold the lattice.

Screw the rear seat plank (Y) in place, butted against the lattice strips (T) on the posts. Screw the front seat plank in place overhanging the front seat support 3/4 inch. Space the remaining seat planks equally between these two and screw them in place.

Now sand, fill, and prime as described in the archway instructions.

Arbor Seat

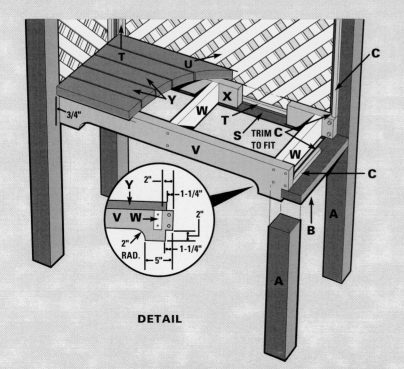

DETAIL

Shopping List

In addition to the basic archway materials:

Quantity	Item
5	2x4 x 8' cedar
1	2x6 x 4' cedar
2	1x4 x 8' cedar
1	4' x 8' lattice panel

Cutting List

For the seat

Key	Pcs.	Size and Description
S	2	2x4 x 41" stretchers
T	8	Approx. 3/4" x 3/4" x various lengths; lattice-mounting strips
U	1	40-3/4" x 56-3/4" lattice
V	1	2x6 x 43-1/2" front seat support
W	3	2x4 x 14" seat blocks
X	1	2x4 x 43-1/2 rear seat support
Y	5	2x4 x 41" seat planks

A Post-and-Beam
Pavilion

Don't let rain or hot sun steal your summer days by keeping you inside. Beat the elements by building this pavilion. It's a challenge, but it could become your yard's outstanding feature.

Outdoor relaxation and enjoyment are the prime pleasures of the late spring, summer, and early fall. During those pleasant months, few things are more disappointing than having outdoor plans foiled by the weather. This patio-based pavilion can let you turn the tables on the weather. Whether it rains or the sun beats down fiercely, you can enjoy your lunch, a quiet conversation, reading, or a hundred other activities in the protection a pavilion provides. And when the weather is fine, the pavilion is a comfortable place to sit and appreciate your yard and garden. All in all, it is likely to become the base for all sorts of outdoor activities.

The beauty of this pavilion is a product of the materials used as well as its simple but graceful design. The wooden structure and roof are all cedar, which is handsome when new, resists the elements well, and weathers to a rich, mellow appearance. The base is patio stones laid over concrete outlined with timber frames, which provide a transition between the wood and stone and the surrounding yard. The posts and beams that support the roof are not difficult to erect. The design creates a solid structure that provides a maximum of open space under the protection of the roof.

If you have ever built a deck or a similar project, you should have no problems building this pavilion. There is plenty to do, enough for two or three full weekends, but the only really tricky part is cutting the rafters for the roof. The specific plans and instructions on the following pages will guide you through all the stages of construction, without difficulty. Don't rush the job, and don't skip any details. You'll be immensely proud of the final results.

Post-and-Beam Pavilion

Tools Required

Wheelbarrow*

Foot-powered sod cutter* (optional)

Hammer drill*

Trowel

Shovel

4-ft. level

Hammer

3-lb. hand sledge

Large sledgehammer (optional)

Tape measure

Chalk line

Framing square

Socket wrench

Hacksaw

Chain saw* (optional)

Handsaw

Circular saw; 32-tooth carbide blade
and plywood blade

Utility knife

12-in. Speed square

Two 6- or 8-foot stepladders

* Rental item

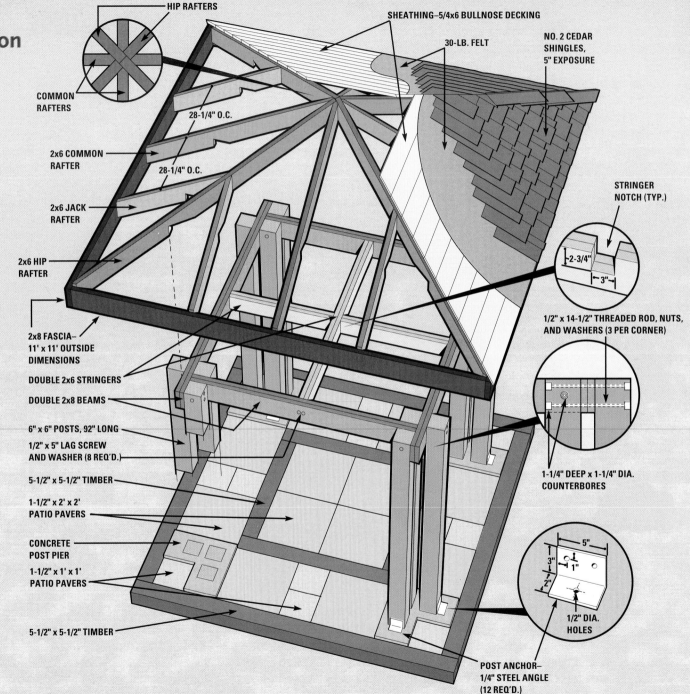

HIP RAFTERS

SHEATHING–5/4x6 BULLNOSE DECKING

30-LB. FELT

NO. 2 CEDAR
SHINGLES,
5" EXPOSURE

COMMON
RAFTERS

28-1/4" O.C.

2x6 COMMON
RAFTER

28-1/4" O.C.

2x6 JACK
RAFTER

2x6 HIP
RAFTER

2x8 FASCIA–
11' x 11' OUTSIDE
DIMENSIONS

DOUBLE 2x6 STRINGERS

DOUBLE 2x8 BEAMS

6" x 6" POSTS, 92" LONG

1/2" x 5" LAG SCREW
AND WASHER (8 REQ'D.)

5-1/2" x 5-1/2" TIMBER

1-1/2" x 2' x 2'
PATIO PAVERS

CONCRETE
POST PIER

1-1/2" x 1' x 1'
PATIO PAVERS

5-1/2" x 5-1/2" TIMBER

STRINGER
NOTCH (TYP.)

2-3/4"

3"

1/2" x 14-1/2" THREADED ROD, NUTS,
AND WASHERS (3 PER CORNER)

1-1/4" DEEP x 1-1/4" DIA.
COUNTERBORES

5"

3"

1"

2"

1/2" DIA.
HOLES

POST ANCHOR–
1/4" STEEL ANGLE
(12 REQ'D.)

Shopping List

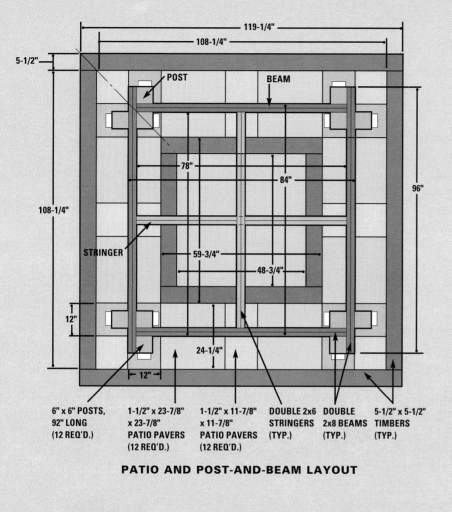

| 119-1/4" |
| 108-1/4" |

POST **BEAM**

78"
84"
96"

108-1/4"

STRINGER

59-3/4"
48-3/4"

12"

24-1/4"
12"

6" x 6" POSTS, 92" LONG (12 REQ'D.) — **1-1/2" x 23-7/8" x 23-7/8" PATIO PAVERS (12 REQ'D.)** — **1-1/2" x 11-7/8" x 11-7/8" PATIO PAVERS (12 REQ'D.)** — **DOUBLE 2x6 STRINGERS (TYP.)** — **DOUBLE 2x8 BEAMS (TYP.)** — **5-1/2" x 5-1/2" TIMBERS (TYP.)**

PATIO AND POST-AND-BEAM LAYOUT

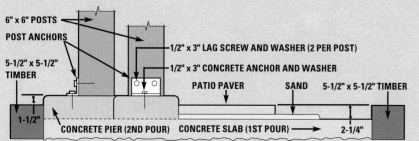

6" x 6" POSTS
POST ANCHORS
5-1/2" x 5-1/2" TIMBER
1/2" x 3" LAG SCREW AND WASHER (2 PER POST)
1/2" x 3" CONCRETE ANCHOR AND WASHER
PATIO PAVER **SAND** **5-1/2" x 5-1/2" TIMBER**
1-1/2"
CONCRETE PIER (2ND POUR) **CONCRETE SLAB (1ST POUR)** 2-1/4"

TYPICAL PLATFORM CROSS SECTION

Quantity	Size and Description/Use
4	Wood stakes
6	5-1/2" x 5-1/2" x 10' treated timbers; patio frames
16	12" spikes; patio frames
1/2 sheet	3/4" plywood; pier forms
12	2' x 2' patio stone pavers
12	1' x 1' patio stone pavers
1 cu. yd.	Concrete, ready-mix
4 60-lb. bags	Sand
1	62" long 3" x 3" x 1/4" steel angle; post bases
24	3" x 1/2" lag screws
12	3" x 1/2" concrete anchors
2	2x6 x 8' pine; screed boards
12	6" x 6" x 8' cedar; posts
8	2x8 x 8' cedar; beams
4	2x8 x 12' cedar; beams
4	2x6 x 7' cedar; stringers
6	1/2" x 36" threaded rod
24	1/2" nuts
56	1/2" washers
8	5" x 1/2" lag screws
2	3" galvanized deck screws; long hip rafters
4	2x6 x 10' cedar; hip rafters
4	2x6 x 7' cedar; common rafters
4	2x6 x 8' cedar; jack rafters
30	5/4 x 6 x 12' cedar; roof decking
1 roll	30-lb. roofing felt
2 squares	No. 2 cedar shingles (200 sq. ft.)
40	Preassembled cedar roof caps
10 lbs.	10d galvanized common nails; rafters, roof deck
8 lbs.	8d galvanized common nails; jack rafters
10 lbs.	3d galvanized box nails; shingles
2 lbs.	16d galvanized common nails; fascia

Project Overview

Building the post-and-beam pavilion shown in the photo on page 157, and in the plans on the preceding pages, involves several stages. These stages are preparing the site and the patio frames; pouring the concrete base; setting the patio stones; installing post bases; erecting the frame of posts, beams, and stringers; cutting the roof rafters; framing the roof; and completing the roof with decking and shingles. Detailed instructions for constructing the pavilion are given on the following pages. However, to help you follow them easily, the following overview provides information about the components and procedures involved at each stage.

Site and Patio Frames

The ground must be cleared of grass and leveled. A base of sand may be needed for good drainage. There are two patio frames, each built from 5-1/2 inch timbers spiked together. Each frame is a square, one with inside dimensions of just over 9 feet, the other with dimensions of just over 4 feet.

The smaller frame is centered inside the larger one.

Concrete Base

The frames are filled with concrete up to 2-1/4 inches from the tops of the timbers. This depth allows for bringing the patio pavers flush with the frames. At each corner of the large outer frame, a raised pier for the posts is poured in special forms and troweled to a smooth finish.

Patio Stones

The finished surface of the patio consists of 1x1-foot and 2x2-foot pavers, or patio stones. They are laid dry—that is, without mortar—on a shallow bed of sand poured over the concrete base. The depth of the sand is adjusted as necessary so the surface of the pavers is even with the surface of the timber frames.

Post Bases

Metal angle irons to hold the posts are bolted to the piers, using concrete anchors in holes made with a hammer drill. These post bases must be placed precisely, because they determine the spacing of the posts from corner to corner, and consequently the dimensions of the upper structural frame, which must be square in a plan view.

Posts, Beams, and Stringers

There are three 6x6 by 92-inch cedar posts at each corner. They are held in position by lag screws driven through holes in the metal angle-iron post bases. The bottoms and tops of the posts must be cut square so they will stand plumb (vertical) and not protrude above the beams.

The beams are doubled 2x8 cedar boards. Each beam fits between two posts and is held by threaded metal rods that run all the way through the posts. The rods are secured by countersunk nuts.

Doubled 2x6 stringers are installed to connect the midpoints of opposite beams to brace the structure.

Rafters

The roof frame is built of common, jack, and hip rafters. All must have angled notches to rest on the beams at the proper slant, and angled end cuts to join properly at the center peak of the roof. Specific plans (page 165) show exactly what length and angles are required in cutting each kind of rafter.

Roof Framing

Nailing the rafters in position to form the roof framing is not difficult—if you have cut the rafters precisely and install them in the proper sequence. However, there is no question that these two procedures are the most complex part of the project. Once the rafters are in place, their outside ends are joined by fascia boards—the vertical facing boards of the eave overhang.

Decking and Shingles

The roof framing is covered with cedar decking for a handsome appearance from inside the pavilion, and for strength. The decking is covered with roofing felt for waterproofing, and then cedar shingles are nailed in place. The seams from each corner to the peak of the roof are covered with preassembled cedar roof caps.

Preparing the Site and Frames

The pavilion's patio base is easier to build if you have a level site. If not, you can build up the low side with extra timbers using the techniques explained in Building a Timber Retaining Wall (pages 136–145).

Site Layout

Use stakes and string to lay out a square that is 11 feet on each side. To make sure the area is in fact square, measure the diagonals. They must be equal to give you a square perimeter. Because the stakes and string will get in the way of your work, mark the outline on the ground with spray paint *(below),* then remove the string.

Skin off the sod in this entire area, using a flat-nosed shovel or foot-powered (kick) sod cutter. You can rent the cutter, which makes the job easier. Dig the area down to a depth equal to the thickness of your frame timbers if you have firm, good-draining soil. In soil that does not drain well, dig a few inches deeper and pour a bed of sand. Check the entire area with a level on the edge of a long, straight 2x4. Set the 2x4 parallel to the edges at 4-foot intervals, and also diagonally from corner to corner. Add soil or sand as necessary to get a level base.

Frame Construction

Cut the pressure-treated timbers for the two frames to length. The dimensions given in the patio and post-and-beam layout detail on page 159 may not be precise, depending on the thickness of your timbers. Adjust as necessary so the large frame will measure 9 feet 1/4 inch on each inside edge and the small frame will measure 4 feet 3/4 inch on its inside edges. Use a chain saw or circular saw followed by a handsaw; wear eye and ear protection and a face mask. Timber-cutting techniques are explained on page 141.

Nail the timbers together with 12-inch spikes and a hand sledgehammer *(below).* To avoid splitting the timber ends, drill pilot holes somewhat smaller than the spike diameter. If the timbers shift as you hammer, stand on them. Measure to make sure the small frame is located exactly in the center of the large outside frame. Measure the diagonals of each frame and whack one corner or another with a sledgehammer to make the frame square.

Marking Paint
Digging Perimeter

Stake out an 11-ft. square and mark the ground with spray paint. Dig out the area to the depth of the frame timbers, or deeper if you need to add sand for drainage.

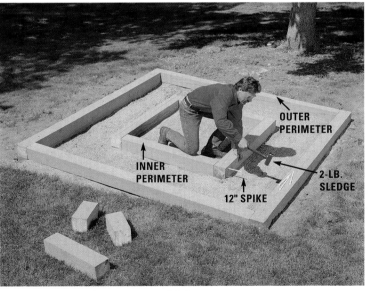

Outer Perimeter
Inner Perimeter
2-LB. SLEDGE
12" SPIKE

Construct the frames of pressure-treated timbers. Predrill for 12-inch spikes to avoid splitting at the ends. The tops of the frames must be level; fill beneath as necessary to make adjustments.

Pouring the Concrete Base

There are two phases to pouring the concrete base for the patio. One is preparing the items you need for the job. The other is the actual pouring. When you pour, you must level the concrete at the proper depth in the frames for sand and patio stones to go on top, and then you must build piers at the corners to support the wooden posts of the pavilion. You'll have to work fast to do all this before the concrete begins to set. A helper or two will be very valuable.

Preparation

You need some special items for the pouring: two screeds for leveling the concrete, and four sets of forms for the piers.

A screed is a board notched so its ends can rest on the timber frames and its center tongue extend down between the frames. For one screed use a 3- or 4-foot long 2x6 and

cut notches 2-1/4 inches deep in each end, leaving a tongue that just fits between the inner and outer frames, as shown in the photo *(right)*. For the inner frame, use a 6-foot long 2x6 and notch each end 1 foot, to make a tongue 4 feet long.

You'll need a pier form at each corner of the patio. There are four pieces in each form *(diagram, below left)*. Cut the forms from 3/4-inch plywood and have them ready to nail in place as soon as the concrete has been leveled.

Making the Pour

You would have to hand-mix 50 bags of concrete to have enough for this job, so instead order a delivery of 1 cubic yard of ready-mix from a concrete company. Ask for a sidewalk mix.

Have a wheelbarrow at hand, shovels, and a helper or two. Fill the small frame first, and screed it to depth immediately. Two people can handle the long screed easier than one. Then fill the space between the two frames and screed it to depth too *(right top)*.

As soon as each corner is screeded, you or a helper should nail the pieces of the pier form in place. Immediately shovel in concrete to fill the form *(right bottom)*. The concrete in the piers needs to bond with the concrete underneath, so work fast. You'll have only about an hour on a hot, dry day. Level the concrete off at the top of the form, then use a trowel to smooth the surface and round the exposed edges. Finished piers are shown on the opposite page. Leave the forms in place until the next day.

Screed off the concrete 2-1/4 in. below the tops of the timber frames. Don't worry about making the surface smooth; it will be covered with sand and patio pavers.

Install forms for the post piers at the corners while the concrete below is still moist. Fill the forms to the top, then trowel the surface smooth and round off the exposed open edges.

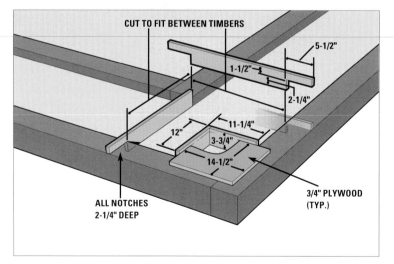

Concrete pier forms

Setting the Patio Stones

When the concrete base has cured for a day you can set the patio stones or pavers on it. Pavers are available at many home centers and patio supply outlets. Choose colors to suit your floor design; two colors were used in this project. Check the thickness to determine how much sand to put down.

Cut new screeds or add thickness to the "handles" of your concrete screeds so a sand bed will put the surface of the pavers flush with the framing timbers. Pour sand on the concrete base and screed it smooth. Then put the pavers in place *(below)*. Butt their edges together and add sand as needed to adjust leveling. If a line is too long to fit in the frame, trim equal amounts from the two corner pavers to fit. Use a masonry blade in your circular saw; wear goggles and gloves.

Screed a layer of sand over the dry concrete deep enough to put the pavers flush with the timbers. Lay the pavers without mortar. Add sand as needed to level each paver.

Installing Post Bases

The posts are held by brackets cut from 2 x 3 x 1/4-inch steel angle iron. Welding and metal-working shops and industrial hardware outlets carry this kind of material. You can cut a long piece of stock into 5-inch lengths with an aluminum oxide metal-cutting blade in a circular saw, but it's a lot easier to have a shop do it for you. Most have a shear that easily cuts the steel. Typical cost is about $1 per cut.

It's also worthwhile having the shop drill 9/16-inch holes for the mounting bolts and the 1/2-inch lag screws that go into the pavilion posts. If you do this yourself, use a heavy-duty electric drill. Start with a 1/4-inch hole, then enlarge it with a 9/16-inch bit. File any sharp edges on the cut and drilled metal and clean it with mineral spirits. Then spray each bracket with two coats of rust-inhibiting paint.

Use cut-off post ends to mark the positions of the posts and the base support brackets *(right top)*. Set the inner posts first, with their outside edges 78 inches from one another (see plan detail, page 159). Set the outer posts 3 inches farther away. Mark the post and bracket hole positions in pencil.

Drill 1/2-inch holes into the concrete to accept the concrete anchor bolts *(right bottom)*. A rented hammer drill is probably the best way to make the holes; a masonry bit in a heavy-duty drill will take a long time. The anchors *(far right)* grip the concrete as you tighten a bolt into them. Hammer the anchors into the hole, place the support bracket over them, and drive bolts with washers into the anchors with a wrench.

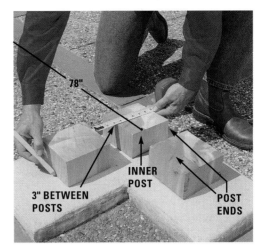

Mark post positions accurately, using scrap ends as guides. Outer edges of the inside posts must be 78 in. apart. Spacing in each post group is 3 in.

Concrete anchors

Drill holes for post base supports with a hammer drill. Install concrete anchors *(right)* in the holes. Then bolt the supports in place.

Erecting the Frame

The basic frame of the pavilion is constructed by erecting the posts and long beams on one side first, then the posts and long beams on the opposite side. Short beams are added to the open sides, and finally the stringers between beams are installed.

Put Up Posts

Check one end of each post with a square from two adjoining sides; if it is not square, mark and cut it accurately. Then measure the length—92 inches—mark the other end square from two sides, and cut it. Recheck and use the squarer end as the post base.

While a helper holds each post against its steel base bracket, drill 3/8-inch pilot holes into the post. Then use a wrench to install 3 x 1/2-inch lag screws to hold the post.

Install the Beams

Nail two cedar 2x8s together for each beam and cut them to length. With a helper, clamp a beam into position flush with the top edges of its posts *(below left)*. Do the long beams first. For fasteners, cut 1/2-inch threaded rod 1/2 inch shorter than the thickness of the two posts plus the beam.

Drill countersink holes 1-1/4 inches into the posts, then drill 1/2-inch holes all the way through. Keep the drill straight. Drill for two fasteners through the long beams, one fastener through the short beams *(below)*. If you can't find a long-shank bit, use a 1/2-inch spade bit with an extension.

Put a washer and nut on one end of the rod, and drive it through the hole with a hammer. Slip a washer and nut on the other end and tighten each side.

Install the Stringers

Nail two cedar 2x6s together for each stringer. Don't nail in the center, where you will cut notches. Before cutting the stringers to length, check to see that the corner posts are plumb (vertical). If they need to be adjusted, cut a 2x4 brace to reach from the bottom of one post to the top of an opposite post. Nail it at the bottom, get both posts plumb, then nail it at the top. Leave the brace(s) in place until the roof is completed.

Cut the stringers to fit between the midpoints of opposite beams and notch them in the middle (plan detail, page 158). Temporarily nail one stringer in position and fasten it with two 5 x 1/2-inch lag screws and washers driven through pilot holes in the beams *(below)*. Put the other stringer in position and fasten it in the same way.

Clamp beams in position to drill holes all the way through the posts and beam for 1/2-in. threaded rod. Tighten the nuts and washers in countersunk holes with a socket wrench.

Install the short beams after both long beams are in place. Use two fasteners in each long beam, but only one in the short beams.

Center the stringers between the beams. Bend over 16d nails above and below to hold them while you drill holes for lag screws.

Cutting the Roof Rafters

Use 2x6 cedar boards for rafters. Follow the plans at the right and cut the rafters to exactly the lengths and angles specified. Some of the rafters have compound end cuts: the end is cut at an angle with a 45° cheek cut (bevel) on one or both sides. Set your adjustable square or miter guide to the angle shown in the plans, then tilt the base of your circular saw for the 45° bevel *(below)*. Some bevels will have to be cut with a handsaw. Note that all the rafters are also notched to rest on the beams of the pavilion.

Cut the two longer hip rafters (A) first and install them (see Framing the Roof, page 166). Then cut and install the other two hip rafters (B). They are 3/4 inch shorter to make up for the thickness of the two already in place. Do the common rafters next and the jack rafters last.

Cut rafters with an adjustable square or guide to make the end angle precisely right. Tilt the saw blade 45° to cut bevels at the same time.

Pavilion Rafters

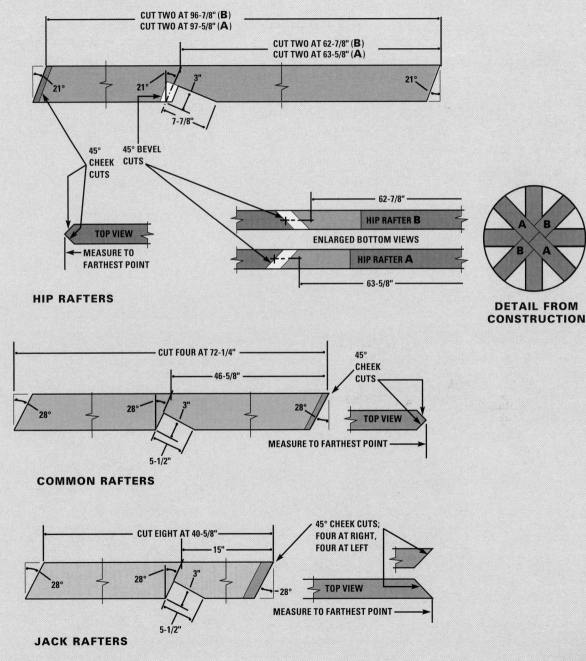

CUT TWO AT 96-7/8" (**B**)
CUT TWO AT 97-5/8" (**A**)

CUT TWO AT 62-7/8" (**B**)
CUT TWO AT 63-5/8" (**A**)

21°   21°   3"   21°

7-7/8"

45° CHEEK CUTS   45° BEVEL CUTS

TOP VIEW

MEASURE TO FARTHEST POINT

HIP RAFTERS

62-7/8"
HIP RAFTER **B**

ENLARGED BOTTOM VIEWS

HIP RAFTER **A**
63-5/8"

DETAIL FROM CONSTRUCTION

CUT FOUR AT 72-1/4"   45° CHEEK CUTS

46-5/8"

28°   28°   3"   28°

TOP VIEW

5-1/2"

MEASURE TO FARTHEST POINT

COMMON RAFTERS

CUT EIGHT AT 40-5/8"   45° CHEEK CUTS; FOUR AT RIGHT, FOUR AT LEFT

15"

28°   28°   3"   28°

TOP VIEW

5-1/2"

MEASURE TO FARTHEST POINT

JACK RAFTERS

Framing the Roof

It is best to frame the roof by installing the rafters in pairs as you cut them (page 165). Begin with the two longest hip rafters (A, *below left*). On the ground, fasten their top, flat ends together with two 3-inch galvanized deck screws. The ends with the cheek cuts will form corners at the eaves. Then with a helper walk the assembly up two ladders and position it so the rafters fall directly over the intersections of the beams at the corners *(below)*. Nail each side with two 10d galvanized common nails.

Next install the two shorter hip rafters (B, *below left)* using 10d galvanized nails. Nail their flat ends to the first two hip rafters at the peak and nail them at the beams. The ends with cheek cuts are at the eaves.

The four common rafters run from the midpoints of the beams to the peak of the roof *(below right)*. The ends with double cheek cuts go at the peak, to fit between the intersections of the four hip rafters. Nail them there, and also at the beams, again with 10d galvanized nails. The flat-cut ends of the common rafters are at the eaves.

The jack rafters run from the beams to the sides of the hip rafters. Note the direction of the bevels in the compound cuts at the upper ends. Four are right-sided and four left-sided in order to fit against the hip rafters. The flat-cut ends are at the eaves. Use 8d galva-

nized nails to fasten the jack rafters to the beams and to the hip rafters.

Complete the roof framing by installing the fascia boards across the eave ends of the rafters. Cut 2x8 cedar boards to length for the fascia. Make butt joints at the four corners, not mitered joints (see plans, page 158). Nail the fascia boards into the rafter ends with 16d galvanized common nails. Do not set their top edges flush with the tops of the rafters. Instead, drop the fascia board 3/4 inch so the roof decking running off the rafters can rest on their outside edges.

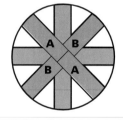

Rafter ends at dome top

Join the long hip rafters on the ground with screws. Then carry them up and fasten them over diagonally opposite corners of the pavilion.

Install common rafters after all four hip rafters are up, then add the jack rafters. Be sure to cut them with left and right angles to fit against the hip rafters.

Completing the Roof

The last steps in building the pavilion roof are to cover the rafters with decking, and then to lay shingles over the decking.

Lay the Decking

The plans call for 12-foot lengths of 5/4 cedar decking. It will be handsome to look at from inside the pavilion and is thick enough so shingle nails won't poke through.

Starting at the bottom on one side, place the first board so it hangs over the fascia 1-1/4 inches. Nail it into the rafters with 8d galvanized common nails. Place the nails carefully. If you miss any rafters, you'll be able to see the mistake from inside.

Butt the next board against the first and nail it with two nails into each rafter. Continue this way up to the peak, getting the boards tight against one another so they look good from inside. Each board can be cut a bit shorter than the one below, but let the ends overhang the hip rafters. When you reach the top, snap a chalk line on the decking along the middle of the hip rafter at each end *(right top)*. Set your circular saw to the thickness of the decking and trim along the chalk lines.

When you do the two adjoining sides of the roof, angle-cut one end of each board to fit against the decking in place. Snap a chalk line and trim the other end when the side is covered to the peak. For the last side of the roof you will have to angle-cut both ends of each board to fit it in place.

Lay the Shingles

When the decking is finished, staple 30-pound roofing felt over the entire roof as waterproofing under the shingles. For a roof that harmonizes with the natural wood structure of the pavilion, use No. 2 cedar shingles. They have a few knots but are rustic and will add charm to the structure.

As with the decking, do one side of the roof at a time. Using 3d galvanized box nails, lay the first row at the bottom, overhanging the edge of the decking 1/2 inch. Then nail another row directly over this course, offsetting the seams with those below.

Start the next course 5 inches above the first. You can align the bottom edges for an even reveal, or stagger them for a more rustic, hand-built look *(right bottom)*. Place the nails so they will be covered by the course above. Stagger the seams from course to course, and trim the shingles at the hips as you go with a fine-toothed plywood blade in your circular saw. You can also shave the edges to fit with a utility knife or plane.

When all four sides of the roof have been shingled, finish off the seams above the hips by nailing on preassembled cedar roof caps, sold at lumberyards. Work from eave to peak along each hip, overlapping the caps.

Finally, it's a good idea to seal the entire pavilion with a deck sealer. This will keep the shingles, beams, and posts from cracking in the sun. After two or three months, check the bolts, nuts, and lag screws. As the wood dries and shrinks, they may need tightening.

Install roof decking with the ends running long. When one side is covered, snap a chalk line along the middle of each hip and cut the decking to length. Then go on to the next side.

Lay shingles over 30-lb. roofing felt. The first course is two shingles thick, with offset seams. Lay succeeding courses with either an even or a staggered reveal. Cover the hip seams with preassembled roof caps.

A Graceful
Wooden Bridge

This attractive and practical bridge can span a stream, help you across a backyard pond, or provide a charming transition from one garden area to another. You may enjoy building it almost as much as walking over it when you're finished.

For a homeowner who enjoys construction projects, the idea of building a bridge is especially intriguing. The design of an arched bridge like the one in this project is unlike that of almost any other home-improvement structure. There are some unusual, but not difficult, construction techniques to be learned. And there should be satisfaction in knowing that an arched bridge will be a unique landscaping feature.

You can build this 9-foot bridge in about four days if you want to devote yourself entirely to it. The work is not hard, but it will be a lot more enjoyable if you take your time to savor the completion of each stage and the satisfaction of mastering techniques such as laminating beams.

The bridge is not a particularly expensive project. The wood and hardware specified could cost about $250 to $300, but that can differ greatly in various areas, or if you choose to use a different kind of wood. You don't need any special tools, and the plans and instructions on the following pages show you just what to do. So go to work, and in a short time you'll have the pleasure of using your bridge as well as a very justifiable pride in your accomplishment.

From the simplicity of planks laid on timbers to the strength and energy of stone and reinforced concrete arches, to the graceful curves and lacy intricacy of suspension cables, bridges are fascinating and beautiful structures. In our world of high-speed, long-distance transportation where bridges carry multiple lanes of traffic, it is easy to forget how pleasing a small-scale footbridge is, both to look at and to use.

This project will bring you into contact with an essentially simple but clever design, one that is the result of refinements and improvements produced by craftsmen over many generations—the kind of evolution that results from practical experience.

A Graceful Wooden Bridge

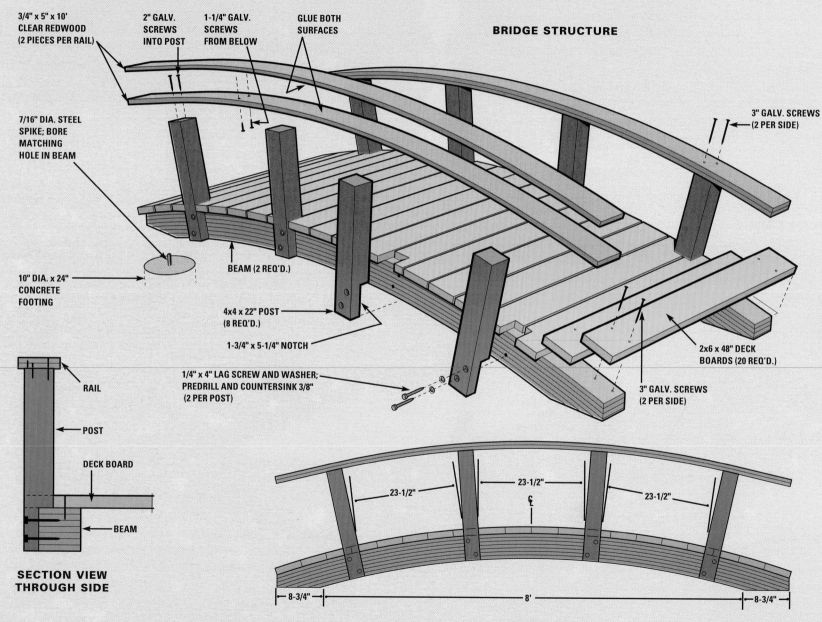

3/4" x 5" x 10'
CLEAR REDWOOD
(2 PIECES PER RAIL)

2" GALV.
SCREWS
INTO POST

1-1/4" GALV.
SCREWS
FROM BELOW

GLUE BOTH
SURFACES

BRIDGE STRUCTURE

3" GALV. SCREWS
(2 PER SIDE)

7/16" DIA. STEEL
SPIKE; BORE
MATCHING
HOLE IN BEAM

BEAM (2 REQ'D.)

10" DIA. x 24"
CONCRETE
FOOTING

4x4 x 22" POST
(8 REQ'D.)

1-3/4" x 5-1/4" NOTCH

2x6 x 48" DECK
BOARDS (20 REQ'D.)

1/4" x 4" LAG SCREW AND WASHER;
PREDRILL AND COUNTERSINK 3/8"
(2 PER POST)

3" GALV. SCREWS
(2 PER SIDE)

RAIL

POST

DECK BOARD

BEAM

**SECTION VIEW
THROUGH SIDE**

23-1/2"

23-1/2"

23-1/2"

8-3/4"

8'

8-3/4"

ELEVATION VIEW

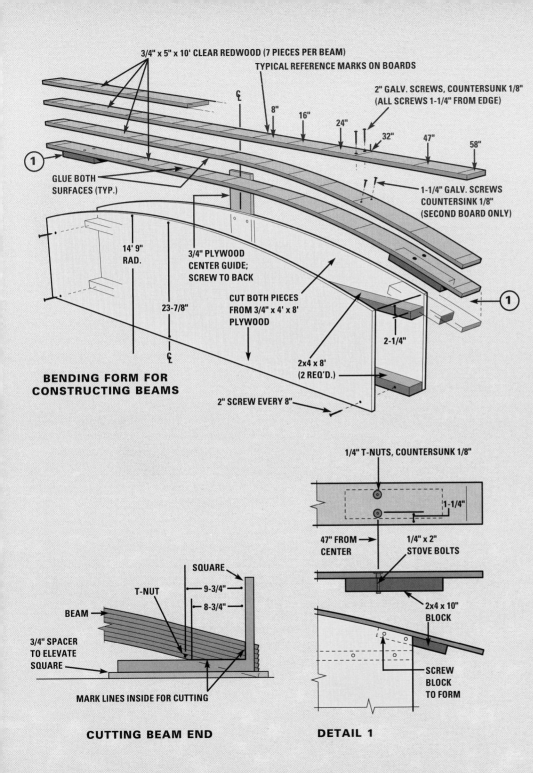

3/4" x 5" x 10' CLEAR REDWOOD (7 PIECES PER BEAM)

TYPICAL REFERENCE MARKS ON BOARDS

8" 16" 24" 32" 47" 58"

2" GALV. SCREWS, COUNTERSUNK 1/8"
(ALL SCREWS 1-1/4" FROM EDGE)

GLUE BOTH
SURFACES (TYP.)

1-1/4" GALV. SCREWS
COUNTERSINK 1/8"
(SECOND BOARD ONLY)

3/4" PLYWOOD
CENTER GUIDE;
SCREW TO BACK

14' 9"
RAD.

CUT BOTH PIECES
FROM 3/4" x 4' x 8'
PLYWOOD

23-7/8"

2-1/4"

2x4 x 8'
(2 REQ'D.)

2" SCREW EVERY 8"

BENDING FORM FOR CONSTRUCTING BEAMS

1/4" T-NUTS, COUNTERSUNK 1/8"

1-1/4"

47" FROM
CENTER

1/4" x 2"
STOVE BOLTS

2x4 x 10"
BLOCK

SCREW
BLOCK
TO FORM

SQUARE

T-NUT

9-3/4"

8-3/4"

BEAM

3/4" SPACER
TO ELEVATE
SQUARE

MARK LINES INSIDE FOR CUTTING

CUTTING BEAM END

DETAIL 1

Shopping List

Quantity	Size and Description/Use
14	1x6 x 10' clear redwood; beams
4	1x6 x 10' clear redwood; handrails
2	4x4 x 10' redwood; posts
20	2x6 x 4' construction-grade redwood; decking
16'	Flexible steel wire
1 sheet	4' x 8' x 3/4" CDX plywood; beam form
1	2x4 x 8' pine; beam form
1	2x4 x 10' pine; beam form, blocks
2 lbs.	1-1/4" galvanized deck screws
5 lbs.	3" galvanized deck screws
6 lbs.	2" galvanized deck screws
16	1/4" x 5" lag screws
16	1/4" washers
8	1/4" T-nuts
8	1/4" x 2" stove bolts and washers
4	12" landscape spikes
1 gal.	Exterior-grade wood glue
4	10" dia. x 24" cardboard tubes; footing forms
5	60-lb. bags concrete mix; footings
1 gal.	Deck sealer

Tools Required

Jigsaw (saber saw)

Circular saw

Handsaw

Drill with 1/4", 7/16", 7/8", and screwdriver bits

Hand screwdrivers

Socket wrench

Clamps

Tape measure

Framing square

Belt sander

Post-hole digger

4-ft. level

Concrete mixing pan/board

Shovel

Warning: This bridge is designed for walking use only. Do not use it for heavy equipment or more than four adults at a time. It is not a children's play piece. The railings do not meet code requirements for attached decks.

Project Overview

Before starting to build your wooden bridge, you should understand its basic construction and the stages in which the work will be done. This will help you avoid making mistakes that would waste materials and will save you effort. It also will let you plan how much to do each day, whether you intend to build the bridge in a concentrated period or do it in two or three weekends.

Basic Construction

The key elements in the design of this bridge are the arched support beams. The grace of their curves is accentuated by matching curved handrails. The plans call for using redwood for the beams, rails, posts, and decking because it has such a handsome appearance in its natural state. But you could use cedar instead, which is also a handsome-looking wood and weathers equally as well as redwood. Choose materials according to your preference, as well as by cost and availability in your area.

The beams are not only graceful, they provide strong support without a complex structure of cross-beams and braces, and they make it easy to assemble the bridge at its site. Their strength is a result of the way in which you build them: they are laminated from separate boards. This is much cheaper and easier than buying huge solid beams and trying to cut them to shape—an almost impossible task with homeowner's tools. And a laminated beam is not likely to check or develop grain-line splits the way a large solid piece of wood often does.

The 1x6 (actually 5-1/2 inch) boards that you buy for the beams must be ripped to 5 inches wide. You could do that yourself, but it would be easier to have them cut at the lumberyard. To make a beam, you bend the boards on a bending form that you construct from 3/4-inch plywood and 2x4s. You build up the laminated piece by gluing and screwing each board layer to those below. The glue must dry completely before the first beam can be removed from the form and the second one made.

The beams are installed on concrete footings that are 12 inches in diameter and 24 inches deep. Landscape spikes in the centers of the footings anchor the beam ends so the assembled bridge cannot shift position.

The walkway decking on the bridge is made of 2x6 boards screwed into the tops of the beams. The handrail posts are notched to be fastened to the sides of the beams. Because they are all cut to the same length, their tops follow the curve of the beams. So when the handrails are screwed to the posts, they assume the proper curve; no prebending or shaping is required.

Project Stages

The actual work in building the wooden bridge falls into the following four stages, which are explained in detail on the following pages.

Building the form. To make the curved beams you need to first build a bending form. The curve must be accurately marked and cut on the plywood sides of the form in order to shape the beams correctly.

Constructing the beams. Each beam is built up by gluing and screwing seven boards together in the form, one at a time, for an overall thickness of 5-1/4 inches. The glue should dry for at least 48 hours before a beam is removed from the form. During that time you could do some of the work for the next stage.

Installing the beams. At the bridge site you must dig holes and pour footings that are properly spaced and have their tops level with one another, so that the beams will be correctly aligned and firmly supported. Then you place the beams on top of spikes embedded in the footings.

Completing the bridge. In the last stage of construction you attach the posts to the beams, install the decking, and fasten the rails to the posts. Finally, you coat the structure with deck sealer to protect the wood.

Building the Form

The bending form that holds the boards in a curved position as you build up each laminated beam is built of two plywood sides separated by 2x4s.

To mark the required curve, fasten a pencil to one end of a long piece of flexible steel wire and securely fasten the other end exactly 177 inches away. This will let you mark a curve with a radius of 14 feet 9 inches on a board for the first form side.

The curve must be centered on a 4x8-foot sheet of 3/4-inch CDX plywood. An easy way to do this is to fasten the end of the wire on the pencil exactly 4 feet out from a side wall and butt one end of the plywood against the same wall *(below left)*. Another way is to draw a line dividing the plywood into two 4-foot halves and make a mark on that line 23-7/8 inches from one edge. That allows for the kerf wastage when you cut on the outside of the curved line you will draw.

Position the plywood so that the pencil is exactly at the center when the wire is pulled taut and swing the pencil right and left to draw a curve from one end of the plywood to the other. Cut the curve with a jigsaw to make one side of the form, then trace its shape on the remaining piece of plywood and cut out the second side.

Join the two sides of the form by screwing them to two 8-foot lengths of 2x4 *(below right)*. Use 2-inch galvanized screws spaced every 8 inches. Fasten one 2x4 along the bottom of the form, and the other exactly 2-1/4 inches below the corners of the curve at each end (see Bending Form plan, page 171). This spacing allows room for support blocks on the bottom of the beam.

Mark the form's curve with a pencil and a steel wire 177 inches long (string would stretch). Draw an arc on one half of a plywood sheet. Cut it out and use it to mark the other half.

Assemble the form by screwing the sides to 2x4s. The upper 2x4 must be 2-1/4 in. below the ends of the curve, to allow room for support blocks in constructing the beams.

Constructing the Beams

There are six steps in constructing each beam: mark the boards; attach support blocks; fasten the first board; laminate the boards; sand the sides; and cut the ends.

Each step is described below and shown in the photos on the opposite page.

Mark the Boards

Stack seven 10-foot 3/4- x 5-inch redwood boards and align their ends and edges. Mark the middle of the stack down the edges on one side *(Photo 1)* and then mark the edges at 8, 16, 24, 32, 40, 47, and 58 inches from the middle toward each end of the stack. These will help guide screw placement later. The 47-inch marks show where to fasten support blocks.

Attach Support Blocks

To attach support blocks, you must install T-nuts (detail photo, opposite page) in the board that will be the bottom layer of the beam. At each end of the board, 47 inches from the center, drill two 1/4-inch diameter holes for the shanks of the T-nuts. Locate the center of each hole 1-1/4 inches from the edge of the board (see Detail 1 in the plans, page 171). With a 7/8-inch spade bit, mortise the holes 1/8-inch deep from the top of the board so you can countersink the bases of the T-nuts below the surface *(Photo 2)*. They will remain in the finished beam. Now drill matching 1/4-inch holes in two 10-inch 2x4 blocks. Locate the holes so the blocks will be centered in the width of the beam. Attach the blocks by driving 1/4 x 2-inch stove bolts with washers up into the T-nuts in the beam board.

Fasten the First Board

At each end of the bending form, clamp the bottom 2x4 to a sawhorse or other support that will put it at a convenient height. Then use the mark at the center of the beam board to center it on the form. Because it is wider, the board will rest on the curved edges of the form. Push one end down so the support block on the bottom of the board is between the form sides and fasten it with three 2-inch galvanized screws on each side *(Photo 3)*. Push the support block at the other end of the board into the form and fasten it in the same way. You may want a helper to hold this end down as you drive the first screws.

Laminate the Boards

Spread waterproof (exterior grade) wood glue on the surface of the board in the form and on the underside of the board that will be the next layer in the beam. Screw this board to the board in the form, starting at one end and working to the other *(Photo 4)*. Keep the edges aligned, and have a helper hold up the free end of the board. Use 1-1/4 inch galvanized screws in this layer. Predrill the holes and countersink them so the screws will get a good bite and their heads will be below the surface. Space them according to the reference marks on the edge and countersink them 1/8 inch. Use two screws at each interval, set in about 1-1/4 inches from the edges. Continue gluing and screwing each layer, but use 2-inch screws in layers three through seven for better holding power. The bridge decking will conceal the screwheads in the top layer. Let the glue dry 48 hours before removing the beam from the form.

Sand the Sides

After removing the beam from the form, use a belt sander to remove the glue squeeze-out and edge irregularities on each side *(Photo 5)*. You could wait to sand the first beam until you have laminated the second beam and it is drying in the form.

Cut the Ends

After both beams have been sanded, unscrew the stove bolts and remove the support blocks from the ends. Then mark the beams for cutting. Use a framing square resting on a 3/4-inch thick board spacer *(Photo 6)* to mark the side of the beam. Set the square so that the T-nut location in the beam is at the 9-3/4 inch mark on the inside edge of the framing square blade. Mark the inside horizontal and vertical lines. When you cut on these lines you won't hit any screws or T-nuts in the beam. Make the cuts to square off the ends and the undersides of the beam using a circular saw, followed by a handsaw to cut through the part the circular saw blade doesn't reach. Finally, give each beam a coating of deck sealer. You won't be able to get at them once the bridge is completed.

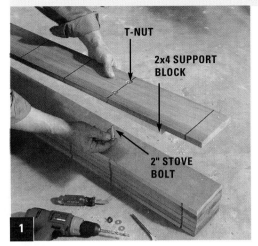

1 Mark the boards for each beam on the edges. Mark the middle first, then make marks at intervals of 8, 16, 24, 32, 40, and 58 in. toward each end for screws, and at 47 in. for T-nuts.

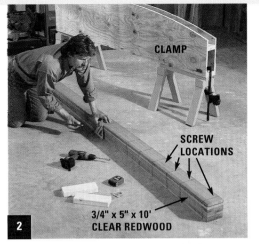

2 Attach support blocks at each end of the first beam board. Drill and countersink holes for T-nuts *(far right)* at the 47-in. marks. Attach 2x4 blocks with 2 in. stove bolts and washers from below.

T-nut

3 Fasten the first board in the form by first centering it lengthwise. Drive three screws into the support block from both sides at one end, bend the board, and fasten the other end.

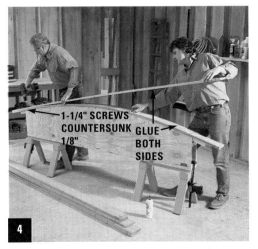

4 Laminate the boards one at a time with glue and screws. Spread glue on both facing surfaces. Drive screws from one end to the other. Use the reference marks to help you stagger the screws.

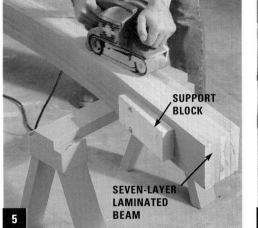

5 Sand the sides of the beam after letting the glue set for 48 hours before removing it from the form. Use a belt sander to remove glue squeeze-out and smooth any edge unevenness.

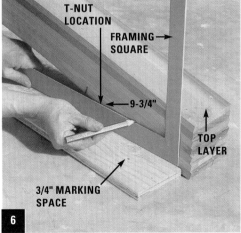

6 Cut the ends of the beams along lines marked with a framing square. Put the square on a 3/4-in. spacer as shown, with the 9-3/4 in. mark aligned with the T-nut in the bottom layer.

Installing the Beams

At the site where you will construct the bridge, clear away any interfering growth and drive stakes to mark the centers of the locations for concrete footings. The distance between stakes at opposite ends of the bridge span should be 102 inches (8 feet 6 inches). The spacing between the stakes at each end should be 39-1/2 inches.

With a post-hole digger, dig 10-inch holes 24 inches deep *(below)*. In firm soil you won't need forms, but in sandy or crumbly soil insert a cardboard form tube—available at home centers—in each hole to keep the sides from collapsing and to shape the footing. Form tubes are also helpful in making height adjustments, because the tops of the forms must be level with each other.

Fill the holes or forms to the top with concrete. You'll need about 1-1/4 60-pound bags of concrete mix for each hole. While the concrete is still wet, insert a 12-inch land-scaping spike in the center of each footing, extending 3-1/4 inches above the surface.

Let the concrete set for at least a full day. Then measure the exact span distance between opposite spikes *(below center)* and drill corresponding 7/16-inch diameter holes in the flat undersides of the beams. Center the holes in the width of the beams.

Install the beams by placing the holes over the spikes *(below right)* and pushing them down until they rest firmly on the footings.

Dig holes for footings after driving accurately placed markers (red) where their centers are to be located. Footings must be 10 in. in diameter, 24 in. deep. Insert spikes in the wet concrete.

Measure the span between the spikes in opposite footings after the concrete has cured for at least a day. Drill 7/16-in. diameter holes in the beams at exactly the same distance from one another.

Install each beam by lowering it onto the footings with the spikes going into the holes in the bottom of the beam. Push or step down on the beam ends until they rest firmly on the concrete.

Completing the Bridge

With the beams installed on their footings, mark the locations for the handrail along each side *(below)*. Follow the spacing shown in the plans (Elevation View, page 170). The posts are 22 inches long. Cut them to length, and then notch the bottom ends to fit over the beams (Section View in plans). Use a circular saw and handsaw to cut the notches.

Predrill the posts and beams for 1/4-inch lag screws (Bridge Structure in plans). Offset the holes from one another, and countersink them 3/8 inch in the posts for the screw heads and washers. Drive the lag screws with a socket wrench.

Attach a temporary spacer at each end of the beams to keep their outside edges 44-1/2 inches apart. Then cut and install the 2x6 decking *(below center)*. Cut the decking to fit snugly around the posts, and fasten each end with 3-inch galvanized screws. Predrill and countersink holes for the screws.

The handrails are two layers of 1x6 boards ripped to 5 inches wide. Screw the first board to the post tops. Spread glue on the top of this board and the underside of the upper board. Screw the upper board in place by driving 1-1/4 inch galvanized screws up from underneath *(below right)*. Clamp the ends of the rails until the glue has dried.

Finally, sand the edges of the handrails to soften the sharp corners and remove any glue squeeze-out. After a few days, apply a coat of deck sealer to all accessible surfaces to keep the boards from cracking.

Mark the post positions on the side of each beam according to the plan spacing. Notch the posts half their thickness to fit the beam. Fasten each one with two lag screws and washers.

Fasten the decking to the tops of the beams with 3-in. galvanized screws. Keep the beams aligned with temporary spacers at the ends. Cut the decking to fit around the posts.

Screw the bottom handrail board to the posts, then fasten the top board with glue, clamps, and 1-1/4 in. screws from below. Sand the edges and sides after the glue dries. Apply deck sealer overall a few days later.

A Domed *Gazebo*

This charming gazebo will not only embellish
the beauty of your outdoor space, it can be
a perfect retreat for reading a book, having
lunch, or just enjoying a summer day.
Using a new, flexible wood/plastic material
makes it easy to form the curves
in the dome.

Project Overview

A gazebo is a small summer house with an open design that provides a view of beautiful surroundings and allows fresh air to flow through. The decorative features of the gazebo shown in this project may make it look rather complicated, but it is really a combination of elements that individually are not difficult to build.

The various elements make up two basic sections of the gazebo: the open framework of sides or "walls," and the dome. Here are the important features of each section.

The Framework

The plan of the gazebo is an octagon. The framework is built of eight posts set in concrete, joined by rails and balusters at the bottom and spandrels with short slats at the top. A clever jig simplifies placing the posts so they are equally spaced around the perimeter. The jig also holds the posts in position as concrete is poured into holes around their bases.

The rails and balusters are preassembled before attaching them to the posts. In this project, two sides were left open *(photo, opposite page)* for access from different directions. You might choose to have three openings or only one.

The spandrels between the tops of the posts are also preassembled, using a time- and work-saving jig to make the spacing of the short slats equal. They are installed between flat top caps and supporting arches. Each arch is simply a flat board with a curve cut in one side.

The detail at the top of each post is a ball-shaped finial—a stock item, you don't have to do any lathe work—mounted on a flat piece called a "lookout" that is supported by the post and a wedge-shaped corbel.

The Dome

The curves of the gazebo are both striking and graceful in appearance. In the old days, a skilled craftsman would have had to soak or steam each piece to bend it to shape. You aren't faced with that problem, because you can use a new, highly flexible wood-and-plastic product called TREX *(sidebar, right)*. It can be cut, drilled, and sanded like wood, and it can be bent without special treatment to curves that would cause real wood to splinter or snap.

The dome is constructed of eight rafters attached to the posts and fastened between two round plates at the top center. The openwork roof is constructed of slats that run horizontally between the rafters. The detail at the top of the dome is a ball-shaped finial on a post-and-cap hub with curved support pieces. Keep in mind that because TREX is a nonstructural material, you should not hang hammocks, swings, or other heavy objects from the dome.

The plans on page 180 and the photos and instructions on the following pages show you how to build each of the elements that go into both sections of the gazebo, and how to assemble them into the finished structure. The entire project will take two or three full weekends.

About TREX

TREX is a product that marries many qualities of wood and plastic in a single material. It is available at lumberyards and home centers.

Manufactured by Mobil Corporation, TREX is made from waste wood fibers and recycled plastic. It is a durable material for exterior use: It won't split, crack, or rot when exposed to the elements. It also is a good-looking product. When left unfinished, it weathers to a pleasing gray after about a year, much the same as natural cedar but without a visible grain pattern. If a different appearance is preferred, it can be stained or painted like wood.

TREX is molded into standard lumber dimensions. Although it is superior to real wood for certain applications, it lacks the structural integrity of wood. Therefore, you can't use it for construction elements, such as deck joists, headers, or framing. TREX posts were used here on an experimental basis. You should use stronger material, such as cedar, redwood, cypress, or treated wood.

The primary uses for TREX outdoors are for decking, compost bins, planters, lawn edging, and similar applications. You can saw, nail, and screw pieces of TREX together, or join them to real wood or other materials. When driving screws, always drill a countersink and pilot hole or else the fibers will tend to mushroom to the surface. Conventional glues do not hold TREX as securely as they do real wood, but epoxy seems to work well with this material.

Because it can be bent much more than wood, TREX is an excellent material for curved structures such as the dome in this gazebo project. However, it bends much less readily when cold than when warm. To get the most flexibility, choose days when the temperature is in the mid-70s F. Look for this product at a lumberyard or home center.

Domed Gazebo

Fastener Schedule

Plan key	Fastener
①	1-1/4" screw
②	2" screw
③	3" screw
④	4" screw
⑤	Finish washer
⑥	7/8" staple
⑦	No. 6 nail
⑧	No. 8 nail
⑨	No. 10 nail

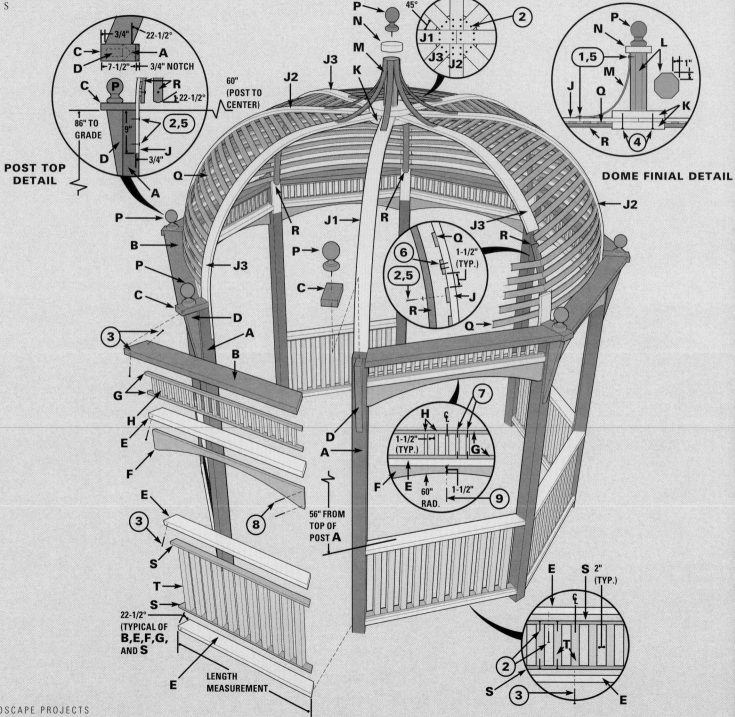

POST TOP DETAIL

DOME FINIAL DETAIL

Cutting List

Plan Key	Quantity	Size and Description/Use
A	8	3-1/2" x 3-1/2" (4x4) x 10' posts
B	8	1-1/2" x 5-1/2" (2x6) x 47-3/4" top caps**
C	8	1-1/2" x 3-1/2" (2x4) x 7-1/2" post lookouts
D	8	1-1/2" x 3-1/2" (2x4) x 20" corbels
E*	20	1-1/2" x 3-1/2" (2x4) x 45-3/8" rails**
F	8	3/4" x 5-1/2" (1x6) x 45-1/4" arches**
G	16	3/4" x 3/4" x 45-1/4" spandrel rails**
H	152	3/4" x 3/4" x 4-1/2" spandrel slats
J1	2	3/4" x 3-1/2" x 86-3/4" rafters
J2	2	3/4" x 3-1/2" x 87" rafters
J3	4	3/4" x 3-1/2" x 86-5/16" rafters
K	2	1-1/2" x 11-1/4" dia. (2x12) rafter support disks
L	1	3-1/2" x 3-1/2" (4x4) x 12" center hub
M	8	1/4" x 1-1/2" x 17" curved hub supports
N	1	1-1/2" x 5-1/2" dia. (2x6) hub cap
P	9	3-1/2" ball-shaped finials
Q	128	3/8" x 1-1/2" x 48" dome roof slats (trim to fit; use waste for shorter slats)
R	8	3/4" x 1-7/8" x 74" slat trim
S*	12	3/4" x 1-3/4" x 44-1/2" subrails**
T*	66	1-3/4" x 1-3/4" (2x2) x 22-1/2" balusters

* Quantities for parts E, S, T are for six railing assemblies. Increase or decrease quantities appropriately for seven or five assemblies.

** These parts have 22-1/2° end cuts; lengths given are from long point to long point.

Shopping List

Quantity	Item (Plan Key)
15	1x6 x 12' TREX (F, G, H, J1, J2, J3, R, S)
3	2x6 x 12' TREX (B)
4	2x6 x 16' TREX (M, N, Q)
9	2x4 x 12' TREX (C, D, E)
33	2x2 x 4' TREX (T)
8	4x4 x 12' cedar, redwood, cypress, or treated wood (A, L)
1	2x12 x 2' treated pine (K)
9	3-1/2" ball-shaped finial* (P)
3 lbs.	2" galvanized wood screws
2 lbs.	3" galvanized wood screws
1 lb.	1-1/4" galvanized wood screws
2	4" galvanized wood screws
80	No. 8 finish washers
1 box	7/8" rust-resistant pneumatic staples
1 box	1-1/2" rust-resistant pneumatic nails
1 lb.	8d galvanized casing nails
8	3" x 3" steel angles (for jig-post connection)
1	3' length 1/2" EMT electrical conduit
8	60-lb. bags concrete mix

* If not available at a home center or lumber-yard, look for a mail-order supplier. One source is Boston Turning Works (617) 482-9085.

Tools Required

Shovel

Post-hole digger

Hammer

Wood chisel

Screw gun

Measuring tape

4-ft. level

Framing square

Try square

Wheelbarrow

1/4" crown air stapler[†]

16-gauge finish nailer[†]

Air compressor for stapler, nailer*

Circular saw

Sawhorses

Two 6-ft. or taller stepladders

Jigsaw (saber saw)

Table saw

[†] Rental items.

Laying Out the Octagon

Select a level site for the gazebo, one that slopes no more than 3 inches in 10 feet, and stake out the corners of a 10-foot octagon. To do this, make a two-part jig. Each part has two 10-foot, straight 2x4s crossing at right angles *(below)*. Notch the 2x4s for a half-lap joint in the center *(diagram, right)* and keep them aligned at a right angle with a framing square as you screw them together. Screw a crossbrace between two legs of each jig to maintain the right angle. Drill a 3/4-inch diameter hole through the center, and screw a 3-inch x 3-inch steel angle at the end of each leg, on top.

Drive a length of 1/2-inch conduit in the very center of your site as a pivot and slip the two jigs over it. Adjust the jigs so there is a 45° angle between adjacent legs. Measure to make sure the distance is the same between the ends of all legs—this is essential in order to have a symmetrical octagon—and screw each crossbrace to the leg it crosses, to keep the alignment *(right)*.

Now pound a stake 1-3/4 inches away from the end of each leg to mark where the posts will go. Rotate the jig out of the way, but don't take it off its center post, and dig a post hole centered on each stake. Make each hole 8 inches in diameter and 2 feet deep.

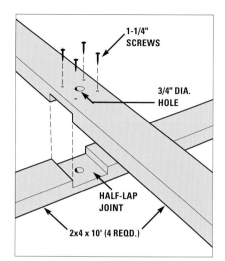

Center joint of jig crosses

Use a jig to lay out an octagon with equal sides. Set up two crosses of 10-ft. 2x4s, pivoted on a 1/2 in. conduit at the center. A brace keeps each cross at a right angle.

Drive stakes 1-3/4 in. from the ends of the screwed-together jig to mark the post locations. Rotate the jig out of the way and dig 8-in. diameter holes 2 ft. deep.

Erecting the Posts

Use solid wood, not TREX, for the gazebo posts. They must be set in concrete, cut to height, and notched to support the rafters.

Set the Posts

Rotate the jig back to line up with the post holes and dig out the sides of any holes as necessary so they are centered with the jig ends. Then stand a post in each hole and screw the angle bracket on the end of the jig leg into it *(below)*.

Mix up concrete—you'll need about one 60-pound bag of concrete mix for each hole—and pack it around the post bases. Have a helper hold the post plumb (vertical) while you fill each hole. Use a level to check the post, and don't be careless. The posts must be equally spaced and plumb or you will have lots of construction problems.

Cut and Notch the Posts

Let the concrete set overnight, then start at the post at the highest point of the site and mark it 86 inches above the ground *(below)*. Using a 4-foot level, mark all the other posts at that same height. With a square, extend the mark to all four sides of each post. Cut off each post top with a circular saw, using the marked lines to get the cut square and level.

Mark the inside face of each post 9 inches down from the top, set your circular saw to cut 3/4 inch deep, and cut a series of kerfs across the post, down to the mark. Remove the wood between the kerfs with a hammer and chisel *(right)*. The resulting notch will support the bottom end of the rafter that runs to the top of the dome.

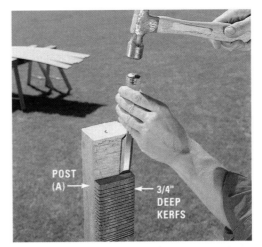

Cut kerfs 3/4-in. deep for 9 inches down the inside face of each post. Chisel away the kerfed sections to make a notch for the bottom end of the dome rafter.

Fasten the posts to angles on the jig to keep them centered in their holes for pouring concrete. Unscrew the angles and remove the jig after the concrete has hardened overnight.

Mark the posts 86 inches above the highest spot of land. Use a level to extend the mark from post to post. With a circular saw, cut off each post top square and level.

Connecting Post Tops

To connect the posts at the top, first install the lookouts, corbels, and top caps. Then build and install the spandrels and arches.

Lookouts, Corbels, and Top Caps

Cut and screw a lookout (C) to the top of each post, extending past the outside face *(below)*. Mark a line on each side of the lookouts 3/4 inch from the end. Then cut and install the triangular corbel (D) under each lookout.

Cut the top caps with their ends angled 22-1/2°, making the length given in the cutting list the longest, outside edge dimension. Predrill the front edge and the top near the rear so you can drive screws at an angle into the lookouts. Align the front corners of the top caps with the 3/4-inch marks on the lookout edges as you install them.

Spandrels and Arches

Use your table saw to precut all the spandrel rails (G) and slats (H) from 1x6 material. Angle the rail ends 22-1/2°. Build a jig from scrap plywood to assemble the spandrels *(below)*. Put a stop block at one end of a base that is 48 inches long and about 8 inches wide. Fasten 1-1/2 inch wide spacer blocks every 1-1/2 inches along the jig. Cut the spacers 1/2 inch shorter than the slats to allow room for alignment.

Lay the spandrel rails (G) and the slats (H) in the jig and nail them together as shown. You could hand-nail the parts, but it would take hours to make all eight spandrels. Instead, use an air-powered nailer loaded with 1-1/2 inch nails. Wear eye protection, and keep your fingers clear of the nail path.

When you install the spandrels, use the nail gun to fasten it to the top cap and posts.

Then cut the rails (E) with angled ends that go under the spandrels. Push each rail snug against the bottom of its spandrel while you drive screws through it into the posts.

Finally, cut the arches (F) with angled edges at each end to fit against the sides of the posts. Use the wire-and-pencil technique shown on page 173 to mark a curve with a 60-inch radius. Cut the curve with a jigsaw and sand it. Drill pilot holes and angle-screw through the face of the arches to hold them at the ends *(below)*. In the very center of each arch, drill a pilot hole and drive a nail up into the rail under the spandrel, as shown in the plans (page 180).

Working Tip

If your ball-shaped finials are not supplied with a mounting screw in the base, drill a hole in the center of the bottom and epoxy the head of a 1-1/4 inch screw in the hole. Then you can install a finial by drilling a pilot hole in the support piece and turning the finial screw into it.

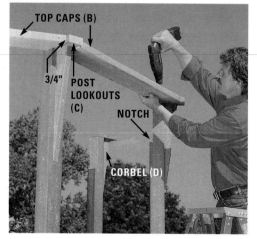

Install lookouts and corbels, then add top caps. To align the octagon correctly, cut the caps to exact length and move the posts to them. Set the top caps 3/4 in. from the ends of the lookouts.

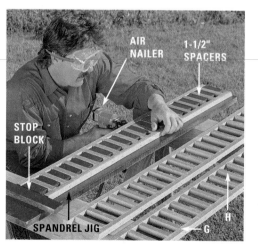

Build the spandrels by using an air-powered nailer and a plywood assembly jig, to avoid hours of tedious hand-nailing. Wear safety goggles and use the nailer with great care.

Nail the arches to the posts after fastening the spandrels to the posts and top caps and installing the rails under the spandrels. Also nail the center of each arch into the rail above.

Installing the Rafters

The rafters (J1, J2, J3) are the key elements in forming the graceful shape of the dome, so it is important to be careful and precise in the two steps of installing them. First you cut them and—to make completing the dome easier—mark them for the slats. Then you and a helper can attach them to the posts and fasten them to a top disk at the center.

Cut and Mark the Rafters

On your table saw, rip eight 1x6 TREX boards to a width of 3-1/2 inches. Then cut them to the lengths given in the cutting list (page 181). The bottom ends of all the rafters, and the top ends of the J1 and J2 rafters, are cut square. The four J3 rafters are cut to 45° points at the top ends so they will fit into position between the others as shown in the detail in the plans.

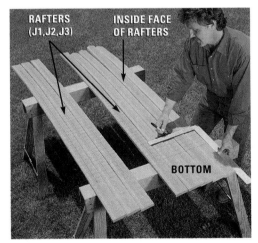

Cut the rafters to width and length, then mark locations for the dome slats on the inside surfaces. Starting 12 in. from the bottom, mark every 1-1/2 in. for a total of 23 slats on each rafter.

Lay the cut rafters side by side and mark the inside faces so later you can space the dome roof slats properly *(below left)*. Start 12 inches from the bottom ends and draw a line every 1-1/2 inches. Use a framing square so the marks will match on all the rafters.

Attach the Rafters

Let the rafters warm in the sun before installing them, so they will be flexible. During this time you can predrill pilot holes for 2-inch galvanized screws in their ends. When you are ready to install them, screw a top disk (K) to one end of a J1 rafter, seat the other end in the notch on one post, and screw it to the post. Then screw the bottom end of the other J1 rafter into the notch in the post directly opposite. Working on stepladders, you and a helper can now bend the rafters and butt their ends together *(right top)*. While the helper holds things in position, screw the end of the second rafter to the disk from below.

Install the other rafters in opposite pairs to form the dome. Do the J2 rafters first. Fasten them at the bottom to the posts midway on each side between the J1 posts, then butt them against the sides of the J1 rafters at the top and fasten them to the disk. Finally, install the four J3 rafters *(right bottom)*. Place screws as shown in the plan detail: four screws in the top ends of J1 and J2 rafters, and two screws in the J3 rafters.

Screw the J1 rafters into the notches on opposite posts. One should have the top disk attached to it. Bend them until their ends butt together, then screw the second one to the disk.

Install the other rafters in pairs. The tops of the J2 rafters butt against the sides of the J1 rafters. The J3 rafter ends are angle-cut to 45° points to fit between the others.

Completing the Dome

Once the rafters have been installed, there are three more steps to complete the dome. First, build and install the decorative finial at the top of the dome. Second, install the roof slats. Third, install trim to hide the ends of the slats on the undersides of the rafters.

Build and Install the Finial

The finial *(below)* has an octagonal center hub or post, a hub cap, a ball-shaped finial, and eight curved hub supports; the hub rests on the top disk of the dome.

Cut the hub (L) from 4x4 scrap from the posts. Set your table saw blade at 45° and cut 1 inch from each long edge to form an octagonal cylinder (Dome Finial Detail, page 180). Cut the round hub cap (N) from 2x6 scrap with a jigsaw; screw it to the top of the hub,

leaving the center clear. Drill a pilot hole in the center of the hub cap and screw a ball-shaped finial (P) into it.

Center the hub on the top disk above the dome rafters, turn it so the flat sides line up with the rafters, and fasten it in place by driving two 4-inch screws up through the rafter ends and top disk from below.

Cut the hub supports by ripping 1/4-inch thick strips from the edge of a TREX 2x6. Predrill holes in both ends. Hold one end of each support against a side of the finial hub, snug against the hub cap, and drill into the hub. Then drive screws to fasten the support. Now gently bend the supports so they rest on the tops of the rafters and secure them with 1-1/4 inch screws and finish washers. Finally, screw the lower disk (K) to the underside of the rafters *(below)*.

Install the Roof Slats

Cut 2x6s into 4-foot lengths on your table saw and then rip 3/8-inch thick strips from the edges for the roof slats (Q). Don't use the first strip, because TREX has factory-rounded edges. Cut the slats to length as you install them *(below)*.

Start at the bottom between two rafters. Hold the bottom edge of a slat against the spacing marks you made earlier on the rafters. Bend the slat flat against the rafters, mark and cut it to length (to the midpoint of each rafter), and fasten each end with two 7/8-inch staples. Use an air-powered stapler; a light-duty stapler can't do the job. Work up to the top. When the first section is done, do the opposite section in the dome. Continue, doing opposite pairs of sections to ensure that the dome stays straight.

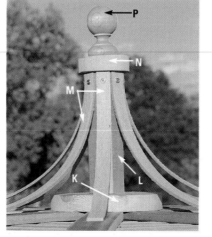

Install the finial after the rafters are done. Mount the hub, cap, and ball-finial assembly on the top disk (K). Then screw the supports (L) to the hub and the rafters.

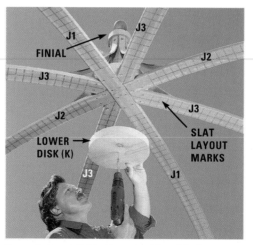

Screw the lower disk to the undersides of the intersecting rafters at the top of the dome after installing the finial assembly. The slat layout marks are used in the next step of construction.

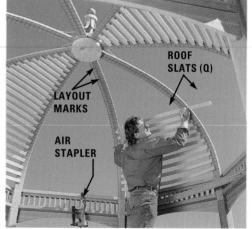

Install slats from bottom to top in one section at a time. Cut each slat to fit between midpoints of its rafters. Power-staple the ends to secure them. Use trim pieces for short upper slats.

Install the Trim

The ends of the slats butted together on the undersides of the rafters make the dome look rough and unfinished from inside. The final step in completing the dome is to install trim that hides them.

Rip trim strips (R) 1-7/8 inches wide and 74 inches long from 1x6s. Trim the corners at one end of the strip with 22-1/2° cuts (see Post Top Detail, page 180).

To install the trim, butt the square end of a strip against the edge of the lower disk at the dome top, and work downward fastening it to the rafter with 2-inch screws and No. 8 finish washers *(below)*. Drill pilot holes and drive one screw about every 12 inches. Make sure the screws go through the roof slats, not the spaces between them.

Installing Railings

The final construction stage is to install railings between the posts of the gazebo. As noted with the cutting list (page 181), the quantities listed for each railing part are for six railing assemblies. You may want to make more or less. Another important point: The lengths given in the cutting list for the rails (E) and subrails (S) are ideal dimensions. There will be some variance in actual construction, so measure each space and cut the parts to fit. The key to getting the subrails the right length is to note that they are centered in the width of the rails to which they are fastened.

Construct each railing assembly on a flat spot. The balusters (T) should be set with 2-inch spaces between. If you could not get 2x2 balusters (actually 1-3/4 x 1-3/4 inches) at a lumberyard, cut pieces from 2x6 lumber and adjust the spacing as necessary. Since the railings are like the spandrels, you could build a similar, larger construction jig (photo, page 184) to make the railings.

Screw the balusters to the subrails with 2-inch galvanized screws. Begin in the middle with the center baluster and work toward each end. Next, screw the subrails to the top and bottom rails. Drill pilot holes and use 2-inch screws.

To connect each railing assembly to the posts *(below)*, measure 56 inches down from the top of each post and align the top of the railing with marks at that height. Drill angled pilot holes and countersinks in the front and back edges at each end of both the top and the bottom rail. Drive 3-1/2 inch galvanized screws to fasten the rails to the posts. If you paint the railings, cover the screwheads with wood putty.

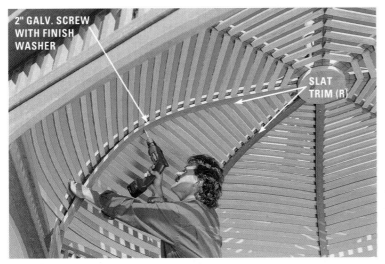

Hide the slat ends from view inside the dome by covering them with trim strips. Fasten the trim with 2-in. galvanized screws and finish washers. Screw through slats, not the spaces between.

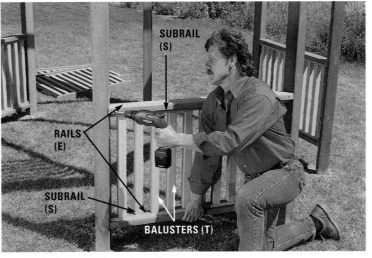

Preassemble the railing for each section. Measure carefully and cut the rails and subrails to fit; the distance between posts will vary a bit from one section to another. Install with screws.

Index

Acknowledgments

The Family Handyman editors, writers, designers, and illustrators

John Baskerville, Jan Boer, Sam Brungardt, Darrell Bush, Spike Carlsen, Ron Chamberlain, Kathleen Childers, Lee Christiansen, Bill Faber, David Farr, Ron Finger, Duane Johnson, John Keely, Doug Oudekerk, Don Prestly, David Radtke, Bill Reynolds, Art Rooze, Julia Schreifels, Mike Smith, Dan Stoffel, Eugene Thompson, Mark Thompson, Bob Ungar, Gregg Weigand, Mac Wentz, Michaela Wentz, Gordy Wilkinson, Marcia Williston, Mary Worcester

Consultants

Breck Bulbs; Deb Brown; Joe Christenson, Southview Design; Don Christianson; Bob Dahm, Southview Design; Mervin Eisel; Steve Evenson; Freeman & Associates; Dave Frober; Mike Frober; Gene W. Grey, Society of American Foresters; Anne Halpin; Cindy Jamieson; Dave Kopfmann, Yardscapes; John Lehn; Jeraldine Mordaunt; Jerry Odash, North Star Turf; Donald T. Olson, University of Minnesota Extension Service; Steven Shurson, American Society of Landscape Architects, Landhabitat Inc.; Gregg Thompson, Yardscapes; Liz Walton, Landhabitat Inc.

Photographers

David Cavagnaro; R. Todd Davis; Thomas E. Eltzroth; Derek Fell; Grant Heilman (Lefever/Grushow); Horticultural Photography, Corvallis, OR; Jackson & Perkins; Mike Krivit; Michael Landis; John Lehn; Phil Leisenheimer; Ramon Moreno; Lynn Steiner/ Minnesota State Horticultural Society; Michael S. Thompson; Wayside Gardens; Bill Zuehlke

This book was produced by Roundtable Press, Inc.,
for the Reader's Digest Association
in cooperation with *The Family Handyman* magazine.

If you have any questions or comments, please feel free to write us at:

The Family Handyman
7900 International Drive
Suite 950
Minneapolis, MN 55425